# Creativity in pre-school education

Edited by

Antonio Gariboldi and Nicola Catellani

Printed in Italy

ISBN-13: 978-8890487842

First Edition 2013

14 13 12 11 10 / 10 9 8 7 6 5 4 3 2 1

www.sern.eu
www.creativityinpreschool.eu

CREATIVITY IN PRE-SCHOOL EDUCATION

# Acknowledgments

This book was produced thanks to the support of the European Union and to the work and engagement of all partner organizations:

Municipality of Scandiano (IT)
Sweden Emilia Romagna Network (IT) (Project Coordinator)
University of Modena and Reggio Emilia (IT)
Landratsamt Enzkreis(DE)
University of Jyväskylä (FI)
University College Lillebaelt (DK)
Municipality of Norrköping (SE)
Escola Superior De Educação Politecnico De Beja(PT)
Klaipeda University – Faculty of Pedagogy (LT)
Liepaja University (LV)
University of Murcia (ES)
Verteneglio Municipality(HR).

Special thanks    also to all the associated partners, the pre-schools and the teachers who have been involved in the research activities    .

# Contents

# Notes on the Contributors

**Maria Do Céu Lopes Da Silva André** holds a Med in Educational Supervision; Diploma in Pre-School Didactics (João de Deus Methodology). From 1979 till 1996 worked as a Pre-School Teacher in different institutions (private and public).Since 1997 works as a Lecturer in the field of Pre-School Education, most particularly linked to the practical training, in initial, in-service and master degree courses. Member of the Coordination team of Elementary and Early Childhood Education Course.

**Chiara Bertolini** holds a PhD and she is assistant professor-on contract at the Department of Education and Humane Sciences (University of Modena and Reggio Emilia, Italy). She studies and researches about teachers competencies, conflict management, text comprehension and creativity in particular with reference to pre-school-age children. About these topics, she wrote books and articles and she discussed in international conferences.

**Roberta Cardarello** is full professor of General Didactic at the Department of Education and human Sciences in the University of Modena and Reggio Emilia (IT) . Member of scientific committee of Italian Society of Teaching Research (Sird) , she is also committee member of the editorial board of journals (Italian Journal of Educational Research) and academic books.Her main research areas are the educational processes involved in the following topics: promoting children's reading and reading comprehension; the mass media experience (tv, comics and movies); the quality of infant school; creativity, and documentation in education; teachers education.

**Nicola Catellani** holds a Phd in International relations awarded by the London School of Economics and Political Science. He has published internationally in the field of international relations and EU studies. He has been Visiting research Fellow at several research instituties in Europe and Canada. Since 2006 he has been working as coordinator of SERN and director of its Secretariat. Over the years he has been engaged in the planning and management of many EU funded project. He is the coordinator of the CREANET project.

**Maria Teresa Pereira Dos Santos** holds a PhD in Educational Psychology; Med in Special Education; Diploma in Educational Psychology.

From 1981-1989, worked as an Educational Psychologist in schools and services for handicapped children. From 1989 is a Lecturer in the field of Education, Special Education and Psychology in initial, in-service training, specialized and master degree courses for teachers and other professionals. Integrated the Organisational Committee of the 3 editions of the Congresses on Creativity. Was the Coordinator of the Early Childhood Teacher's Course. She has been developing various seminars and workshops using creative and dynamic strategies applied to education and other fields.

**Carmen Ferrándiz**, is professor at Murcia University. She had a pre-doctoral FPU scholarship funded by the Department of Education (MEC). She has been invited researcher in different universities: Yale University, USA (under Dr. Sternberg supervision), Coimbra University, Portugal, under Dr. Morgado supervision. Her Doctoral Thesis was focused on Multiple Intelligences and was awarded with both extraordinary award of doctorate Studies and First National award of research. Her Publications verse about emotional intelligence, multiple intelligence and cognitive profile of students with high abilities. Currently she is director of an I+D project about academic, creative and practical intelligence in G&T students.

**Mercedes Ferrando**, Teacher of Educational Psychology at Murcia University. She was pre-doctoral research fellow sponsored by the Spanish Department of Education. Her doctoral training included research stays in different universities:(Universidad do Minho, Portugal; Warwick-University, UK; Canterbury-University, UK). she obtained a post-doctoral Grant sponsored by Fundación Séneca to work at Tufts and Yale Universities. She has obtained the research contracts both "Saavedra Fajardo" and "Juan de la Cierva" to work with the high abilities research group. Her research is focused on creativity, intelligence giftedness and talent.

**Antonio Gariboldi** is Associate Professor in General Didactics and Special Pedagogy at the Department of Education and Human Sciences of the University of Modena and Reggio Emilia. He's a member of the PhD School in Human Sciences at the same university. He conducts research on the topics of early childhood education and educational evaluation. Among his most recent publications: Thinking creativity. Researches in pre-school contexts (2012) and Support, connect, promote: the pedagogical coordinator in educational services for children (2013).

**Inka Kotsalainen** has been working as a researcher and research assistant at the Agora Center, University of Jyväskylä, Finland. She became a part of the CREANET research team when she started to do her Master's thesis on creativity in the early childhood education in 2011. In addition to the early childhood education background, she is also studying to become a primary school teacher.

**Rasa Jautakyte** is Associate Professor of the department of Education at Klaipeda University (Lithuania). Before joining Klaipeda University she graduated from Lithuanian Conservatoire grand-piano specialty, taught at the School of Arts. She received her PhD from Vilnius University in 1994. Her main research interests have focused on the early childhood music education, music training in pre-school and primary school and music therapy. She is also interested in teacher training and professional identity of teachers. She is author of numerous articles in academic and professional journals, the book Music in the Early Years.

**Anne Lindegaard** is Senior Lecturer at University College Lillebaelt - Department of Social Education. The Main subject taught are Nordic Languages and Literature, emphasis on didactics, theory of science, institutions, and children's language acquisition. She holds a bachelor in linguistics with the emphasis on children's language and a second Bachelor in Pedagogy and Psychology with the emphasis on action research and children's reading of literature.
Her various continuing educations, include: Conflict-managing, supervising, various development projects, global entrepreneurship (in South Africa), mother tongue and second language.

**Ilaria Mussini** holds a laurea degree in science in education. She is an expert in clinical pedagogy, professional counselor and care expert. She has worked for 13 years in the field of education with particular attention to the coordination and the management of educational services for children and young people (0-14 years) and families, staff training and pedagogical-educational counseling.She is currently responsible for the educational services of the town of Scandiano (Reggio Emilia - Italy) and works as a consultant and trainer for public and private entities.

**Tuula Nousiainen** holds a Ph.D. in information systems. She works as a post-doctoral researcher at the Agora Center, University of Jyväskylä,

Finland. Her main research areas include technology-enhanced education and user involvement. She is interested in the various ways in which children can be active participants in the use and design of technology. Her doctoral thesis (2008) dealt with the involvement of children in the development of game-based learning environments.

**Linda Pavitola** is associate professor in Liepaja University, Latvia, where she acts as a Deputy Dean of the Faculty of Education and Social Work. She is director of teacher education study programmes at bachelor and master levels. Her research interests are connected with cultural aspects and the possibilities to develop creative potential and self-expression in the sphere of education.

**Antonella Pugnaghi** holds a PhD in Human Sciences awarded by the Univeristy of Modena and Reggio Emilia, she has conducted workshops in General Didactics at the Department of Education and Human Sciences, University of Modena and Reggio Emilia. She has carried out research on topics such as early childhood education and the quality of the educational relationship.

**Nelson Santa Eufemia** is International Relations Officer at the Municipality of Norrkoping. He holds a Bachelor of Arts with French, English and Pedagogy as core subjects. Language teacher background at upper secondary level, initiated transnational work in 1995 when Sweden joined the European Union. Extensive experience as project coordinator under Socrates and Lingua, Comenius, Leonardo da Vinci and Grundtvig programmes.

**Henriette Vognsgaard** is Senior Lecturer at University College Lillebaelt - Department of Social Education.
She holds a Degree from University of Southern Denmark in Philosophy and Cultural Studies, 2000, Specialization in Children- and Youth Cultural studies and Childrens Playculture.
Her main interests and research fields are: an interdisciplinary focus (e.g Cultural Antropology, Sociology of Childhood and Play Phenomenology) on the issues on childrens' creativity, play and informal competences in childhood education: Creativity, communication and expressive languages Aesthetic education and medias.

# Introduction

*Nicola Catellani*

Creativity in pre-school education is the result of the work carried out between 2010 and 2013 by a pool of researchers in the context of the Comenius Network "CREANET" – a project co-financed by the European Commission through the Lifelong Learning Programme.

CREANET has had as its main purpose the construction of a European context for discussion, research and exchange of best practices that promote creativity in the field of early childhood education and care. Unlike other types of projects co-financed by this program, the network is a tool to promote European co-operation and innovation in specific thematic areas of particular importance to school education in a European context.

More specifically CREANET has aimed:

1) to create a framework for discussion and exchange on the topic of European creativity among different actors in the world of pre-school education such as universities, teacher training colleges, local authorities and pre-schools.

2) to create opportunities for deepening some aspects related to creativity through the production of a research and new partnerships among actors active in Early Childhood Education and Care (ECEC).

The network-building process has led the promoters  to create a partnership with organizations from ten  different countries providing specific expertise on creativity in ECEC: The Sweden Emilia Romagna Network (SERN), the Municipality of Scandiano, the University of Modena and Reggio - Faculty of Education (Italy), the Province of Enzkreis (Germany), the University of Jyvaskyla (Finland), University College Lillebaelt Odense (Denmark), the Municipality of Norrköping (Sweden), the Polytechnic Institute of Beja - School of Education (Portugal), the University of Klaipeda (Lithuania), the University of Liepaja (Latvia), the University of Murcia (Spain), the Municipality of Verteneglio (HR). In addition to these organizations, forty-one associated partners were invited to attend the activities of the network.

CREANET has been by far the largest process of cooperation that has been carried out in Europe over the last decade with a focus on creativity in pre-school education. Paradoxically, despite the centrality and the attention that the theme of creativity has attracted no pan-European attempt to approach the issue had been done before. One of the reasons is probably due to the fact that creativity in the pre-school context as a subject has proved to be a broad theme difficult to tackle due to its many (often differing) interpretations and definitions. Furthermore, it should be added in the ten countries of the partnership the broad involvement of stakeholders with different educational backgrounds, cultures and roles has added further complexity to the process of identifying a common European approach to the issue.

In order to achieve the objectives of the network, it has proved essential to define a research strategy framing creativity in a manner sufficiently clear and definite. In this respect, the research work has unfolded in parallel to, and has connected on several occasions with, the exchange of good practices among the pre-school teachers and pedagogues. This close interaction between researchers and practitioners has proved to be a great added value that it is expressed through this book as well as the other publications produced by the network.

## The structure of the book

The structure of the book follows to a large extent the research plan that has been developed over the three years of the project.

The first step, reflected in Section 1, consisted of the analysis of the national literatures on creativity. The chapter by Mercedes Ferrando provides an overview of the work done on a national basis. The researchers have focused mainly on primary sources in national languages of the countries represented in the research group: Italy, Spain, Portugal, Latvia, Lithuania, Denmark and Finland. From Section 1 it emerges that creativity is a broad term that is being used in our societies to describe aspects pertaining to economics, communication, and of course education. It is a concept that is permeating our daily lives, but for which a definition is not always clear, to the point that its meaning emerges as intuitive rather than based on scientific assumptions and definitions. Therefore, in order to be able to contextualize through common lenses pre-school teachers' good practices in countries like Finland or Germany as opposite to the practices conducted in Portugal or Italy, or the practice in Lithuania and Latvia, it was necessary to understand their specific context and their traditions and approaches in the study of creativity.

This first phase was concluded by the analysis of thematic international literature on some specific themes related to creativity. In particular, Linda Pavitola provides an overview of the theme creativity and arts; Roberta Cardarello focuses on creativity and scientific thinking; Mercedes Ferrando analyses the work of scholars who have dealt with creativity in children vs. creativity in adults; Tuula Nousiainen provides an overview of the research work on Creativity and technology with specific attention dedicated to the pre-school context. Henriette Vognsgaard illustrates the main scholars who have dealt with the theme of creativity and expressive languages while Maria Teresa Dos Santos provides an analysis of the international literature dealing with creativity and teaching. Finally, Pugnaghi analyses the literature on creativity as a teacher's conception.

Out of the analysis of the national literature reviews and the international thematic literature a (non-exclusive) set of keywords featuring creativity in the pre-school context were identified as most relevant and recurrent in the sources examined. Such keywords, or features of creativity, such as novelty, self-expression, independence, curiosity, risk, self-esteem, and inventiveness were then used by the practitioners to describe their daily practices presented in the context of the transnational working group meetings. This process, which lasted for almost one and a half years, was geared to provide the teachers with some analytical tools facilitating the work of description of their activities. At the same time, the keywords resulted in valuable elements for the analysis of the results of the practices at a later stage of the research activities.

The second phase of the research process focused on the identification of the perspective of the teachers on creativity by focusing on the nature of the activities, methodologies and attitudes contributing to the promotion or inhibition of creativity in pre-school settings.

Such work, illustrated by Tuula Nousiainen in Section 3 of the book, has involved the whole partnership and it has been carried out through different methodologies: questionnaires, focus groups and interviews with the practitioners.  This part includes a general illustration of the methodology used followed by specific contributions on the outcomes of the research carried out in the different countries as a result of the methodology chosen. The principal tool for gathering data was a survey targeting a total of 425 pre-school teachers in Finland, Germany, Latvia, Lithuania, Portugal, Spain and Sweden. Focus groups were carried out in Italy, Denmark and Portugal. In Italy, there was a series of ten focus group sessions involving a total of 75 teachers while in Portugal the focus group consisted of eight pre-school teachers meeting regularly every two months. In Denmark, the pedagogues involved in the focus group activities totalled 18 while it should also be noted that the fieldwork activities were also implemented as an additional qualitative tool to identify the perspective of the teachers on creativity.

The large amount of qualitative and quantitative elements collected by the researchers have provided indeed a complex picture. However, despite different ideas of what creativity is, or what the most appropriate ways of stimulating its development could be, what emerges clearly from the teachers' point of view is the importance and the educational value of creativity.

Section four of the book builds on the results of the work of analysis carried out through the national and international literature review as well as the analysis of the perspectives of the teachers but above all it is centered on the daily practices on creativity presented by the pre-school teachers in the context of the working group meetings.

As a result of the outputs described above, the research group identified two complementary levels of analysis through which approaching the practices in the field creativity.

On the one hand, a set of assumptions or basic principles, outlined in the contribution of Henriette Vognsgaard and Anne Lindegaard, such as democracy, social inclusion and child-centred perspectives emerged as common to most practices in the European countries fostering creativity, and therefore they constituted a substantially shared framework of values of reference within which all Early Childhood Education and Care actors operate.

On the other hand, a set of more specific elements were identified as significant for planning and organizing educational contexts, functional to the promotion of creative processes. Antonio Gariboldi and Roberta Cardarello underline therefore the link between creativity and the centrality of the five elements in stimulating, giving value and supporting the free expression of children's original ideas. In particular, the elements were: exploring/experimenting with different spaces and materials, the importance of an extended and relaxed time for the children, the centrality of social collaboration among children in open problem-solving situations, the combination of different symbolic languages and codes and last but not least the role of the educator.

The section ends with the analysis made by Chiara Bertolini of the 36 practices presented in the context of the meetings showing the multiplicity and variety of concrete contexts and practical actions put in place by the teachers to foster creativity in pre-school aged children.

Finally, as pointed out in the conclusions by Gariboldi and Cardarello, this work does not provide final answers but indeed sets out important questions to be deepened and at the same time frames issues that are crucial not only for future research but also for the daily work of practitioners and policy makers. In particular, the question of which contexts provide the best conditions to foster (and educate) to creativity in pre-school settings emerges as the key question to look at both in terms of the future challenges that lie ahead and the quality of early childhood education and care in the European Union of the twenty-first century.

# Part 1

# National literature reviews on creativity

# CREATIVITY IN PRE-SCHOOL EDUCATION

# 1 The national narratives about creativity
*VV AA* [1]

The first section of this work is dedicated to the contextualization of the term creativity in the different participant countries. This was the first step in our research process; in order to achieve it  the research examines the roots and traditions of creativity in their own countries. This was (probably) a challenge for all the researchers for two reasons: 1) sometimes we are accustomed to working around our own concept of creativity; and 2) sometimes we are turned into the practice of others countries (especially English speakers) and we forget to look at what is being done in our own context.

As the reader will verify, there is not a unique definition of creativity that is widely and totally accepted by all the scientific community, although a simple and popular definition is that creativity is what is "novel and valuable" (Amabile, 1983). Novel in the sense of original, statistically infrequent; and valuable in the sense of useful, and appropriate to the task, that is, something that can solve the problem at hand. But this definition is not totally accepted and as it will be shown, there are contexts in which creativity is not identified with the product, but with the person, and then creativity appears linked to self-expression, extroversion and self-concept, rather than to a way of thinking. In some other contexts, there is no a special focus on just one of its facets, but rather different studies focus on different aspects of creativity.

Through the different chapters that review the literature analyzing the evolution in the meaning of creativity, two main issues emerge. Firstly, an element is common to many European countries: During the last years there have been substantial reforms in the educative systems that have promoted more open systems, more focused on the student and in his/her global and integral education, centred more on the achievement of competences than on the mere transmission of contents. This is the case in Portugal, Denmark, Latvia, Lithuania and Spain.

The second issue regarding the research on creativity concerns the fact that there is a great diversity among the countries participating in this review, thus some countries have oriented their research and their actions following their own traditions as culture (i.e. Denmark, Italy, Finland and Lithuania), while others have make incursions on the creative field following the international (mainly American) point of view, influenced by authors like Guilford, Torrance and other relevant researchers who initiated and promoted the study of creativity from a scientific and educative approach, departing from the philosophical or sociological approach (i.e. Italy,

Portugal and Spain). There are also some countries in which institutions only recently have been interested in creativity (i.e. Lithuania).

Something that seems to be common among the countries is an increasing interest to foster creativity in society, for instance this has been one of the goals of education in Lithuania since the independence of the country in the early nineties. In Latvia a big effort to disseminate the research on creativity (hosting and giving impulse to many international conferences and events on creativity, inviting researchers all over the world and offering a multifaceted approach that swings from sociology to economics) is being made; and in Finland a creative strategy that covers all aspects of life – not just connected to business – is being implemented by the Ministry of Education.

The considerations presented on the following pages, provide an overview of all the countries participating in this research with an eye to the specificities characterizing each of them.


## Italy

The Italian studies represented in the following paragraphs offer a review of national academic and other types of research on the issue of creativity, focusing particularly on pre-school children.

The definition of the concept of creativity emerging from Italian literature, in line with international literature, is rich and varied, some focusing on the features of a finished product, others on cognitive processes. The variety of possible methods used by Italian scholars to interpret creativity underlines the multi-faceted and transient nature of the concept itself.

Many interesting Italian studies have explored the psychological conditions and cognitive processes of the generation of creative thought. Some research works have considered creativity as a feature of personality (Rocchi, 1998), demonstrating the mutual influence of creativity and the need for cognitive closure conceptualised by Kruglanski (1989). Some Italian development psychologists have on the other hand explored the relationship between child development and creative skill, stating that creativity emerges manifestly in pre-school age (Pinto et al., 1977; Tallandini, Varesano, 2003). There are, on the other hand, many more cognitivist studies which examine individual cognitive mechanisms associated to creative thought. In particular, many research projects, influenced by the works of Karmiloff-Smith (1992) and Finke and Slayton (1988), have demonstrated a link between creative behaviour and the ability to manipulate personal mental representations (Boschi et al., 1997; Levorato et al., 1997). Finally, Italian psychometry has innovatively explored the issue of creativity, on one hand developing instruments to measure creative thought and on the other debating standardised instruments (Cerioli,

Antonietti, 1992b; Molteni, 2009).

In the field of studies into the education of creative thought, it would be hard not to consider the contribution of three Italian 20th century intellectuals: Bruno Munari (1907-1998), Gianni Rodari (1920-1980) and Loris Malaguzzi (1920-1994). Their thoughts are indeed considered innovative, as they anticipated many important discoveries in academic research. For Munari and Rodari, creative skills – possessed by all humans and not merely a chosen few – consist of establishing original links between known elements in a context governed by rules. Both Munari in the artistic field and Rodari in the linguistic field saw how creative invention derives from the adoption of rules, which represent both constraints and boundaries but equally resources for its genesis. In particular, according to Munari (1977), adults wishing to stimulate creativity in children should start by introducing them to the rules of creativity – the techniques and instruments used by artists – allowing them to know how to use them and autonomously discover new directions of doing. Rodari's rule-technique of the fantastic binomial (1973), used to invent infinite stories, is famous. The thought of Malaguzzi, which greatly influenced the pedagogy of the Reggio Emilia pre-schools and which is renowned throughout the world today, partly stands apart from the theories of the previous authors. According to the pedagogista from Reggio Emilia, every act of learning is a creative act, not in terms of product but rather in terms of process, as it involves running through "non-conventional" paths for the first time, recombining and processing knowledge.

Today, Italian research in education shares some fundamental theoretical assumptions. On one hand, it confirms the pedagogical and social recognition of the value of creativity as a positive and desirable quality of thought. On the other hand, it accepts and confirms the definition of creativity as a cognitive act that allows individuals to effectively solve problems by adopting new strategies compared to those usually used. This allows us to consider creativity as a thought skill we all possess, which can be stimulated, improved and educated (Andrich, 2001; Petter, 2010).

Italian literature offers many indications on the strategies and organisational factors used to foster creative thought in children at school. It is fundamental to offer an accepting environment, in which children are able to act freely. This non-judgmental context also constitutes the ideal conditions for stimulating curiosity and the desire for discovery among students (Griéger, 2003). It is also considered useful to place children in open problematic situations, inviting them to be active, discover and associate knowledge from different disciplines (Bocci, 1999; Petter, 2010). And it is precisely interdisciplinarity that offers a key for teaching creativity, helping to overcome the widespread prejudice that only the aesthetic environment is pertinent to creative manifestations. The dominating approach in Italy today in fact insists not so much on artistic expression as the sole vehicle of creativity, but rather on the work of art as a teaching material, a "pretext" for educating children to creativity (Dallari, Francucci, 1997; Munari, 1977). Other ingredients also help to foster creative thought. For example, it is deemed useful to make available a variety of formal and informal materials (Rinaldi, 2009). Another teaching principle that has been stated as important by many authors, refers to peer dialogue, which could facilitate the co-construction of creative processes and thoughts (Andrich, 2001; Malaguzzi, 1983).

Some Italian scholars, like their foreign colleagues, have also highlighted the role played by both the social representations held by teachers on the issue of creativity (Limone, 2001; Sironi, 2005), and that of teacher training in this area (Cascino, 1997).

Finally, in academic educational research, we should remember two training methods identified and developed by Antonietti's group, the effectiveness of which has been tried and tested: ASCI (Giorgetti et al., 2009) PSCI (Antonietti, Pizzingrilli, 2009). Both consist of several experience units targeting children aged between 4 and 10. They are based on two methodological principles: on one hand, the intention to stimulate a multitude of expressive codes. And on the other, each of the language activities were designed to stimulate the free production of ideas, the association of ideas (meaning the ability to associate stimuli even from different categories in order to produce something new) and the restructuring of thought (meaning the ability to decontextualize stimuli and change one's viewpoint).


## Denmark

In order to understand the Danish tradition first we need to frame their understanding of creativity. There are 6 main points of what defines creativity that are the basis of the Danish tradition.

• Creativity: The ability and the will to imagine things different than they usually are – and to act according to that.

• Creativity can be nurtured by the occupation with arts and artistic processes –but that is not the only way.

• A creative approach makes more out of less – things get new, surprising and convincing expressions and solutions are created.

• Creativity is closely connected to play, exploration, experiments, chaos. Chaotic thinking is a way to enter the world and children possess chaotic thinking in their play.

• The concept of creativity is a key word within aesthetic education, aesthetic processes and aesthetic expressions.

• So creativity is important and necessary these days when we face great challenges, ecological as well as economical and educational.

Taking all these considerations into account, we also need to review the background of the day care system in order to understand the way in which creativity has been translated into Danish day care. In Denmark we have a specific tradition concerning small children in day care. It was born long before day care became an everyday experience for nearly all Danish children, and it was part of the anti-authoritarian grass-root movements during and between the two European wars in the last century. "Following orders" was seen as one of the causes of the disasters of the two World Wars; therefore, war is a result of the authoritarian upbringing of small children. – So perhaps war and violence could be avoided if children were encouraged towards creativity instead of obedience.

Of course this answer was related to other phenomena in the period and in the culture: Scientifically it was inspired by the dawn of psychological knowledge of the great impact of childhood – i.e. the consequences of a highly authoritarian upbringing (Freud, Mahler, Eriksson, Miller). And of course by the great pedagogical philosophers and practitioners: Pestalozzi, Rousseau, Fröbel, Montessori and Neill. And probably it also was inspired by some specific Danish circumstances such as the experiments in public schools during the 20's.

Especially two dimensions were regarded essential in pedagogical thinking and practice:

1. A huge respect for small children's specific way of living and learning: Playing, dreaming, inventing, experimenting, imitating – and being ever so slow. Not rational in the grown-up way.

2. Great emphasis on the aesthetical and the creative as it was regarded as an access to one's personality as well as a basis for the development of empathy - and as a necessary condition for relevant changes in society.

This was the beginning of the "Education for Small Children's Pedagogues" in 1928 which main characteristics were non-restricted admission and work using students' presentations. This was due to the conviction that knowledge and personal development could only grow in freedom – and could never live in a strictly governed curriculum. In these schools, students did a lot of arts and music, especially experimental, based upon the assumption that human beings need to express themselves in a lot of different ways, and that it would be a huge failure to restrict oneself (and others) to the verbal language. Creativity weighed highly in this part of the education.

In the 60's when women became wage-earners, these day care schools became public, counting with economical support and lots of regulations, making it obvious that small children were becoming school-children, and that day care institutions should prepare for that. Till now this development has continued, and it has gained momentum with the PISA reports and the Bologna process.

During the last years, the day care institutions have become more and more strictly regulated, thus leaving as well the former aim of creativity, self-assurance, and cooperation as the strong tradition of self-determination. An obvious sign of this was the law of curriculum in 2004. The curriculum stresses that day care centres are committed to "making space" for play, learning and development. Thereby the day care centres are submitted to comprehensive management by objectives. Furthermore, in the latest government bill for instance "creativity" is not mentioned – the nearest concept mentioned is "aesthetical" which is only mentioned once. The focus of this law is on "learning" and in "preparation for school". Even so, it is possible to find fragments of the creative tradition: some arts, handicrafts, some creativity, and a certain respect for the small child. And you also see signs of it in day care institutions when you meet: Respect for children's ways of living and learning, i.e. not trying to teach them as you do with older children, but giving them instead room for playing and creating; singing, dancing, painting, rhyming, etc, both planned and spontaneously; a lot of outdoor living in day care centres, emphasizing the significance of snow suits, rain clothes, sand pits, adventure playgrounds, outdoor kindergartens, etc.

Currently, in Denmark, two trends regarding day care education can be found:

(a) The public, dominant trend, the main stream: Pre-school learning programmes which are highly intellectual and rational.

(b) The counter movement, still deeply inspired by The Danish Tradition, still trying to provide conditions for small children developing creativity.

During the last 30 years there has been a pronounced focus on child culture and children´s culture in Scandinavian child culture research. Two approaches have dominated: 1. A sociological approach and 2. An anthropological approach. Both approaches contribute to ongoing reflections about creativity and aesthetic education in day care centres.

The concept of child culture stresses that children are active beings in their everyday lives trying to contribute to meaning and sense in what they do in their informal learning processes – within their own culture. That is their singing, drawing, stories, their rhyming, their play, their bodily learning. Also it stresses how children are experimenting with different materials, how they interpret different medias, how they creatively contribute to participation in their everyday lives (Juncker, Mouritsen, Kampmann).

The concept of children´s culture traditionally includes classical and modern media and the importance of artistic activities – as well as the importance of children´s interaction with artistic activities and the arts (children´s literature, children´s theatre, storytelling, art, music, architecture and dance). These traditions have been (and still are) connected to the understanding of the Danish Traditions – as well as the child culture research stems from the Danish Reform Pedagogy.


## Finland

Creativity has been a widely discussed subject in Finland for quite some time now. Fostering creativity has become a nationwide top goal, which can be seen in many different projects. Creativity has mostly been connected to the business and technological world but in 2003, The Ministry of Education established a team to make a proposal on how to prepare and assign a creative strategy that would cover all aspects of life. The goal of this Creativity Strategy is to transform Finland into a creative nation and to advance creative thinking in all aspects of life and in every field (for example in education, science and the arts), create wealth, and increase people's happiness. This strategy also had an aim to support current projects that are trying to foster creativity, to start new projects and to make it possible for creativity to shine in every aspect of life and society. In addition, the target of the Creativity Strategy is also to remove the factors that prevent creativity from growing (Opetusministeriön julkaisuja: 2004; 2005; 2006).

The Creative Strategy Opetusministeriön julkaisuja (2005) also pointed out an important fact concerning the well-being of Finnish children and youngsters. Finland has faced a problem with children and young people's mental health issues. Mental health problems as well as the need for special education have increased rapidly. This means that a great deal of creative resources and other useful resources are not being used and developed because most of the resources go into resolving problems. This is one of the challenges that we have to overcome in order to make Finland a more creative nation. Various studies, such as a study made by Liikanen (2010) for The Ministry of Education, show that creativity has been seen to prevent mental health problems; hence, in the enhancement of the well-being of children, creativity plays an important role.

Creativity has also been pointed out in the field of education. One of these creativity researchers is Professor Kari Uusikylä (200, 2001, 2005, 2006), who concentrates on many aspects on creativity. There is also some literature which touches on particular methods for fostering creativity and giving children a say. Liisa Karlsson (2003) has researched and developed a method called story-crafting, which allows the children to use creativity and imagination. It was designed to increase the voice of children. Child-focused education is also present when children are story-crafting, and child focused education is considered a key element in the early childhood education in present day Finland. Both child-focused education and story-crafting also rose strongly from the research materials produced in Creanet.

## Latvia

In Latvia the concept Creativity has been used in different contexts with different meanings. Creativity (in Latvian called radošums) can be viewed from three aspects: as a feature of personality (individuality), as a process and as a product. As a feature of personality it represents originality, innovation, anti-conformism, courage, etc. As a process it represents creative intuition, rich fantasy, divergent thinking, inspiration, plasticity of the psyche, activities of sub-consciousness and superego. A creative product in various spheres (art, science, technology, etc.) is characterised by novelty and public significance.

Creativity has often been mentioned together with innovation with the aim of contributing to economic prosperity as well as to social and individual well-being. The awareness of the importance of creativity and innovation for personal, social and economic development has been raised by the dissemination of good practices, stimulating education and research, and promoting policy debate on related issues.

The issue of diagnostics of creativity is also very significant. Some of the most researched areas include:

- Creative personality development,
- Creativity as a feature of a personality,
- Creativity as a process and a result,
- Pedagogical and psychological aspects of creativity,
- Creativity in education.

Most researchers agree that creativity is a complex result of various factors, including personal characteristics, social, cultural and environmental aspects. Therefore, a multidimensional complex approach in the field of creativity has been used.

The tendency to focus on some particular dimension has had an impact on research results: a particular characteristic (for example, cognitive processes) has been perceived and interpreted as creativity on the whole, while other important characteristics (for example, motivation and cultural context) have been ignored.

The most widely studied topics in the sphere of creativity and the authors who have studied them can be mentioned as follows:

- R. Bebre (YEAR) analyses the structure of a creative personality.
- A. Lasmane analyses correlations between creativity of a personality and identity.
- J. Raipulis focuses on genetic preconditions of a creative personality and the characteristics that certify about creativity and giftedness.

- D. Rumpite researches on creativity theories as well as on the models of creative thinking, creative process and development of creative individuality.
- I. Strazdina analyses creativity, personality self-development and creative self-realization. Development of creative thinking, perception of artistic images, and the role of art in creativity development, creative self-expression and self-realization.
- I. Mikelsone has emphasized that creative activity and self-actualization is promoted by psychological security (awareness of the value of creativity), psychological freedom and freedom of choice.
- L. Pavitola reveals the issues on creative self-expression possibilities in the process of education.
- R. Garleja believes that the creative pedagogue is a creative artist, whose task is to investigate the pedagogical process, subject-subject relations as well as to activate creative cognitive activity and empower students to do research activities.

The research proves that childhood is especially favourable for developing creative potential.

It can be concluded that it is necessary to have knowledgeable and professional pedagogues, who are able to apply skilfully different and interest-provoking methods, thus promoting creativity and self-expression of children and also ensuring qualitative study processes at school.

In the school it is recommended to a) improve the content of the study process that is based mainly on acquiring knowledge, thus raising interest and creating a need to use acquired knowledge for their personality development. b) to have knowledgeable and professional pedagogues who are able to apply skilfully different and interest provoking study methods, thus promoting creativity and self-expression of children and also ensuring qualitative study processes.

During recent years a great interest for promoting creativity has emerged in Latvia: in schools many projects such as the "Creative Education-Pilot Project" (2011, promoted by the British Council") have been conducted; and many international conferences on creativity which have reached their 15th edition, each edition focusing on a specific topic have been held.

Creativity also has been of interest for industries, and the government is promoting different actions. Creativity is one of the main focuses on the national plans and programs for development (i.e. National Development Plan 2007-2013, Lisbon Programme 2005-2008, National Strategic Reference Framework Document 2007-2013)

Of interest regarding creativity in society is the project "Creative Cities" carried out by the British Council the aim of which is to share experiences across Europe on the way that creativity, entrepreneurship and innovation can help to improve people's live.

## Lithuania

In Lithuania, before the process of Restoration a context that supported the individuality of people did not exist. Therefore, the soviet contexts offered few opportunities to develop children's creativity. There were no school programmes oriented to foster creative thinking, independent elections or problem resolution. Since the Educational Reform in 1992 the Lithuanian systems have experienced several changes, one of particular importance has been the focus on children's creativity as one of the goals of education. In 2002 the long-term development strategy for the country was approved in the parliament. This has been the guideline for the entire education system; increasing the students' and teachers' motivation for autonomous learning and teaching how to learn, so that each learning child would experience success.

This same trend is seen in the pre-school stage, where teaching oriented towards content of knowledge is being replaced by the content oriented towards the child's needs. It is relevant to mention two of the main programmes, which have contributed to this vision: the pre-school Education programs "Virinelis" ("the string of beads", 1993) and the guidelines for pre-school education (1993). The conception of pre-school education of Lithuanian children states that direct systematic teaching of a subject must be discarded, that care, upbringing, education and teaching of the child may not be a dissociated process. The form of teaching – a lesson - was rejected and education of the child via activity was chosen.

As seen above, the Lithuanian pedagogy is more closely related to learning by doing and to have active children in classroom. In line with this philosophy the contributions of different authors aim to foster children's creativity using their activity and learning and try to make this experience as enjoyable as possible for children, while meeting the standards of education. Among the pedagogues that have explored the area of creativity we can mention the following:

• V. Jonyniene (1987, 2009) who is one of the first authors that analyzed the problems, blocks and issues in developing young people's creativity;

• K. Kaluinaaite (2002,2003,2006,2010) who conducted a doctoral thesis which argues that stimulating and fostering self-expression does improve young people's creativity. His model of education is based on the development of creativity through art teaching. His research revealed that the dynamic differentiated teaching of art affected development of creative thinking effectively;

• J. Almonaitiene (1997) is one of the first authors that studies creativity, and he focuses on the internal factors of the individual. According to his work, creativity is composed of two main elements: both the abilities and the personality of the person who creates. With personality being more determinant than abilities for creative achievement. Therefore rather than teaching abilities and the form of divergent thinking skills as well as the techniques of creative thinking, more attention should be paid at development of the individual's authenticity and formation of interest, values and motivational orientation.

• M. Bredikyte (2000) focuses her doctoral thesis on pre-school children's creativity and how to improve it using different activities that involve fairy tales and puppets drama representation. When preparing for their representation students found different challenges and problems that needed to be solved using their own strategies and resources.

• V. Kazragyte (2000) also focuses on pre-school students and the use of acting performance. The acting allows children to experience: symbolisation of the character, symbolisation of the circumstances, evaluation of the circumstances, development of actions, theme of actions and it also helps to improve the children's oral expression;

• K. Stankeviciené (2002) turns the focus to national folk-art, creating a new model of pre-school children's creativity development through folk art. This is based on the enrichment of general programs by folk art and the connection of purposefully selected folk art content and technologies. This promotes creativity in the education process as well as involvement of children into acts expanding their folk art expression: visual creative activity, communicative and verbal creative expression, creative games, cognition through investigation and close to fold art activity.

• V. Schoroškienė (2001) conducted a doctoral thesis focused on creativity and language, particularly examining the relationship between language and the development of thinking that impacts the creativity shown by students. This author contributes with a proposition to foster creativity through assignments on language;

• R. Girdzijauskiene (2001, 2003, 2004) has studied how to foster creativity through music. In her studies she has focused on different aspects of: a) fostering creativity by the accumulation of different experiences and stimulating a child's musical independence and self-expression; b) examining the impact of the emotional experience during the act of creation; c) examining teachers' pedagogical skills as a factor that can boost students' creativity; d) analysing the problems involved when assessing students' musical creative achievements; e) and recently focusing on the role of new technologies to foster autonomous and independent learning of music;

• D. Grakauskaite's-Karkockiene (2002, 2006) is the first Lithuanian author to present a programme which fosters students' creativity based on both the cognitive and personal components of creativity. The cognitive components focus on the main dimensions of fluency, flexibility, and originality. Whereas the personal components focus on recognizing and belief in one's own creative potential. This author has been linked to the study of gifted and talented development;

• N. Braziene (2004) focuses on the early stimulation of creativity with fairy tales, which can foster the cognitive complexity of students;

• G. Bersnevicius (2010) conducted a doctoral thesis about the educative dimensions of creative thinking. In this thesis the influence of different factors are analysed, such as: motivation, personality traits, abilities, thinking, the scope of inertia of thinking, special and general knowledge, reproductive and creative imagination, intuition, behavior, emotions, physiological state as well as social and physical environments.


## Portugal

Even when creativity invades the daily discourse of politicians, enterprises and society, there is not a translation of this speech into coherent practice in the social field of education (Morais Azedo, 2008). In the following lines, we will examine the different studies that have been carried out in Portugal in the field of creativity. They are diverse and focus on different areas, this is not an exhaustive review of the Portuguese outcomes, but rather an overview.

Most of the authors referred here agree about the importance of creativity for everyone's life and the development of society, recognizing creativity as part of human nature.

Concept definition and evaluation of creativity (based on an international literature review) are themes for reflection for Portuguese researchers in the fields of Psychology and Education. The emphasis is that creativity is a complex, multi-dimensional and systemic construct, which cannot be analysed if we tend to separate personal characteristics from context, processes and product aspects (Morais, 2001, 2003; Bahia & Nogueira, 2005; Bahia, 2007a, 2008; Candeias, 2008). In these studies attention is put into the clarification of different theoretical frameworks and the evolution in the ideas about the concept of creativity since the beginning of humanity and particularly its scientific approach from the 50s, with Guilford's proposal (Morais, 2001, 2003; Martins, 2004; Bahia & Nogueira, 2005). The relation of creativity to intelligence, the characteristics of creative thinking, creative personalities and the role of creativity for the development of personality are other issues which interest academic research (Fonseca, 1990; Borges, 1998; Ribeiro, 1999; Pereira, 2001; Bahia, 2007b).

Among the topics and contributions made by Portuguese researchers we found:

- Differences in the perception of the relationship between Creativity and Intelligence. In this area, especially relevant are the works of Bahia (2007b, 2007c, 2002) who studied the preconceptions about creativity and intelligence; and Morais, (2001, 2003); and Morais & Azevedo (2008) who focus on the study of creativity as a gifted identification, finding that not only gifted children show creativity and that therefore, some independence can be traced between those two concepts.

- Evaluation is another important topic of investigation crossing different approaches (Morais, 2001, 2003; Bahia 2007a, 2008; Candeias, 2008; Neto, 2009; Melo and Almeida (2008). For instance, the work of Bahia (2007c and Bahia & Nogueira, 2006) has focused on the study and comparison of different instruments of evaluation, mainly the TTCT (Torrance Test of Creative Thinking) and the TCT-DP. And they review the reliability of such measures. Other studies focus on people's recognition of creative potential. Azevedo (2008) aimed to study the creativity of middle school students, as perceived by them and their teachers. It was verified that the students' and teachers' perceptions were not in tune with what concerns expression and recognition of creativity, with students having difficulty in recognizing it in themselves. Other studies focus on the relationship between creative evaluation and school success (Neto, 2009).

- Creativity and education. Much of the literature stresses the meaning of creativity in education and how this relation can contribute to breeding authors instead of only reproducers of knowledge (Amaral, 2005).

In this regard, some programmes to foster creativity have been developed, a number of which have been applied among high ability children and youngsters. Some examples are: a) Miranda & Almeida, (2008) applied the "Odyssey" Enrichment based on Renzulli's model (1976, 1986); b) Nogueira and Pereira (2008) reflect on three models of international programmes, the authors of which are Betts, Treffinger and Renzulli. They give many ideas to apply them in different contexts but particularly in school settings, reflecting on the school educational project and on teachers' attitudes and practices.

This last issue is also analysed by Bahia (2008), who gives examples of two programmes, one developed with gifted children and youngsters and another with a group of young people with intellectual difficulties which took place during free-time occupation activities. They intended to develop discovery, fluency, flexibility, communication, collaboration, and creative problem-solving. In both there was an ethos towards risk-taking and doing things that are appreciated by the actors themselves and by the others. Evaluation was made both in qualitative and quantitative terms, but as Bahia states (2008: 250) "the most relevant factor when intervening in the creativity field is the auto-telic involvement of all participants and responsible person" and any programme "will surpass expectations if we give them wings, promote creative ethos".

Martins (2010) developed an experimental teaching programme to be used in the Arts subject, in middle school, integrating the sample, children with cerebral palsy and mild intellectual difficulties. The theoretical framework was based on three levels of the self-learning method - affective aspects, meta-cognitive and creative processes. Both quantitative and qualitative data showed the improvement of students in taking risks and increasing their fluency and energy, in regulating their creative processes and emotional expression.

Another line of work focuses on Creativity and Teachers' Perceptions, Practices and Training. A considerable number of studies are concerned with teachers' characteristics, personality traits and behaviours, their teaching methodologies and classroom management skills which either favour or inhibit the development of creativity in children. The access to teachers' perceptions of creativity are of utmost importance for the development of their creative skills and the effect they can have on the school curriculum, embedding in it creative teaching and learning. Studies that should be mentioned are those of Morais and Azevedo (2008 ) and Pequito (1999) Oliveira (2009)

We would argue that it is important to reflect upon how to educate free and creative thinkers, therefore it seems evident that we also need free and creative educators and this requires a whole transformation of models of teacher training and actual society. The project Creativity and School Improvement ("CRIA-SE – Criatividade e Sucesso Escolar") conducted by Ribeiro, Lopes and Pereira (2001) from 1993 to 1996 in pre and elementary schools, involving four teachers of both contexts, following an action-research model, is an example of a participative methodology, where researchers and practitioners can discuss and find solutions together on the possible transformations from an education for conformity to an education for creativity.

Reflecting upon the excess of discourses (from different voices: political; experts; scientists; educational researchers and teachers) leading often to the poverty of practices in all those domains, Nóvoa (1999) points out that only the construction of innovative pedagogical practices by teachers through the reflection of their own experience can contribute to enrich the field of educational action.


## Spain

This section has been structured following the development of the study of creativity in this country. We thus present, as accurately as possible, the studies that are being conducted in the field of creativity and education. This review covers the 80's to the year 2011.

It is not rare that in Spain, Psychology research goes in tow of what is done in the United States context; research on creativity is not an exception. The majority of Spanish authors have published sporadic and casual works and few of them have been working consistently in this field, among them Manuela Romo, Maite Garaigordobil, Clemente Franco Justo, Maria Dolores Prieto, and less prevalent, Javier Corbalán and M. Angeles Gervilla. Here, we comment the topics related to education and more relevant authors and research on each one:

A) The concept of creativity: bibliographic revisions. The first works being published about creativity were mainly an effort to extend the research already conducted in other countries. Example of this are the works of Manuela Romo (1997); Carlos Alonso Monreal (2000); Genovard et al (2006). Recently periodic publications have emerged aimed at the dissemination of the research on creativity, such is the case of "Creatividad y sociedad" ["Creativity and Society"]. Among the uncountable websites about creativity, the neuronilla.com deserve a special mention as it counts with many summaries and reviews by experts in the field dealing with different subjects from economics to education.

B) Creativity and Giftedness. A very close research line linked to creativity is gifted and talented education, especially in recent years it has been stressed in Spain. This line of research has supposedly a strong impulse to the basic research on creativity: its concept, its assessment, and its training. Important here are the works of Castelló (2008), the research conducted by Lola Prieto and her team (Prieto et al, 1999), pioneer in the study of giftedness in Spain, the works of Arquiles and his collaborators (Artiles Hernandez & Jimenez Gonzalez, 2005, 2007) as well as others.

C) Fostering Creativity. Spanish researchers have intended not just to promote activities that develop creativity but, also, to assess the efficacy of these activities and to what extent creativity can be improved. Here feature the works of the Murcia University team who adapt materials from the English language and also design their own material (Ferrando, 2009, Prieto et al, 2003; Prieto et al 2010). Similarly in the Canary Islands programmes to foster creativity are being funded by the local government such as the PREPEDI (Artiles Hernandez & Jimenez Gonzalez, 2005, 2007). A special mention is deserved for the works of Maite Garaigordobil and her team (Garaigordobil 1995; Garaigordobil , 2003; Garaigordobil, 1999; Garaigordobil & Perez, 2001) who, after years of research have published their programme, oriented to develop creativity and collaborative learning in the school ages. Also the work of Franco Justo (Franco Justo, 2009; Franco Justo & Justo Martinez, 2009) which promotes creativity through many methods: by using tales covering both the cognitive and affective dimension; by trying out programs of corporal creativity in children; and by bolstering students' self-perception. Other contributions are those of

Berlanga Jiménez, & Argueda Carmona, (1993) who try to foster creativity using dramatized tales.

In the aim of fostering creativity other authors have been carrying out pedagogical experiences that sometimes are not noticed, and rarely are published in academic journals. These experiences are usually conducted in Primary and Secondary Education. Among them we can mention the guidelines offered by Isabel Agüera (1997). And particularly the activities designed for the math curriculum that are being published on the Internet by Claudí Alsina (http://www.upc.edu/ea-smi//personal/claudi), and by Jose Ángel Murcia (http://www.tocamates.com)

D) Assessment of creativity. The assessment of creativity is necessary to quantify it, mainly with two aims: Diagnosis of high ability and the assessment of the efficacy of the programmess to foster creativity. In Spain, the majority of the tests designed are strongly inspired by the North-American trend. In 1978, Francisco Rivas adapted the Mendick test of remote association, in 1985 Martinez Beltran published a self-report assessment of creativity, in 1991 De la Torre published the test Abre-acción aimed at measuring divergent thinking. In 2006 Garaigordobil presented her scale of the creative personality. Cenizo Benjumea & Fernández Truan (2004) designed an instrument to assess psychomotor creativity.

Interesting are the works that have produce standard scores for the Spanish population, such as the adaptation of Torrance Test of Creative Thinking (Ferrando et. al. 2007). The design of the CREA test (Corbalan et al, 2003), and the PIC (Artola et al, 2004) as well as the test for pre-school child creativity designed by Romo et al.(2008).

E) Creativity and its relationship with other psychological constructs. Creativity has been related to intelligence, (Gonzalez & Campos, 1994, Ferrando et al. 2005, Sanz de Acedo Lizarraga & Sanz de Acedo Baquedano, 2008; Garaigordobil & Torres 1996); to academic performance, (Garaigordobil, 1996; Campos et al 1997; Garaigordobil & Torres, 1996 ; Campos, & González, 1993a); to self-concept (Armesto, 2001; Franco Justo, 2006, 2008a); to personality traits (Chacón Araya & Moncada Jiménez, 2006; Garaigordobil & Perez Fernandez, 2002; Garaigordobil, 2005); to bilingualism (Atucha, 1981); to play (Aquino Casal y Sanchez de Bustamante, 1999; Garaigordobil, 1995a), and to teachers' expectations (Franco Justo, 2008b).

F) Teachers' own creativity is supposed to make lessons easier and more enjoyable for the students. Within this line of research it is worth mentioning the works of De Miguel Badesa (1994) who reflects about the importance of creativity training in a teaching degree, the works of Barahona (2004) who designed a questionnaire about teachers practices on creativity, Alsina (2006) who established the difference between the creative profile of music teachers and more recently Ruiz Gutierrez (2010) who examined the relationship between creativity and educational praxis.

G) Studies of creativity in early childhood. Even when the pre-school classroom is more indicated to work with creativity, it is not common to find works about pre-school children's creativity. Among them are Garaigordobil and Perez (2002) and Franco Justo (2004) who have studied different training programmes. Barcia (2006) has contributed with reflections about the relationship between infancy, family and creativity, and Sánchez Corral (1993) and Barahona (2004) have studied the effects of children's language and creativity.

The issue is not whether creative actions are being conducted in the pre-school classroom, but that only a few of them are published and acquire a "forma character". In fact, when just googling the word "creatividad infantil" many forums, blogs, etc. can be found. Those websites are addressed to change teachers' experiences in an intuitive way, many times at a beginning level, and are more intuitive than research-based, nevertheless those websites are evidence of teachers' efforts and interest to introduce creativity into their classrooms.

## Conclusions

The research on the field of creativity has been concerned about substantial topics like a) how creativity is defined and which factors compose it, this line of research take the extensive literature review on the topic and broadly has touched upon the personal approach to creativity, to the systemic approach in which creativity is not just confined within the person but in the context, recognizing that creativity can be found in any person and in any domain; in Lithuania for instance, creativity is defined as essentially related to art; whereas in Italy, the recent tendencies see the arts as a vehicle of creativity; b) the psychological factors that correlate or influence creativity; in this line of research the relationship between creativity and intelligence or giftedness (especially in Latvia, Portugal and in Spain have acquire special relevant in the last years) has been of interest, the search of the creative personality −extroversion, self-concept, etc. − (especially in Latvia, Denmark and Finland, seems to be a great interest on the creative personality and how to develop it, linking pre-school creativity to self-expression and self-actualization); c) the assessment of creativity, in the beginning adapting the American test, and then making our own attempt in the evaluation of creativity with tests like the Urban and Jellen (1998) in Germany, Cereioli and Atonietti (1992) in Italy; Morais (2001), in Portugal and Romo et al. (2008) in Spain; d) The study of creativity in the classroom comprises at least three facts:

1. The study of the pedagogical roots of the educative systems that support and encourage creative teaching, especially in Italy, Lithuania and Portugal;

2. How creativity is fostered in the classroom, by two mean ways: by publishing a structured programme (i.e. 'Activities for the development of children's creativity' and 'Programme of development of childhood creativity' in Italy; 'Programme odyssey' in Portugal and 'Bright challenge' and 'MARK' programs in Spain; the program designed by Strazdina in Latvia and the fostering of creativity through music by Girdzijauskiene; and the work of Bredikyte and Kazragyte to foster verbal creativity using drama in Lithuania) or by using teachers own material, which sometimes is more flexible, less structured and has less diffusion being almost isolated experiences.

3. There is a concern about what teachers think about creativity, their attitude as a facilitator of creativity in the classroom, in Italy particular attention has been given to the social representations held by teachers on the issue of creativity (Limone, 2001; Sironi, 2005); e) The development of creativity during the life-span focusing on early childhood, in this sense in Italy (i.e. Pinto et al, 1997; Tallandini, Varesano, 2003) and Portugal the research is concerned about when creativity emerges in the child, while in Spain creativity in early childhood has focused on the study of its characteristics, not being different from the studies with older children.

In addition to the research lines followed in the field of creativity it is important to mention that for some countries more than for others, creativity is not merely a cognitive action, rather it is more linked to the person and the well-being of the student.

Among the countries for which creativity represents the student well-being and happiness and therefore they try to foster personality characteristics linked to self-realization, self-awareness, self-confidence; thus, the educative experience approach mainly works on students' self-expression, rather than focusing on the specific skills related to problem-solving. From the Finland tradition creativity is understood to cover all aspects of life and thus to be manifested in the everyday lives of people of all ages across all kinds of contexts. In this country the role of creativity in schools is linked to the enhancement of children's well-being, therefore creativity is seen as a means of children's education: an education focus on the children giving them voice. In addition in Denmark, creativity is seen as a way to achieve democratic values in the school, stressing the values of inclusion, appreciation, child-centred perspectives, participatory cultures and play. This humanistic approach is also shared in the Lithuanian society, for which the school should foster the development of social skills and abilities including critical thinking and creativity, following a methodology of learning by doing.

**Notes**:
1 The paragraph about Spain was written by Mercedes Ferrando and Carmen Ferrandiz, the paragraph about Italy was written by Chiara Bertolini, the paragraph about Latvia was written by Linda Pavitola, the paragraph about Lithuania was written Rasa Jautakyte, the paragraph about Finland was written by Tuula Nousiainen and Inka Kotsalainen, the paragraph about Portugal was written by Maria Teresa Pereira Dos Santos and Maria Do Céu Lopes Da Silva André, the paragraph about Denmark was written by Henriette Vognsgaard and Anne Lindegaard.

**References**

Agüera, I. (1997). Ideas prácticas para un currículo creativo. Madrid: Narcea de Ediciones.

Almonaitienė J. (1997). Moksleivių kūrybingumo psichologiniai veiksniai [Rankraštis] : daktaro disertacija : socialiniai mokslai, psichologija. Vilnius.

Alonso Monreal, C.(2000),Qué es la creatividad?. Madrid: Biblioteca Nueva.

Alsina, M. (2006). Competencias profesionales y creatividad docente en los futuros profesores de musica de secundaria: un estudi a partir del contexto universitario ingles. Revista electronica omputense de investigación en educación musical. 3, 2

Amabile, T. M. (1983). The social psychology of creativity: a componencial conceptualization. Journal of Personality and Social Psychology, 45(2), 357-376.

Amaral, M.E.R.A.G. (2005). Criatividade e educação artística: lugares de arte, estética, formação e criatividade. Tese de Doutoramento. FPCE, Universidade do Porto. Available in pdf: http://hdl.handle.net/10216/22895.

Andrich, S. (2001), Creatività e lavoro di gruppo: una proposta didattica per creare un clima cooperativo in classe, Difficoltà di apprendimento, 6, 353-367.

Antonietti, A., & Pizzingrilli, P. (2009), Come sviluppare la creatività nei bambini: le indicazioni di un programma di ricerca, Synergies Europe, 4, 151-166

Aquino Casal, F.; & Sánchez de Bustamante, I. ( 1999) Algunas reflexiones acerca del juego y la creatividad desde el punto de vista constructivista. Tiempo de educar , 1 (2). 131-153

Armesto, María C. (2001): Creatividad y autoconcepto [Creativity and self-concept]. R. interam. Psicol. 35(1), 79-95 (esp.).

Artiles Hernandez, C. y JIMÉNEZ Gonzalez, J. E. (coord.) (2005) La respuesta educativa para el alumnado con altas capacidades intelectuales (vol. III) Las Palmas de Gran Canaria: Universidad de las Palmas de Gran Canaria.

Artiles Hernandez, C., Jimenez Gonzalez, J. (Coord).(2007)Programa de enriquecimiento extracurricular: Actividades para estimular el crecimiento divergente en el alumnado de Educación Primaria (PREPEDI). Dirección General de Ordenación e Innovación Educativa de Canarias.

Artola, I., Barraca, J., Mosteiro, P. y Pina J. (2004). PIC. Prueba de Imaginación Creativa. Madrid: TEA

Atucha Zamalloa, K. (1981).- Ministerio de Educación y Ciencia. INCE - Influencias del bilingüismo familiar y escolar en el desarrollo de la creatividad. Revista de educación Madrid 1981, n. 268 ; p. 63-76

Azevedo, M. I. P. (2008). Criatividade e percurso escolar : um estudo com jovens do ensino básico. Tese de Doutoramento em Educação - Área de especialização em Psicologia da Educação. Universidade do Minho: Available in pdf: http://hdl.handle.net/1822/8065.

Bahia, S. (2002). Da educação à arte e à criatividade. Sobredotação, 3 (2), 101-126. Available in pdf: http://hdl.handle.net/10451/2730

Bahia, S. (2007a). Psicologia da Criatividade. Manual de Apoio para a disciplina de Psicologia da Criatividade. Mestrado em Teatro e Comunidade da ESTC/IPL. Available in pdf: http://www.esd.ipl.pt/znew/pdfs/manuaisdeestudo/psicopedagogia2_psic ologiadacriatividade.pdf.

Bahia, S. (2007b). Artistas criativos e cientistas inteligentes: uma dicotomia enraizada ao longo do desenvolvimento. In A. A. Candeias & L.S. Almeida (Orgs). Inteligência humana: Investigação e Aplicações, Volume I (485-495). Coimbra: Quarteto. Also available in pdf: http://hdl.handle.net/10451/2709.

Bahia, S. (2007c). Quadros que compõem a criatividade: uma análise do Teste de Torrance. Sobredotação, 8, 91-120. Available in pdf: http://hdl.handle.net/10451/2728.

Bahia, S. (2008). Promoção do Ethos Criativo. In S. Bahia, & M.F. Morais (Coord.). Criatividade: Conceito, necessidades e intervenção (pp.229-252). Braga: Psiquilíbrios Edições.

Bahia, S., & Nogueira, S. I. (2005). Entre a teoria e a prática da criatividade. In G. Miranda & S. Bahia (Org.), Psicologia da Educação: Temas de Desenvolvimento, Aprendizagem e Ensino (pp. 332-363). Lisboa: Relógio d'Água Editores. Also available in pdf: http://hdl.handle.net/10451/2721.

Bahia, S., & Nogueira, S.I. (2006). "Dez vezes duas" avaliações da criatividade. Revista Recre@rte, 6. IACAT. Available in pdf: http://hdl.handle.net/10451/2756.

Barahona, E. (2004) Estudio de Validez del Cuestionario de Prácticas Pedagógicas Para la Creatividad (CPPC). Psykhe, , vol.13, no.1, p.157-174.

Barcia Moreno, M (2006) La creatividad en los alumnos de educación infantil Incidencia del contexto familiarCreatividad y sociedad: revista de la Asociación para la Creatividad, , N°. 9, 2006 , pags. 43-52

Bebre, R.(2011).Creativity and the teacher`s personality, Retrieved

February 20, 2011 from http://www.lvasa.lv/bebre.html

Beresnevičius G. (2010). Kūrybiškumo ir kūrybinio mąstymo edukacinės dimensijos. Daktaro disertacija. Šiauliai.

Berlanga Jiménez, M.C.; & Argueda Carmona, F. ( 1993) Desarrollo de la creatividad infantil a través de un cuento musical dramatizado. Investigaciones y experiencias en educación infantil / coord. por María Dolores García Fernández, 1993, ISBN 84-7801-205-2, págs. 471-482

Bocci F. (1999), La creatività: cinquant'anni dopo Guilford, Scuola e Città, 50, 11, 449-458.

Borges, I. (1998). Estruturação da personalidade e da criatividade. Saber (e) Educar, 3, 7-15, Available in pdf: http://purl.net/esepf/handle/10000/205

Boschi, F., Biggeri, A., Bigozzi, L., & Sciabetta I. (1997), Aspetti di flessibilità rappresentativa indotta in compiti cognitivo-linguistici di base, Età Evolutiva, 55, 96-106.

Bražienė, N. (2004). Pradinių klasių vaikų kūrybingumo ugdymas pasakomis. Daktaro disertacija. Socialiniai mokslai, edukologija. Šiauliai.

Bražienė, N., Ramaneckienė I. (2004). Jaunesniojo mokyklinio amžiaus vaikų kūrybingumo ugdymas pasakomis, kaip edukacinės diagnostikos objektas. Ugdymo psichologija. Nr. 11.

Brėdikytė M. (2000). Vaidybinis dialogas su lėlėmis – vaikų verbalinės kūrybos aktyvinimo metodas (2000). Daktaro disertacija. Vilnius.

Campos, A y González, M. A. (1993a). Vividness of imagery and creativity. Perceptual and Motor Skills, 77, 923-928.

Campos, A.; Gónzalez, M.A.; y Calderón, M.L. (1997) imagen, creatividad y rendimiento academico. Revista galego-portuguesa de psicoloxía e educación. N° 1(Vol. 1) Ano 1°-1997

Candeias, A.A. (2008). Criatividade: Perspectiva inegrativa sobre o conceito e a sua avaliação. In S. Bahia & M.F. Morais (Coord.). Criatividade: Conceito, necessidades e intervenção (pp.41-63). Braga: Psiquilíbrios Edições.

Cascino, V. (1997), Educare al pensiero creativo: un contributo di ricerca sperimentale, I problemi della Pedagogia, 43. 5-6, 583-587.

Castelló, A. (2008) Bases intelectuales de la excepcionalidad: un esquema integrador. Revista Española de Pedagogía. 66: 203-220

Cenizo Benjumea, J.M. & Fernández Truan, J. C. (2004) Instrumento para evaluar la creatividad motriz del alumnado de educación física en primaria. Educación física y deportes, ISSN 1514-3465, N°. 71, 2004

Cerioli, L., & Antonietti, A. (1992b), Test di creatività infantile (T.C.I.), http://www.erickson.it/erickson/repository/pdf/doc_cre_6.4.1.pdf

Corbalán Berná, F.J., Martínez Zaragoza, F. Donolo, D.S.; Alonso Monreal, C. Tejerina Arreal, M. Limiñana Gras, R.M. (2003) CREA. Inteligencia Creativa. Una media cognitiva de la creatividad. TEA ediciones. Madrid

Chacón Araya, Y. y Moncada Jiménez, J. (2006). Relación entre personalidad y creatividad en estudiantes de Educación Física. Actualidades investigativas en educación, 6 (1), 1-19.

Dallari, M., & Francucci, C. (1997), L'esperienza pedagogica dell'arte, Firenze, Nuova Italia.

De la Torre, S. (1991). Evaluación de la creatividad. Test de Abre Acción para Evaluar la Creatividad TAEC. Madrid: Escuela Española.

De Miguel Badesa, S. (1995). La creatividad como algo valioso en la formacion de maestros .Tendencias Pedagogicas., n° 01 (pp. 67-74).

Ferrando, M. (2009) Proyecto "suelta tu mente". Talleres dirigidos a niños de 1° a 4° de Educación Primaria. Financiado por la Fundación Séneca. www.f-seneca.org/seneca/doc/fichas_talleres2009.pdf

Ferrando, M., Ferrándiz, C; Bermejo, M.R.; Sánchez, C. Parra, J. y Prieto, M.D. (2007). Estructura Interna y Baremación del Test de Pensamiento Creativo de Torrance. Psicothema, 3(19), 489-496.

Ferrando, M.; Prieto, M.D.; Ferrándiz, C y Sánchez, C (2005). Inteligencia y creatividad,Revista Electrónica de Investigación Psicoeducativa, 7(3), 21-50.

Finke, R. A., & Slayton, K. (1988), Exploration of creative visual synthesis in mental imagery, Memory and Cognition, 16, 252-257

Fonseca, A.F.(1990),A Psicologia da Criatividade. Lisboa: Escher Publicações.

Franco Justo, C. (2004). Intervención en la creatividad docente y su incidencia en los niveles de creatividad de los alumnos. Revista de educación de la Universidad de Granada, N° 17, 2004, págs. 37-50

Franco Justo, C. (2006). Relación entre las variables autoconcepto y creatividad en una muestra de alumnos de educación infantil. REDIE: Revista Electrónica de Investigación Educativa, Vol. 8, N°.1.

Franco Justo, C. (2008a). Relajación creativa, creatividad motriz y autoconcoepto en una muestra de niños de educación infantil. Revista electronica de investigación educativa N14 vol6 (1), 29-50

Franco Justo, C. (2008b). Effects of teacher expectations on the development of verbal creativity in childhood education. Actualidades Investigativas en Educación, ISSN 1409-4703, Vol. 8, N°. 3, 2008

Franco Justo, C. (2009). Efectos de un programa de meditación sobre los niveles de creatividad verbal de un grupo de alumnos/as de Bachillerato. Suma Psicológica, ISSN 0121-4381, Vol. 16, N°. 2, 2009, págs. 113-120

Franco Justo, C. y Justo Martinez, E. (2009). Efectos de un programa de intervención basado en la imaginación, la relajación y el cuento infantil, sobre los niveles de creatividad verbal, gráfica y motora en un grupo de niños de último curso de educación infantil. Revista Iberoamericana de Educación, Vol. 49, N°. 3, 2009

Garaigordobil Landazaabal, M. & Perez Fernandez, J.I. (2002) Análisis predictivo y correlacional de la creatividad grafica y verbal con otros rasgos de la personalidad infantil. Revista de Psicología general y aplicada, 55 (3)

373-390.

Garaigordobil Landazabal, M. (2006). EPC: Escala de Personalidad Creadora: Evaluación de conductas y rasgos de la personalidad creativa infantile. Comprender y evaluar la creatividad / coord. por Verónica Violant, Saturnino de la Torre de la Torre, Vol. 2, 2006 (Cómo investigar y evaluar la creatividad), ISBN 84-9700-326-8, págs. 324-332

Garaigordobil Landazabañ. M. (1996). Evaluación de la creatividad y sus correlatos con inteligencia y rendimiento académico . Revista de psicología Universitas Tarraconensis, Vol. 18, Nº. 1, 1996, págs. 87-98

Garaigordobil Landizabal, M. (2005) Evaluación del cambio de conductas y rasgos de la personalidad creadora: efectos de una experiencia con niños de 10-11 años. Infancia y aprendizaje, 28 (1) 51-61.

Garaigordobil, M. y Pérez J.l. (2001). Impacto de un programa de arte en la creatividad motriz, la percepción y el autoconcepto en niños de 6-7 años. Boletín de Psicología, No. 71, Junio 2001, 45-62

Garaigordobil, M. (2003). Programa Juego 8-10 años. Juegos cooperativos y creativos para grupos de niños de 8 a 10 años. Madrid: Pirámide. 263 págs

Garaigordobil, M.; y Torres, E. (1996). Evaluación de la creatividad en sus correlatos con inteligencia y rendimiento académico. Revista de Psicología Universitas Tarraconensis Vol. XVIII (1/1996)

Garaigordobil. M. (1995a). Psicología para el desarrollo de la cooperación y de la creatividad. Descripción y evaluación de un programa de juego para cooperar y crear en grupo (8-10/11 años). Bilbao: Desclée de Brouwer

Garaigordobil. M. (1999). Assessment of a cooperative program of assertive behavior and self-concept. Spanish journal of psychology, , Vol. 2, Nº. 1, 1999, págs. 3-10.

Genovard, C., Prieto, M.D.; Bermejo, R. & Ferrandiz, C. (2006 ) The History of Creativity in Spain. En James Kaufman and Robert. J. Sternberg (Coord) The International Handbook of creativity. NY: Cambridge University Press. PP The History of Creativity in Spain.

Giorgetti, M., Pizzingrilli, P., & Antonietti, A. (2009), Creatività: come promuoverla a scuola, Psicologia e Scuola, 6, 42-48.

Girdzijauskienė R. (2001). Kai kurie I - II klasių mokinių kūrybiškumo ypatumai Tiltai : humanitariniai ir socialiniai mokslai. Klaipėdos universitetas. T. 3

Girdzijauskienė R. (2003), Jaunesniojo mokyklinio amžiaus vaikų kūrybiškumo ugdymo muzikine veikla kryptys Acta paedagogica Vilnensia T. 11

Girdzijauskienė R. (2003). Vaikas. Muzika. Kūryba. Vilnius.

Girdzijauskienė R. (2004). Jaunesniojo mokyklinio amžiaus vaikų kūrybiškumo ugdymas muzikine veikla. Monografija. Klaipėda.

Girdzijauskienė R. (2004). Kai kurie jaunesniojo mokyklinio amžiaus vaikų kūrybiškumui įtaką darantys pedagoginiai veiksniai. Pradinė mokykla :

ugdymo turinys ir socialinė integracija : žurnalo "Tiltai" priedas Nr. 22.

Gonzalez, M.A. & Campos, A. ( 1994). Imagen, inteligencia y creatividad. Psicothema, 6, N°. 3, pp. 387-393.

Grakauskaitė-Karkockienė D. (2002). Kūrybos psichologija (mokslinis metodinis leidinys), (I leidimas). Vilnius

Grakauskaitė-Karkockienė D. (2006). Studentų kūrybiškumo kaitos ypatumai. Daktaro disertacija (socialiniai m.) - Vilniaus universitetas.

Griéger, P. (2003), Lo sviluppo della creatività, Rivista Lasalliana, 1, 37-49.

Ikimokyklinio ugdymo gairės. Programa pedagogams ir tėvams (1993). Vilnius.

Jonynienė V. (1987). Jaunesniųjų moksleivių kūrybinio mąstymo ugdymas. Metodinės rekomendacijos. Vilnius.

Jonynienė V. (2009). Kūrybinio mąstymo ugdymas pradinėje mokykloje. Žvirblių takas. Nr. 21.

Kaluinaitė K. (2002). V – VII klasių mokinių kūrybiškumo raida diferencijuoto dailės mokymo procese. Daktaro disertacija: Socialiniai mokslai, Edukologija. Vilnius.

Kaluinaitė K. (2003). Kūrybinio mąstymo ugdymas dinamiškai diferencijuoto dailės mokymo procese. Pedagogika. Nr. 65.

Kaluinaitė K. (2003). Vaizduotės lavinimas dinamiškai diferencijuoto dailės mokymo procese. Pedagogika. Nr. 68.

Kaluinaitė K. (2006). Kai kurie vaikų kūrybingumo ir vaizdinės plastinės raiškos raidos aspektai. Metodinė priemonė. Vilnius.

Kaluinaitė K. (2010). Diferencijuoto dailės mokymo teoriniai ir praktiniai aspektai ugdant paauglių kūrybingumą. Mokymo priemonė. Vilnius.

Karlsson, L. Sadutus. Avain osallistuvaan toimintakulttuuriin. 2000. Jyväskylä: PS-kustannus.

Karmiloff-Smith, A. (1992), Beyond modularity: A developmental perspective on cognition science, Cambridge, MIT Press.

Kruglanski, A. W. (1989), Lay epistemic and human knowledge: Cognitive and motivational bases, New York, Dell.

Kazragytë, V. (2000). Prieðmokyklinio amþiaus vaikø vaidybos gebëjimø ugdymas : daktaro disertacijos santrauka : socialiniai mokslai, edukologija (07 S). Vilnius.

Kazragytë, V. (2008). Prieðmokyklinio amþiaus vaikø vaidybos gebëjimø ugdymas : teatro edukologija : mokslinë monografija. Vilnius.

Levorato, M. C., & Cacciari, C. (1997), La creatività linguistica: categorie linguistiche e strutture concettuali, Età Evolutiva, 55, 89-96.

Liikanen, H-L. 2010. Taiteesta ja kulttuurista hyvinvointia. Ehdotus toimintaohjelmaksi 2010-2014. Opetusministeriön julkaisuja 2010:1. http://www.minedu.fi/export/sites/default/OPM/Julkaisut/2010/liitteet/OPM1.pdf?lang= 29.4.2011

Limone, P. (2001), La creatività infantile nelle rappresentazioni sociali presenti in un gruppo di insegnanti di scuola materna, 93-104, in Paparella, N. (Eds.), infanzia, apprendimento, creatività, vol. V, Bergamo, Junior.

Malaguzzi, L. (1983), Che posto c'è per Rodari?, in De Luca, C. (Eds.), Se la fantasia cavalca con la ragione. prolungamenti degli itinerari suggeriti dall'opera di Gianni Rodari, Bergamo, Juvenilia.

Martínez Beltrán, J.M. & Rimm, S. (1985). Cuestionario de creatividad. Madrid: San Pío X.

Martins, J.A.L.G. (2010). Metacognição, criatividade e emoção na Educação Visual e Tecnológica : contributos e orientações para a formação de alunos com sucesso. Tese de Doutoramento em Estudos da Criança (área de especialização em Comunicação Visual e Expressão Plástica). Universidade do Minho. Available in pdf: http://hdl.handle.net/1822/10671.

Martins, V.M.T. (2004). Da "sociedade da criação" à "escola da criação" ou de como é urgente a criatividade na nossa escola - breves notas. http://hdl.handle.net/10400.19/570

Melo, A.S., & Almeida, L.S. (2008). Avaliação da precocidade para a entrada antecipada na escola: A negligência da criatividade. In S. Bahia & M. F. Morais (Coord.). Criatividade: Conceito, necessidades e intervenção (pp.197-225). Braga: Psiquilíbrios Edições.

Miranda, L., & Almeida, L. S. (2008). Estimular a criatividade: O programa de enriquecimento escolar "Odisseia". In S. Bahia & M. F. Morais (Coord.). Criatividade: Conceito, necessidades e intervenção (pp.279-300). Braga: Psiquilíbrios Edições.

Molteni, S. (2009), La rappresentazione della creatività: uno studio sul riconoscimento della ristrutturazione nei disegni da parte di bambini con sviluppo atipico, 6, 39-64,

Morais, M. F. (2001). Definição e avaliação da criatividade. Braga: Universidade do Minho.

Morais, M. F. (2003). Os produtos criativos: Introdução a uma alternativa de avaliação no contexto educativo. Sobredotação, 4 (2), 9-24.

Morais, M. F., & Azevedo, I. (2008). Criatividade em contexto escolar: representações de professores dos Ensinos Básico e Secundário. In S. Bahia & M. F. Morais (Coord.). Criatividade: Conceito, necessidades e intervenção (pp.157-196). Braga: Psiquilíbrios Edições.

Munari, B. (1977), Fantasia, Bari:Laterza(Final Edition: Bari: Laterza, 2006).

Neto, N. M. R. C. (2009). Criatividade face ao sucesso escolar e ao raciocínio : um estudo comalunos de diferentes áreas do Ensino Secundário. Dissertação de Mestrado em Psicologia (área de especialização em Psicologia Escolar). Universidade do Minho. Available in pdf: http://hdl.handle.net/1822/10701.

Nogueira, S. M., & Pereira, M. (2004). M.O.R.C.E.G.O.S.: Um programa de enriquecimento da criatividade. Sobredotação, 5, 19-38.

Nóvoa (1999). Os Professores na virada do Milénio: do excesso dos

discursos à pobreza das práticas. Available in pdf: http://repositorio.ul.pt/bitstream/10451/690/1/21136_1517-9702_.pdf
Oliveira, A. I. G. (2009). O lugar e o não lugar da Expressão Plástica/Artes Plásticas nos projectos curriculares e nas acções dos educadores de infância. Dissertação de Mestrado em Estudos da Criança (área de especialização em Comunicação Artística e Expressão Plástica). Universidade do Minho. Available in pdf: http://hdl.handle.net/1822/11049.
Opetusministeriön julkaisuja 2004:4 .Luovuuskertomus. Ehdotus hallitusohjelmassa tarkoitetun luovuusstrategian tekemisen luonteesta, lähtökohdista ja toteuttamisen tavoista. http://www.minedu.fi/export/sites/default/OPM/Julkaisut/2004/liitteet/ opm_188_luovuuskertomus.pdf?lang=fi 29.4.2011
Opetusministeriön julkaisuja 2005: 35. Kolme puheenvuoroa luovuuden edistämisestä. Luovuusstartegian osatyöryhmien raportit. http://www.minedu.fi/export/sites/default/OPM/Julkaisut/2005/liitteet/ opm_300_opm35.pdf?lang=fi 18.4.2011
Opetusministeriön julkaisuja 2006:43. Yksitoista askelta luovaan Suomeen. Luovuusstrategian loppuraportti. http://www.minedu.fi/export/sites/default/OPM/Julkaisut/2006/liitteet/ opm43.pdf?lang= 15.4.2011
Pequito, P. (1999). Representações de criatividade dos Educadores de Infância. Saber (e) Educar, 4, 61-77. Available in pdf: http://purl.net/esepf/handle/10000/218
Pereira, M. (2001). Inteligência e criatividade: Duas trajectórias alternativas para as crianzas sobredotadas? Psicologia: Teoria, investigação e prática, 1, 171-188.
Petter, G. (2010), Ragione, fantasia, creatività nel bambino e nell'adolescente, Firenze, Giunti.
Pinto, G., Bombi, A. S., & Freeman, N. H. (1977) , L'emergere della raffigurazione del volto umano. Flessibilità rappresentativa e modalità esecutive. Età Evolutiva, 55, 82-88.
Prieto, M.D. , Lopez, O. Ferrandiz, C. (2003). La creatividad en el contexto escolar: estrategias para favorecerla. Madrid: Piramide.
Prieto, M.D., López, O., Bermejo, R. (1999) Ingenio, creatividad y superdotación. Murcia: Diego Marín.
Prieto, M.D.; Ferrando, M. Hernandez, D. & Sainz, M. (2010) Program to foster scientific and creative thinking. Founded by Fundación Seneca. (Unpublished)
Ribeiro, A. (1999). A imaginação na Pedagogia. Saber (e) Educar, 4, 11-17. Available in pdf: http://purl.net/esepf/handle/10000/214
Ribeiro, A., Lopes, A., & Pereira, F. (2001). Projecto CRIA-SE ou a criatividade na escola de todos os dias. Psicologia: Teoria, Investigação e Prática, 1, 227-243. Available in pdf: http://hdl.handle.net/10216/6666.

Rinaldi, C. (2009), Creatività come qualità di pensiero, in Rinaldi, C. (Eds.), In dialogo con Reggio Emilia: ricercare, ascoltare e apprendere: discorsi e interventi1984-2007, Reggio Emilia, Reggio Children, pp.136-144.

Rivas. F. (1978). Estudio psicométrico y dimensional de dos test cognitivos de creatividad. Innovación creadora, 7, pp. 40-55

Rocchi, P. (1998), Il bisogno di chiusura cognitiva e la creatività, Giornale Italiano di Psicologia, 1, 153-190.

Rodari, G. (1973), Grammatica della fantasia, Torino; Einaudi (Final Edition: Trieste, Einaudi EL, 2010).

Romo, M. (1997). Psicología de la creatividad. Ed. Paidós. Barcelona, 1997.

Romo, M. Alfonso Benlliure, V. y Sánchez Ruíz, M.J. (2008). TCI: Test de Creatividad Infantil. Madrid. TEA Ediciones.

Ruiz Gutierrez, S. (2010). Practica educativa y creatividad en educación infantil. Tesis doctoral. Universidad de Málaga. http://riuma.uma.es/xmlui/bitstream/handle/10630/4618/TD%20de%20Samuel%20Ruiz%20Gutierrez.pdf?sequence=1

Sánchez Corral, L. (1993) De la creatividad (lingüística) infantil: placer y trasgresión. Investigaciones y experiencias en educación infantil / coord. por María Dolores García Fernández, 1993, pp. 331-348.

Sanz de Acedo Lizarraga, M. L., y Sanz de Acedo Baquedano, M. T. (2007). La creatividad individual y grupal en la educación. Madrid: EIUNSA

Schoroškienė V. (2001). Kūrybiniai teksto darbai - svarbi pradinės mokyklos mokinių kūrybinių nuostatų ugdymo sąlyga: daktaro disertacija : Socialiniai mokslai, Edukologija. Vilnius

Sironi S. (2005), La creatività nelle rappresentazioni di insegnanti di scuola primaria, Imparare, 2, 63-78, www.ledonline.it/imparare

Stankevičienė K. (2002). Vaikų kūrybiškumo ugdymas F. Frėbelio, M. Montessori, R. Šteinerio pedagoginėse sistemose. Vilnius.

Tallandini, M. A., Varesano, E. (2003), Il processo produttivo nella rappresentazione grafica, Età Evolutiva, 76, 64-71.

Uusikylä, K. 2001. Lapsen luovuus elää vapaudessa. In S, Karppinen, A, Puurula & I, Ruokonen. 2001. Taiteen ja leikin luomous. Tampere: Tammer-Paino Oy, 14—22.

Uusikylä, K. 2005. Luova koulu, rokote kouluviihtymättömyyteen. In S, Karppinen, I, Ruokonen & K, Uusikylä. 2005. Taidon ja taiteen luova voima. Kirjoituksia 9—12-vuotiaiden lasten taito- ja taidekasvatuksesta. Tampere: Tammer-Paino Oy, 23—31.

Uusikylä, K. 2006. Hyvä paha opettaja. Jyväskylä: Gummerus Kirjapaino.

Uusikylä, K.2000. Voiko luovuutta opettaa? In P, Kansanen & K, Uusikylä (toim.). 2000. Luovuutta, motivaatiota, tunteita. Opetuksen tutkimuksen uusia suuntia. Jyväskylä: PS-kustannus, 42—55.

Vaikų darželių programa „Vėrinėlis" (1993). Vilnius.

# Part 2

# Thematic perspectives on creativity

# 2 Creativity and arts in pre-school education

*Linda Pavitola and Rasa Jautakyte*

Creativity in education is a topical issue in pre-school educational programmes, but it does not always tend to be experienced in children's lives. There is a lot of passive learning, and aspects of creativity often remain at a theoretical level without becoming a value for everyday life. Creativity is strongly influenced by culture – national and universal – the one that determines our understanding of the concept as well as the ways of creativity expression, and is seen as the core element for creative development. Culture is related to meanings, knowledge, talents and values, and is linked to the ability to think imaginatively or metaphorically, to challenge the conventional, and to call on the symbolic and affective to communicate (The impact of culture on creativity, 2009). Therefore, in the process of education more attention should be turned towards children – their intellectual potential, creativity and development, especially in the initial stage of lifelong learning. Early experiences in arts, including visual arts, dance, music making and song, are one of the most efficient means that fosters creative development, as they provide children with opportunities to respond to each other's creativity and explore boundless possibilities in imaginative, positive, dynamic and innovative ways. Bloomfield (2000) suggests that the nurturing of creativity arises from appropriate environment that is conducive to imaginative, sensitive and artistic development. Strength and confidence in teaching the arts is reflected in the ethos of the educational institution, especially where staff support each other and when they are provided with positive leadership.

The article reveals the essence of creativity and its characteristic features and expressions at pre-school age, as well as the significance of arts education.

## Understanding the concept of creativity

Creativity is a broad concept that is essential on both individual and societal levels, as well as in problem solving within different areas. On the individual level creativity is significant, for example, solving work and everyday life issues, as well as in the process of self-actualization, when fulfilling one's own potential. On the societal level creativity can influence and guide new scientific findings, discoveries, art styles and social programmes (Sternberg & Lubart, 1999).

There are several aspects in explaining the concept of creativity. Sternberg and Lubart (1999) characterize it as the ability to create a result that is innovative and socially significant. Novelty has often been mentioned as one of the most sufficient features of creativity. Grecov (2007) has emphasized that creativity is a totality of abilities, a complex of intellectual and personal characteristics, which also includes the person's attitude towards life.

There are some approaches towards understanding the concept of creativity that can be viewed as:

• Product – ability to create something new, unusual, original; characterized within different spheres by novelty and social significance,

• Process – particular diversity of creative thinking, highly developed thinking, esthetical world perception; characterized by creative intuition, rich fantasy, divergent thinking, inspiration, plasticity of psyche, activity of sub-consciousness, meta-consciousness,

• Personal characteristics – openness to new experience, independence, flexibility, dynamism, originality, singularity of a personality, anti-conformism, courage etc.,

• External conditions – ability to act productively in situations with a high level of uncertainty, when there are no algorithms for action known before that guarantee the preferable result (Elshout, 1996; Grecov, 2007).

These approaches are sufficient also in the process of pre-school education, where the main attention is given to the creative process itself, and not to the result (product), which depends on the characteristics of every person and the external conditions determined by a learning environment.

The awareness of intellectual preconditions of creativity is considered of great significance in the understanding of the concept creativity. Torrance (1988) believes that creativity has to be perceived as divergent or multisided thinking (oriented towards different directions), conceding diversity of searches that leads to unexpected findings. The process of creative thinking is characterized by the following abilities:

• to define and set up a problem;
• to generate many ideas simultaneously;
• to produce ideas of different concepts;
• to put forward uncommon, non-standard ideas;
• to improve the ideas put forward;
• to analyse and synthesize information for problem solving.

Also De Bono (2009) suggests using lateral thinking - a kind of thinking that helps to find a solution to apparently unsolvable problems, applying non-traditional elements and methods of thinking. Vertical (traditional) thinking proceeds by involvement processes of logics, in its turn, lateral (or creative) thinking disarranges the process of logical thinking, coming to a conclusion from another view point, thus making the self-organizing system of our brain alter the traditional thinking sequence.

Since traditional thinking emphasizes the correctness of every step in a problem-solving process, fear of mistakes becomes one of the obstacles in the creative search of new ways. In its turn, in the process of creative thinking the process itself is the most sufficient – not the correctness of every step, but rather how skilfully a person is able to discover diverse solutions that were not known before. The ideas have been evaluated not based on the criterions of "right - wrong", but by their functionality and possibilities to use them in different situations. The majority of learning tasks at school have been created in order to promote the development of traditional thinking. As a result of this, people are often able to solve a specific task, but they are helpless when facing problems in different life situations, because the solution demands a diversity of intellectual strategies. Here the necessity for creative thinking has been put forward (Sternberg & Lubart, 1999).

Creativity along with intellect, morality and physical development is a core value of a personality. The most sufficient characteristics of a creative personality are the following:

- willingness to take a risk,
- perseverance, dynamic progress and devotion to problem solution,
- curiosity,
- openness to new knowledge and experience,
- tolerance for uncertainty,
- wide scope of interests,
- high evaluation of originality,
- intuition and vigorous feelings,
- inner activity, ability to look at the problem "from a distance",
- independence of opinions,
- to orient oneself in novelty,
- logical thinking skills,
- visualization in imagination,
- ability to tear oneself away from restrictions, patterns, etc. (Elshout, 1996; Grecov, 2007).

It is important to be aware that a personality, who cannot be characterized as creative, feels comfortable in a situation of homeostasis – when the internal state is in balance with the outer environment, and there is no impulse to change it on one's own initiative. In the case of changes of the life situation, a person tries not to influence or change the situation, but to adapt to it. On the contrary, a creative personality does not try to be in continuous harmony with the outer environment, because she/he is rather willing to influence and change it actively, and not adapt passively to it. A creative personality feels comfortable in situations when there is no complete information and precise criteria for the activity available, but has an uncertain perspective of the development of events. Personalities with the tendency to express less creativity try to avoid such situations due to feelings of anxiety and discomfort (Grecov, 2007).

Thus creativity, as Grecov argues (2007), includes the following aspects:

• Intellectual pre-conditions for creative activity allowing creating something new, not known before, as well as the acquisition of knowledge and skills necessary for creating this new product.

• Personal characteristics allowing acting productively in uncertain situations, manifesting spontaneity and going beyond that can be foreseen in advance.

• "Meta-creativity" – a person's life position, that facilitates a refusal from patterns and stereotypes in decisions and activity, to perceive and create something new, change oneself and the world around, as well as highly evaluate personal freedom, activity and development.

Creative thinking is not a talent but a skill that can be acquired by anyone. Every child is born with creative potential and the age between three and five are the critical years for the development of creativity. Adults are often amazed by the unique ways in which children express their imagination but children usually need a teacher's support to find the means and the confidence to bring out their ideas. Since the processes that facilitate combinations of different variables for the solution of a problem are based on creativity, then knowledge and experience are also of great significance. Acquisition of basic knowledge and skills gives a possibility to use anyone's creative potential more effectively (De Bono, 2009; Gardner, 1993).

Significance of art education in fostering creativity at pre-school age

Although the philosophical foundation for art education is based on the belief that aesthetic and creative education is the entitlement of every child and that the nature and quality of the provision determines the distinctiveness of cultural life and academic performance, art philosophers, educators, and psychologists have been having regular discussions regarding why art education is necessary for all children (Bloomfield, 2000, p.1). The article shares the understanding that artistic experiences have been viewed as an exploratory process and not as a result of academic learning, and can be used as an excellent tool for enhancing creativity development in children.

Many researchers argue for the importance of the arts in children's education, showing that, since the beginning of history, humans have used their senses to create and interpret codes of representation which symbolize their experiences. They state that the purpose of education is to help children learn both to understand these codes of representation and to use them to "create their own meanings" (Eisner, 1994, p. 19). Also engagement has been recognized as an essential ingredient of the qualitative early childhood curriculum. The research shows that when children are engaged in experiences they demonstrate high levels of focus, intense mental activity and creativity (Laevers, 1996). Creative arts promote these forms of engagement, thus they have an essential role to play in the early childhood curriculum.

Outstanding philosophers – theoreticians of the 20th century, Read and Lowenfeld state that art is a way to educate personality, to foster its internal and external harmony, sensitivity, creativity, and individual expression by non-authoritarian means. In Read's view, education should follow the way of artistic creation. "When I talk of education, I think of an art process, the process of a child's self-creation" (1945, p. 23). Thus, both theoreticians emphasized a child's instinctive need to create, i.e. to transform creative energy into symbols. The symbolic expression is a child's self-expression reflecting a subjective personal world. Therefore, it is very important to create favourable conditions for a child's self-expression, for intuitive and spontaneous activity not regulated by rules, that allows everyone to find one's own way of creation. To quote theoreticians, everyone has the gift of creativity, however, rational intellect, stereotypical thinking, and lack of self-confidence suppresses creative impulses. The value of art activity lies in giving freedom to creative energy.

Authors of a cognitive theory of art education have a different view of children's early art creation. They state that a child is born into a cultural environment that uses significant symbols, therefore, from early childhood, he/she wants to understand them in order to be able to take part in that cultural environment. According to Arnold (1995), the need for self-expression has to be taken into account, however, the goal of education is different: to help a child acquire the knowledge and skills of art on the basis of which a child would provide self-expression with form and meaning. A similar idea was expressed by Lithuanian professor Gaižutis who stated that children have to be introduced to cultural traditions, taught the forms of art, and their creative abilities are to be developed, instead of just trusting " the miraculous power of free self-expression" (1988, p. 26).

As noted by Gardner and Davis, natural artistic development of a child is not systemic. At the age of two to five, a child observes and gets involved in activity, acquires the ability of symbolizing, and learns to create pre-notational symbols. The ability is revealed when a child makes sentences and stories, draws, models, plays role games, and composes and performs simple tunes. Artistic behaviour and inclinations are demonstrated till the age of seven. Later, a child's consciousness records increasingly more details of the environment and he starts to value precise representation. When he finally gets acquainted with symbols of notation – letters, numbers, and notes – he is charmed by their precision: to a child, they seem superior to polysemantic symbols in drawings. Moreover, a child starts to understand the views and values of other people and to pay attention to them. Regretfully, that has a negative impact on the child's creativity: the ability to notice and perceive aesthetical values increases, but the ability to produce creative works having the said values decreases. Therefore, the psychologist proposes interactive education at an early age. Effective art education needs education curricula, good creative teachers, and appropriate methods of assessment (1990).

In 1983, Gardner introduced the theory of multiple intelligences which expanded the idea of intelligence and included arts and musical intelligence. Therefore, once again, art was recognized as a significant part of a child's general education, but not as unnecessary decoration. Not only did Gardner single out autonomous musical intelligence from among the first seven, but he also stated that was the first intelligence to develop. An environment full of musical sounds and proper musical education has a positive impact on a child's musicality and on other fields of his intelligence: linguistic, spatial, kinaesthetic, social, and even mathematical abilities.

In Gardner's opinion, music was the only kind of art that, e.g., allowed for a 10-year-old child to come into contact with the genuine values of art, and under the influence of which the child could have emotional and intellectual experiences identical to those of an adult. In musical activities the inner reactions of the child rise to the peak of aesthetic experiences. Music helps the child to disclose his feelings, to express them, to re-live them. Aesthetic and spiritual experiences "encoded" in music help to shape the child's moral attitudes. Having "caught" the state of feelings, the child is encouraged by artistic values to take the position of inner observer; he empathises with the spiritual state of the lyrical hero. Musical education is based on feelings. According to the outstanding Hungarian researcher, composer and author of the musical education theory Kodaly (1974), the practice of music-making can elevate the child to experience and understand music. Music enables the perceiving person to adopt novel aesthetic and emotional information. The Estonian art sociologist Laidme states that the emotional impact of music is three times greater than that of literature, and five times greater than that of visual arts (Balčytis, 1990).

Music has always been a significant part of education theory and practice. From the time of Antiquity, musical education was related to intellectual, physical, and moral children's education. The world pedagogy presents different views of the proper age to start a child's musical education. Some scholars insist on the age of three, others, on the age of five. However, lately, the idea of early musical education justified by research has been spreading all over the world.

Music in the pre-school period should not merely enable the child to experience and enjoy music, but it should also help to develop child's music abilities and skills. Music activities present an independent form of expressing oneself in music; they encourage a linking for sound, playing, and movements. The level of expressing interest in music activities and the level of development of music abilities are closely linked with child's first experiences in music. For this reason it is important that children are offered a variety of musical experiences already in the pre-school period so that they can form a positive relationship towards music. (Denac, 2008).

As Niland (2007) noted music and storytelling have gone together throughout history. Many ancient cultures use music and dance to tell stories. As young children play together they often create narratives, talking in roles and becoming deeply engrossed in musical/artistic performance. Chants, snatches of song, sound effects and dance are also part of this socio-dramatic arts play. When adults read or tell stories, children respond eagerly to opportunities to be part of the story; they will be more engaged, and think more deeply and creatively, if given these opportunities.

One way to add a musical dimension to a picture book is to create sound effects and dramatic movement. Some picture books can very easily turn into songs. The reader can improvise a tune, perhaps adapted from a simple traditional children's song. Niland (2007) found that the children were most engaged with songs when they were able to respond in a playful way, and that one of their favourite ways of engaging playfully was to dramatize a story along with a song. A story can easily be created around songs about animals or transport.

Moog (1976) provides an extensive analysis of spontaneous songs as they emerge at different age levels during childhood. At ages 2-4, spontaneous singing dominated the musical activities of children. Moog identified three different forms – "imaginative", "narrative' and "pot-pourri" songs. Imaginative songs are spontaneous songs; they bore no resemblance to a known song, and were often hummed or sung to a single syllable. Narrative songs were sung monologues composed mainly of nonsense snatches for words and tunes, and occasionally included excerpts of learned songs. Pot-pourri songs were combinations of learned songs with mixed up words and melodies, and they might contain original improvisations.

Ch. van der Linde (2004) notes that play and movement are interconnected activities and important for the child's development. Play and music are important for the development of children's mental capacity and intellect. They also form the basis of language building. It is therefore very important that music and play should be included in the early childhood curriculum. Movement activity can be a powerful tool to promote children's creativity. Many early childhood educators recognize that children are competent to express themselves through movement activity and there are many movement components that can be used to develop creativity. Capel (1986) indicated that movement activities provide children with the opportunity to move and to create. Many research findings also support the view that motor development and creativity are interrelated and that one area of development connects to the other (Cleland & Gallahue, 1993; McBride, 1991).

Movement should encourage children to experience to discover and to learn by doing. Lloyd (1998) suggested that movement is a form of self-expression which uses the body movement to express ideas, minds and emotions. Gilbert (1992) also described creative movement as being a joyful way for children to explore movement and to stimulate imagination and promote creativity. Movement activity should allow children to use body actions to communicate an image, an idea or a feeling. Therefore, the activities should be designed to provide opportunity for children to use their own body movement to express and communicate.

Pica (2004) suggests that creative movement is an excellent medium for establishing a relationship between mind and body which is critical to unleashing creativity. Movement activity is concerned with expressive movement and it is important to give children practice and instruction necessary to refine their movement skills and expand their movement vocabularies. This aspect engages children in exploring movement skills relevant to the creative task, and through guided instruction allows them to grasp some basic movement skills and know how to use them.

Play and music create an imaginary world in which a child can master a myriad of skills and develop an understanding of his or her environment that would otherwise have been impossible. Play and music can also stimulate a small child's creativity, and small children often make up their own musical instruments while they are playing. For example, a large box may become a drum, a tin may be used as a banjo, a pot could be tapped rhythmically with a stick (Maxim, 1989).

Children's creativity could be developed by letting them move in the way the music makes them feel. Making up the new words for a song by the teacher and the pupils could contribute to pupils' enjoyment and creativity (Maxim, 1989).

Music is a natural and important part of young children's education and has a huge impact on their development. Children's early contacts with music make a positive impact on the quality of their lives. Early musical education is one of the most acceptable manifestations of a child's development. A universally positive education, being holistic in spiritual, psycho-physiological, and social communication aspects; it encourages harmonious development and creativity of a personality.

## Teachers as promoters of children's creative self-expression

Maslow considers the person's need for self-actualization as a driving force of creativity, thus the necessity for creative self-expression is a sufficient need of a personality. These personalities have a heightened disposition to self-realization and manifestation of creativity (Hibnere, 2000; Maslow, 1997). Creative expressions are closely connected with emotional factors, features of interpersonal relations and motivating atmosphere, which promote the expression of creative abilities. It is influenced also by competence, motivation, emotions of the individual and by the environment. The individual can possess all the inner resources to think creatively, but without environmental support his/her creativity cannot be manifested. Therefore, the attention should be turned to the environment that stimulates creative activity, and teachers' support - facilitating the genesis of children's ideas and individual achievement and providing the foundation for a lifelong interest and participation in the arts - is one of the most significant factors in promoting creativity in children. In its turn, facilitating creativity in a particular sphere, is thus manifest also within other kinds of activities. The task of the pedagogue is to help children to become aware of their inner resources, in order to promote their creativity (Downing, 1997; Grecov, 2000).

If children are only instructed to follow adult instruction and imitate adult symbols and conceptualizations, they merely learn to re-produce; and such activities rarely involve creativity. The methodologies like "repeat after me", didactic instruction and mimetic response deny children the opportunity to explore from multiple perspectives. Children must be encouraged to extend beyond the comfortable – as relying on what they already know does not usually lead to discovery. Teachers should engage children in activities that are personally relevant and based on their interests and concerns. Only then can imaginative and creative thinking emerge, which has to be an objective of teaching (Freedman, 2006; Smilan, 2007).

Being a pedagogue also demands creativity, since the ability to loosen the creative potential of children is possessed only by creative teachers with creative thinking, a pedagogical call and love towards children. Thus, there is a necessity to get to know the means to develop a process of education that is motivating for both children and pedagogues. It is believed that personality self-actualization is a professional necessity for teachers.

As stated by Downing (1997), the educational environment should be created in a way every person could reveal his/her creative potential. In their turn, the teachers have to be aware of three steps in applying the creative approach to an education process: 1) to understand the essence of creativity, 2) to develop creativity in themselves and 3) to use teaching and learning strategies that promote creativity in children. Therefore, those who teach for creativity, innovation and divergent response, must have a comfort level in creativity and innovation. As Smilan (2007) believes, didactic instruction towards convergent response does not lead to re-discovery, renewal and motivation to learn.

One of the most important ways of becoming a creative teacher is the use of art, as it can assist in a natural way and encourage children to use their imagination in astounding ways, because art encourages thoughtful attention to discover what it has to show and tell. Freedman (2006) has emphasized the need to teach creativity less as therapeutic self-expression and more as the development of cultural identity. Helping individual children to "draw out" their perceptions and then supporting them as they attempt to crystallise ideas within a symbolic art statement is the teacher's role. Also art connects to social and personal dimensions of life in powerful affective ways (Bloomfield, 2000).

Children have a natural enthusiasm for the arts as major and valid sources of knowledge. Art education in and through the arts is based upon the level of understanding, knowledge and skills that are acquired by children and which they experience in an imaginative and creative way. A special, dynamic and sensitive relationship exists between what the teacher knows, how the teacher provides an appropriate learning environment, and how the child responds to what is taught.

The application of the principles of good practice in teaching the arts means that teachers will demonstrate in the classroom the relationship of educational theory and teaching practice by a clear understanding of what is intended and why. Judgements about technical aspects of specific art forms and ongoing decision-making reflect the understanding of the child's relationship between skill acquisition and how they were used in the art making process. The following key areas will be covered in a reflexive way:

• A balance in the relationship between teaching technique and creativity;

• A clear definition of the teacher's role as facilitator of the arts using creative teaching approaches that offer security to children;

• A clear definition of the child's role in experiencing the arts in relation to peers/teacher and received works;

• An effective use of resources and materials by teachers and children.

Teaching through arts recognizes the importance of each individual and the teaching approaches take account children's wide-ranging abilities, especially in relation to the acquisition of skills where some children may encounter difficulties while others display special gifts. The arts are the means of exploring multiple perspectives, developing creative sensibilities and breaking down the formal boundaries of achievement and under-achievement in tested academic areas, since all children are empowered by the use of their imagination and the ability to express themselves emotionally through the arts, often achieving sensitivity and poignancy in their work. The knowledge, skills and understanding of the arts programme is accessible to all and promotes individual challenge, development and achievement (Bloomfield, 2000; Smilan, 2007).

## Conclusions

Creative work grows out of each individual arts discipline and its combination with another. The experience children acquire in different contexts can become the illustrative content of their dances, musical compositions, paintings, sculptures or dramatizations. Thus, children's learning takes on a holistic dimension that brings unity and order to their lives, as it draws upon and develops interrelationships of the various forms of children's innate intelligence by awakening linguistic, mathematical, spatial, kinaesthetic and musical modes. It also extends children's creative insights by combining ideas or encouraging them to interpret information in new ways. This permits individual children to conceptualize and understand by using their strength areas to compensate or overcome weaknesses in other areas. It also has the impact of motivating children, sustaining their interest and improving their self-esteem. It provides in-depth study and develops all-round skills (Bloomfield, 2000). The same important aspects of using arts in pre-school is emphasized by Penny Egan , who believes that with so many subjects requiring "right" answers, only the sphere of arts is the one, which allows children to be experimental and creative.

## References

Arnold, P. J. (1995). Objectivity, Expression and Communication in Dance as a performing Art. The Journal of Aesthetic Education. Vol. 29 (1). 61-68.

Balčytis E. (1990). Tauta, muzika, mokykla. Kultūros barai Nr. 1. Vilnius.

Bloomfield A., & Childs J. (2000). Teaching Integrated Arts in the Primary School: Dance, Drama, Music and the Visual Arts. NY: David Fulton Publishers.

Bridges, D. (1994). Music, young children and you: A parent/ teacher guide to music for 0 – 5 year olds. Sydney: Hale & Iremonger.

Capel, S. (1986). Educational gymnastics meeting physical education goals. Journal of Education, Recreation and Dance, 57(2), 34-38.

Cheung, R. H. P. (2010). Designing movement activities to develop children's creativity in early childhood education. Early Child Development and Care. Vol. 180. No. 3, 377-385.

Cleland F. E., & Gallahue, D. L. (1993). Young children's divergent movement ability. Study 1. Perceptual and Motor Skills, 77, 535-547.

De Bono, E. (2009). Lateral Thinking: a textbook of creativity. London: Penguin Books Ltd.

Denac, O. (2008). A case study of pre-school musical interests at home and at school. Early Childhood Education Journal. Vol. 35, No. 1. , pp 439-444.

Downing, J.P. (1997). Creative teaching: ideas to boost student interest.

Englewood, CO: Teacher Ideas Press.

Edwards, C. P., & Springate, K. W. (1995). The Lion Comes Out of the Stone: Helping Young Children Achieve Their Creative Potential. Dimensions of Early Childhood 23 (4, Fall): 24-29.

Eisner, E. W. (2002). The Arts and the Creation of Mind. New Haven and London. New Haven, CT: Yale University Press.

Eisner, E. W. (1994). Cognition and curriculum reconsidered. New York: Teachers College Press.

Elshout J. (1996). Creativity. In E. De Corte & F.E. Weinert (Ed.). International Encyclopedia of Developmental and Instructional Psychology (pp. 391-393). Oxford, UK: Pergamon.

Freedman, K. (2006). Leading creativity: responding to policy in art education. Retrieved from http://portal.unesco.org/culture/en/files/29857/11386135391kerry_freed man.htm/kerry_freedman.htm

Gaižutis, A. (1988). Vaikystė ir grožis. Vilnius: Šviesa.

Gardner, H. (1990). Art Education and Human Development. California, Los Angeles: Getty Publications.

Gardner, H. (1993).Frames of Mind: the Theory of Multiple Intelligences. New York: Basic Books.

Gilbert, A. G. (1992). Creative dance for all ages: A conceptual approach. Reston VA: American Alliance for Health, Physical Education, Recreation and Dance.

Hibnere V., Grasmane L. (2000). Bērna vizuālā darbība [Visual activities of a child]. 2.daļa. Rīga: RaKa.

Kodaly Z. (1974). Music in the Kindergarten. The Sellected Writtings of Zoltan Kodaly. London: New York: Boosey & Hawkes.

Laevers, F. (Ed) (1996). The Leuven involvement scale for young children LIS-YC manual. Experimental Education Series, No. 1. , pp 53-68.

Linde Ch. (1999). The relationship between play and music in early childhood: educational insights. Education, Vol. 119, N. 4. , pp 610-615.

Lloyd, M. L. (1998). Adventures in Creative movement activities: a guide for teaching. Dubuque, Iowa: Eddie Bowers.

Lorenzo-Lasa, R., Ideishi, R. I, & Ideishi, S.K. (2007). Facilitating Pre-school learning and movement through Dance. Early Childhood Education Journal, Vol. 35, No. 1. , pp 25-31.

Lowenfeld, V., & Brittain W. L. (1957). Creative and Mental Growth. New York: Macmillan.

Maxim, G. M. (1989). The very young: Guiding children from infancy through the early years. Third edition. London: Merrill.

Mang, E. (2005). The referent of children's early songs. Music education research. Vol. 7, N 1., pp 3-20.

Moog, H. (1976). The musical experience of the pre-school child. London:

B. Schott.

McBride, R. E. (1991). Critical thinking an overview with implications for physical education. Journal of Teaching in Physical Education, 11, 111-125.

Niland A. (2007). Musical stories: Strategies for integrating literature and music for young children. Australian Journal of Early Childhood. Vol. 32, n. 4, pp7-11.

Pica, R. (2004). Experiences in movement: Birth to age eight (3rd ed.) Clifton Park NY: Thomson Delmar Learning.

Read, H. (1945). Education through Art. New York: Pantheon.

Sharp, C., & Le Métais, J. (2000). The Arts, Creativity and Cultural Education: An International Perspective. London: Qualifications and Curriculum Authority, ISBN 1 85838 463 X

Smilan C., (2007). The creative art of education. International Journal of Social and Human Sciences I, 399-406.

Sternberg J. R., & Lubart, I. T. (1999). The Concept of Creativity: Prospects and Paradigms. In R. J. Sternberg (Ed.), Handbook of Creativity (pp. 3-16). Cambridge: Cambridge University Press, ISBN 0 521 57604 0.

The impact of culture on creativity (2009). A Study prepared for the European Commission (Directorate-General for Education and Culture). KEA European affairs. Retrieved from http://ec.europa.eu/culture/documents/study_impact_cult_creativity_06_09.pdf

Torrance E.P. (1988). The nature of creativity as manifestion of its testing. In R.J.Sternberg (Ed.). The nature of creativity (pp. 43-75). Cambridge, England: Cambridge University Press.

Грецов, А. Г. (2007). Тренинг креативности для старшеклассников и студентов. СПб.: Питер.

Маслоу, А. (1997). Психология бытия. М.: Рефл-бук.

# 3 Creativity and scientific thinking
*Roberta Cardarello*

Recent international research has thematised the relationship between creative and scientific thinking, according to two perspectives which will be illustrated here. Reported below for the purpose of the CREANET Research are those aspects which seem most relevant in supporting education of creativity in childhood.

Creativity, Teaching and Science.
The first perspective connects creativity to the teaching/learning of scientific disciplines, both in school and in extra scholastic environments, for which students' results are considered to be unsatisfactory. Scientific learning is considered crucial both in terms of scientific knowledge and concepts and most of all, in terms of attitude and research procedures within science. From this point of view, many authors suggest modernising science teaching by turning to the adoption of tools such as art, music, drama and play intended as the expression of human creativity. These tools stress the importance of imaginative, inventive-functional ability which is self-expressive and suggestive (e.g. understand in a dramatized form the representation of celestial bodies/stellar constellations). A line of research which crosses this position is focused in particular on creative teaching in various areas including the scientific. Traditional teaching, based on the systematic illustration of phenomena and on abstract study is offset by articulated teaching, which includes students' practicality, their 'exposure' to real phenomena and the simulation of solutions to concrete scientific problems. This perspective, which may be summed up as 'laboratory style teaching' is of interest to creativity in two ways: on the one hand it emphasizes innovation and the educational devices invented by the teachers ( new tools, new procedures, the many forms of collaborative learning); on the other hand it means creativity as exercised by the students as a form of problem-solving, investigative practice and of inductive learning of knowledge and concepts (Shanahan & Nieswandt 2009, Kind &Kind 2007, Pramling 2010, Alberts 2010, Craft 2001, De Hann 2009).

**Creativity and personality traits of the scientist.**
A second perspective however, investigates the analogies between scientific and creative thinking, and concentrates on the mental processes required by scientific practice itself. This sector is often based on the

documentation of scientific discoveries derived from the history of science (Ward 2007). This second line represents the focus of the present contribution of the CREANET Project. Indeed, the idea is to contribute to a better and more complete definition of the creative process by highlighting similarities with scientists' thinking. It is also hoped that such a connection favours a perception of creativity as a process which regards both child and adult, in a spirit of continuity, both of development and of education. The first element of interest which comes from research on scientific thinking is the following. Assuming the definition of creativity as the invention of an entity which has the double characteristic of being both new and adequate to the problem (or context), according to the well-known definition (Sternberg&Lubart 1999; Plucker BeghettoDow, 2004,p.90) similarities are recognized with scientific discovery that indicate an invention (or a solution) that is both new and pertinent to a given problem. This first aspect which is at times underestimated, avoids the risk of 'thinking of creativity' as a demonstration of mere fantasy, of pure imagination, indifferent to its ends. One difference is however, understood: the novelty of a solution/product - which in science is absolute - within the ordinary dynamic is however relative to the protagonist, without whom the classification of creativity would be compromised (Chiu 1999). This fact means that we can talk of anew creative invention when it is new for the agent: for a child an idea and /or an action that is not absolutely new can be creative without the fact or idea necessarily losing its characteristics. The second element of importance comes from those scholars who are dedicated to the research of the psychology of the scientist, and in particular from Feist who, in 2006, opened up the branch of psychology known as psychology of science. Following empirical research they have documented the characteristics of creative scientists or of those who have established themselves in their respective fields of research. Such scientists stand out, from the cognitive point of view, for ' their openness,' their interest in the new, their flexibility, and tolerance of ambiguity" and from an emotional view point for being " enthusiastic, ambitious, intrinsically motivated" (2011, p. 298-299). In other words, in the definition of Feist's scientist, some characteristics are recognizable as defining the creative individual tout court. Through specific behaviours a better picture of the creative individual appears, but they do not yet reach the processes that sustain creative thinking.

By following other authors relevant in international literature, other elements for describing the creative scientist are found, particularly the traits of an imaginative individual immersed in their work. The scientist who makes an innovation or a creative discovery is primarily competent in his field and is dedicated to the research activity with great effort and is totally absorbed, also shows the combination of imagination and logical reasoning, according to the lessons of Schwartz and Simonton (Kind&Kind, 2007, p.12; Jalongo Hirsch, 2012). One should dwell on these characteristics. The first two are obviously unanimously pointed out as conditions of scientific discovery, but it would not be difficult to track them down also in tasks in which a musician or painter produces new products and new creations. Innovation, in fact, is not collocated in a cognitive void: Picasso knew the representative norms of his time and the techniques used, just as the scientist knows theories that 'explain' a phenomenon even when inventing alternative hypotheses that undermines that theory or brings about a scientific revolution. The availability of conceptual tools of that field of knowledge is implicit in the explanation of scientific creativity. Similarly for a child, even if their system of knowledge is less articulated and rich, creativity will be exerted by using what he knows and understands. Secondly, their total absorption in the task alludes to a condition implicated not only in scientific discovery, but in all self-motivated activities, as happens for example, to children in play and in problem solving activities (Jalongo Hirsch, 2012 p. 92). Better again, the absorption in a task is all the more likely as it challenges the subject but with a certain level of accessibility. These are the type of tasks that are intrinsically motivating according to Deci (1975), that are collocated at the right level of newness and ease for the agent. It is not difficult to recognize that this condition also has an effect on childhood and characterizes the individuals who dedicate themselves with self-motivated enthusiasm to a task, as also seen in 2 and 3 year old children (Cardarello, Mazza 1982, Lumbelli 1982).

However, the most important data for us, from an educational view point, are not so much the elements of 'personality' detected in the creative individual, that bring us back to the old and inert assumption that certain people are more creative than others, but rather, the mental processes that underlie those performances and accompany them. In fact, if education and school can act effectively to foster creativity, such an action, once again, promotes the contexts in which the processes which nurture creativity (or, in Guilford's words, divergent thinking) are favoured. Thus, exactly in reference to scientists' creative thinking, relevant indications emerge.

The richest approach in such a perspective is the cognitive approach, exactly due to research and analytical descriptions of the mental processes that contribute to its perspective. To this end, it is useful to point out that cognitive models of explanation of intellectual events do not ignore the affective-emotive dimension. In fact, many studies signal the conditions of psychological well-being, or , at least of normal serenity, as the most favourable to cognitive/ solving engagement, whereas depressive states are hostile to creative manifestation: this is based both on investigations   in neuroscience (Leung et al 2008, p.176) and on auto-analytical studies (Baas, De Dreu, Nijstad 2008).

These elements alone would be sufficient to highlight the useful conditions for the activation of creative processes: facilitate the total absorption of the task, that is put a child in the conditions to dedicate themselves to a task or activity in which they can put into play what they know and give them every opportunity and time needed to become absorbed in the task. The data recorded on the emotional conditions of well-being reiterate, if there was ever a need, the necessity of an essential scholastic context which is calm and soothing as a condition for not hindering creativity.

**Science as a process**
Studies on Creativity, like those designed to strengthen scientific teaching, stress the importance of removing a stereotypical representation of science as a mere system of enunciations and rules that explain classes of phenomena. Science is first and foremost a process of continual research, testing, construction and discovery. Such a process is fuelled by the often routine, constant application of knowledge and rules, and of consolidated and convergent procedures, but certainly also of invention, continuous innovation and discovery, which require creative thinking. But it is exactly this noted and innovative dynamic that stresses that scientific discovery implies the adequacy of invention to problems and to the body of consolidated knowledge. It is obvious that the scientist has the solid and articulated knowledge of his field of knowledge, but also that he adopts a way of thinking which implies posing a problem, formulating hypotheses and making repeated tests. Moreover, this is the logic of enquiry. Up to this point this is concerned with normal problem-solving activity. However, are there circumstances in which the solution to the problem is creative? The answer can be positive on the basis of results, i.e. the product: the solution is creative because it is new or innovative compared to the past. However, the interest in the promotion of creativity in childhood, which is at the centre of our argument leads us to ask if that same creativity of the adult scientist has antecedents in thinking and activity in the early years (or childhood) and most of all if we can recognize them and cultivate them in children without altering the childhood dimension. From this point of view the product made by the children cannot be compared to the product of the adult expert. So, the similarity that is recognized between the creativity of the child and of the scientist is of a kind, or rather of two types. There is an analogy of attitude/emotion that can be summed up in the idea of motivated activity (or intrinsically motivated) and in the behaviour that is

generated, and there is an analogy of procedure of thinking, that regards mental processes. The first analogy regards the condition in which the agent is found, one who has to face/resolve a problem and is dedicated intensely to that activity. This attitude is shared by the scientist but also by the artist intent on creating one of his works. The nature of the problem to be solved undoubtedly has different characteristics in the artist, the scientist and the child, but the concentration on the task will be intense in all of the cases.

## Attitude of inquiry and problem solving

In other words the first analogy between creative activity of the child and that of the scientist lies in the common attitude of inquiry, or of research. In this case, scientific inquiry finds a parallel with all human activities guided by the active research of a solution to a problem. This investigative attitude animates the child not only when they explore objects or natural phenomena, contexts that are closer to the natural sciences, but in many activities: from constructive activities to artistic and play based activities, when he is dedicated to them in pursuing the solution to a problem, or the pursuit of a goal (Jalongo Hirsch 2012, p. 98). The indications for a promotional educational context are clear and precise. Creative thinking can be expressed by tasks and contexts that foster inquiry, therefore, in the presence of questions posed autonomously by children, or else posed by adults, but in such a way as to be shared by the children themselves. Real questions, to which they actively seek answers. This means that those who envisage only one correct answer do not induce a genuine procedure of inquiry, and not even pseudo questions, that is, those to which the adult knows how to respond. They are therefore questions which expect a variety of answers and trigger a prolonged research process. Naturally it is always possible that a child provides creative answers even in the presence of closed questions and that they therefore invent new solutions (new at least for themselves and their classmates). Such a condition is similar to that theorized by Gestalt and defined as productive thinking ( the case of different ways in which it is possible to estimate the area of a geometric shape implies the possibility of some to find unexpected procedures going beyond a known rule (Wertheimer 1959). But this is not the most favourable structural condition, if, as we repeat, it concerns setting up activities which, as such, are open to a number of answers or interpretations.

But, as we said, the analysis of activated thinking processes is equally interesting and can provide even more productive indications for the promotion of creative thinking. In the activity of problem solving the scientist formulates hypotheses and looks for evidence for and against such hypotheses (Eshach, Fried 2005, p.320, Kind and Kind 2007, Zoller 2011), but for such a process of inquiry he does not turn only to logical thinking, guided by scientific categories and theoretical knowledge, but also to the imagination (Feist 2011, Runco et al. 2011, Anonietti et al. 2011) that represents a central component of creativity.

### The processes: imagination and combined thinking.

Certainly, imagination is the most widely included process in the definitions both of scientific and creative thinking, intended as the ability to represent fictional worlds guided by rules. Imagination is implicated in possibility thinking that is typically expressed in children's pretending games (Craft et al. 2012, p.49) if we intend it as the ability to figure out, that is to mentally anticipate, what is not yet there, or what does not exist (Craft et al., 2012). Indeed, if imagining means producing in the mind objects that do not exist, or that are not present, two macro conditions can be given. One when we imagine an object that is not present but that has been experienced, and we call this reproductive imagination (Kind Kind 2007, p. 22), the other when we mentally produce a non-existing object, which is therefore completely 'new' and which would be the real and proper creative imagination that uses and combines 'multiple memories of external objects" (Kind Kind 2007, p.22). Even from the point of view of the imagination process that definition of a 'combinatory art' of experiences that Vigotsky has already lucidly theorized, and which cognitive psychologists stress when they analyse mental production processes. For example, from Kind's definition, of imagination as a combination of multiple memories of external objects,a significant step in recognizing the mental processes of creativity emerges, which helps us describe the conditions useful to its promotion (Ward 2007). If the inclusive and eclectic model of Antonietti at al. is adopted (Antonietti et al., 2011) that is defined WCR, we can describe the three principle processes in action in creative behaviour and retrace the passages of imagination itself. In the first place a widening of the mental field is noted, which is even expressed as the production of numerous ideas, the fluidity of thought ( present in Guilford and Torrance), implies calling to mind (from long term memory) other fields or domains with respect to the present one. Secondly, the connection (combining) of knowledge coming from different explored fields, a translation of structures, concepts and configurations from one universe to another; and finally, their reorganization in a new set (restructuring), that can coincide, for the scientist, with the new solution. The three processes, typical of creative production, can be traced precisely in scientific discovery, from Darwin to Fleming, from Maxwell to Leonardo da Vinci (ibid p. 82 and 83). It is exactly this activation of these processes that brings together the scientist and the child.


## Tools for thinking creatively

If we identify those just indicated as the basic processes for creative production, we can note that they intervene spontaneously and jointly in a number of circumstances even in children. The field of application is not exclusively that of invention or scientific discovery: these processes are applied to contexts in daily life, to contexts of play, to contexts of construction. In all cases children set up a process for facing 'their problem' or producing an object and they resolve it in a new way. Multiple examples of creative childhood behaviour, identified in literature (Petter 2010, Esach Fried 2005, etc) can be read precisely through the action of the processes of collecting broad ideas, the combination of differing domains and the restructuring of the object and /or the action. The well-known technique of brain storming, that implies in a first phase the free association of thoughts and intuition (without any censorship) to a given context (DeHann 2009, Mirzaie et al, 2009, p. 83) sustains precisely the activity of the mind that is stretched in a thousand directions in the search for multiple associations. In terms of process this means exploring "different conceptual trees" (Chiu 1999, p.5).Some more precise tools of thought have been identified as characteristic of the creative imagination of the scientist, namely the analogy (Chiu 1999, p.8 and. Kind & Kind 2007, Jalongo Hirsch 2012, Pramling 2010, Feist 2011), metaphor (Cameron 2002, Gibbs 2011, Pramling 2010), and visualization of concepts (Chi 1997, Feist 2011, p. 299.301). In this sense there are many examples in the history of science: among others, Faraday, Lavoisier, Maxwell.

"Analogy has traditionally been viewed as a powerful engine of discovery, for the scientist, the mathematician, the artist, and the child" (Feist, ibid, p.299)

What is analogy if not the recognition of similarities between radically different objects? And metaphor? If not an innovative and unusual relation between a topic and a vehicle that belong to trees of different categories (Contini, 2012). They express the underlying processes of the combination of different fields and jump from one tree to another in view of a reorganization of the data available (Gibbs 2011).

"A label which together with others constitutes a model is actually detached from the original realm of that model, and is applied to categorize and organize an unknown realm" (Goodman 1968, from the Italian translation p. 69). To speak therefore of the sadness of a painting means transferring not a single predicate, but an entire conceptual network; it means operating, in other words, a categorical transgression (Contini 2012, p.152).

## Playing with analogies and metaphors

We can ask ourselves., therefore, how to encourage the conceptual leaps from one ontological tree to another (Chiu 1999) and we can respond that this is encouraged by explicit invitation to thinking by analogy, to look for similarities where they seem improbable, to visualize ideas, which for small children can not necessarily be abstract but empirically concrete concepts.

In general one can act in favour of creativity by making children experience these conceptual leaps: this means giving them the opportunity to see how others have overcome the barriers (e.g. by representation) and therefore widen the range of their knowledge and the combined possibilities. We are thinking of innovative artistic representation in which it is easy even for small children to recognize the violation of the representative norms given by the combination of different codes, most of all when that means leaping from one conceptual tree to another. "Little blue and Little Yellow", a classic of children's literature is a good example of an experience of the 'play' of analogy, or rather, of the visual metaphor. All other synesthetic transformations are of this kind, such as bodily expression of a piece of music, or a drawing.

Secondly, and to a greater extent, is the direct experience of the production of analogy, metaphor and visualizations that calls for the ability of imagining and of assuming a creative posture. We can detect signals even in non-scientific contexts, such as in constructive play in early childhood, but the process of generating ideas and of their combination remains the same. We find traces in pretending games when a little girl, in pre-school, in attempting to enter a playhouse occupied by three classmates who refuse to widen participation to anyone, turns to the strategy of pretending to be an 'old woman from a fairy tale who is looking for shelter (Gariboldi 2012, p. 130): in this case, recourse to the conceptual tree of the fairy tale is used as the solution to a problem based on social relations. Traces are found once again in a pre-school, in whose garden a flower bed for butterflies is made. After having identified an area for the flower bed the children decide to outline it and fence it off with a palisade. The construction of the fence from available material gives to the alignment of a long series of mineral water bottles that look like the poles of a fence. In this case the new configuration assumed by the bottles renders them similar to the desired object (Balzani 2012, p.250).

## Conclusions

The analysis of scientific and creative thinking, ultimately seems relevant because:

-they help to better define the outline of creative thinking.

-they consciously expand the boundaries of early childhood creativity and ward off the risks of reducing it to mere artistic and expressive demonstration.

In conclusion it seems that the aforementioned characteristics of the creative scientist; expertise in their sector, absorbing effort, imagination, logical reasoning - can really be recognized in children intent on a productive activity and typically in play when it is concerned with real and self-motivated play. Moreover, the mixture of logical thinking and imagination finds fertile ground in the numerous activities of childhood. We have attempted to demonstrate the specific nature of the implied thought processes - from WCR to analogies and metaphor - because only knowledge of the implied cognitive process can help adults to promptly recognize the creative processes in the most diverse contexts of activity and to promote them to all children.

## References

Alberts R. (2010), Discovering science through art-based activities, Learning Disabilities, 2,
   79-80.

Antonietti A., Colombo B. , Pizzingrilli P. (2011) , The WCR Model of Creativity. From Concept to Application, The Open Education Journal, 2011, 4, (Suppl 1:M7) 80-89.

Baas M., De Dreu C. K. W., Nijstad B. A. (2008) , A meta-analysis of 25 years of mood-creativity research: Hedonic tone, activation, or regulatory focus? Psychological Bulletin, Vol. 134(6), 2008, pp. 779-806.

Balzani V. (2012), Forlì, una città mezza grande e mezza piccola, in A. Gariboldi, R. Cardarello (eds), Pensare la creatività. Junior, Bergamo, pp. 239-243.

Cameron L. (2002), Metaphors in the Learning of Science: a discourse focus, British Educational Research Journal, vol. 28, n. 5, pp.673- 688.

Cardarello R., Mazza E. (1982), "Novità e motivazione intrinseca", in L. Lumbelli (a cura di), La novità come risorsa educativa, Franco Angeli, Milano, pp.19- 41.

Chi M. T. H (1997), Creativity: shifting across ontological categories flexibility, in T. Ward et al., Creative thought, Washington D-C., American Psychological Association

Chi, M.-H. (1999). Creativity, conceptual revolution, and science learning, in Proceedings for the First Conference on Science Education in Taiwan and Japan. Tokyo, Japan: [s.n.],

Chiu M. (1999), Creativity, Conceptual revolution, and Science Learning, Tokyo, 16-17/ 11.

Contini A. (2012), La metafora come strumento cognitivo, in R. Cardarello A. Contini (eds), Parole immagini metafore. Per una didattica della comprensione, Junior, Bergamo, 147-177.

Craft A., (2001), An analysis of research and literature on Creativity In in Education, www.euvonal.hu/images/creativity_report.pdf

Craft A., Mcconnon L., Matthews A. (2012), Child-initiated play and professional creativity: enabling four-years-olds' possibility thinking, Thinking Skills and Creativity, 7, 48-61.

Deci E. L. (1975), Intrinsic motivation, Plenum Press, New York.

Dehann R. (2009), "Teaching creativity and inventive problem solving in science", in Life science education, 8, 172-181.

Diakidoy I. A., Kanari E. (1999), "Student Teachers' Beliefs about Creativity", in British Educational Research Journal, n. 25, pp. 225-243.

Eshach H., Fried M. (2005), Should Science be Taught in Early Childhood? Journal of Science Education and Technology, vol. 14, n.3, pp. 315-336.

Feist G.J. , (2011, Creativity in Science, in S.R. Pritzker, M.A. Runco (eds), Encyclopedia of Creativity, Elsevier , pp. 296-302.

Gariboldi A. (2012), Creatività e problem solving, in A. Gariboldi, R. Cardarello (eds), Pensare la creatività, Junior, Bergamo, pp. 133-145.

Gibbs R.W.Jr (2011), Metaphors, in S.R. Pritzker, M.A. Runco (eds), Encyclopedia of Creativity, Elsevier, pp. 113-119.

Guilford, J.P. (1950), Creativity, in American Psychologist, 5, pp. 444-454.

Jalongo M. R., Hirsch R. A. (2012), Reconceptualizing creative thought processes in young children, in Olivia N. Saracho (ed), Contemporary perspectives on Research in Creativity in Early Childhood Education, Information Age Publishing, Charlotte (USA), pp. 89-105.

Leung A. K., Maddux W.W., Galinsky A.D., Chiu C. (2008), Multicultural Experience Enhances Creativity. The when and the how, American Psychologist, Vol. 63, No. 3, pp. 169–181.

Lumbelli L. (1982) (ed.),La novità come risorsa educativa, Franco Angeli, Milano.

Kind P. M., Kind V. (2007), Creativity in Science Education: perspectives and Challenges for Developing School Science, Studies in Science Education, 43, pp.1-37.

Mirzaie R.A., Hamidi F., Anaraki A. (2009), A Study on the Effect of Science Activities on Fostering Creativity in Pre-school Children, in Journal of Turkish Science Education , vol. 6, n. 3, pp. 81- 90.

Petter G. (2010), Ragione, fantasia, creatività nel bambino e nell'adolescente, Giunti, Firenze.

Plucker J.A., Waitman G. R. Hartley K. A. (2011), Education and Creativity, in S.R. Pritzker, M.A. Runco (a cura di), Encyclopedia of

Creativity, Elzevier,  pp. 435-440.

Plucker JA, Beghetto RA, Dow G.T. (2004), Why isn't creativity more important to educational psychologists? Potentials, pitfalls, and future directions in creativity research, Educational Psychologist, 39, pp. 83–96.

Pramling N. (2010), Unearthing Metaphors: Figurativeness in Teacher-Child Talk about Soil and Related Matters, Early Childhood Educ Journal, 38, pp. 57–64

Runco M.A., Cayirdag  N., Acar S.( 2011), Quantitative research on creativity, in P. Thompson and J. Sefton-Green (eds), Researching Creative Learning. Methods and issues, Routledge, London and New York, pp. 153-171.

Shanahan MB., Nieswandt M. (2009), Creative activities and their influence on identification in science: three case studies, Journal of Elementary Science Education, Vol. 21, No. 3, pp. 63-79.

Schmidt A.L. (2011), Creativity in Science: Tensions between Perception and Practice, Creative Education, vol.2, n. 5, pp. 435-445.

Sternberg R. J., Lubart T. I. (1999), "The concept of creativity: Prospects and paradigms", in R. J. Sternberg (Ed), Handbook of creativity, Cambridge University Press, New York, pp. 3-15.

Ward T(2007) , Creative cognition as a window on creativity, "Methods", 42, pp. 28-37.

Zoller U. (2011), Science and technology education in the STES context in primary schools: what should it take? Science education technology, 20, pp. 444-453.

Wertheimer, M. (1945), Productive Thinking. New York: Harper.

# 4 Early years' creativity

*Mercedes Ferrando and Carmen Ferrándiz*

"Creative potential may appear in different forms in children of different ages. It becomes important to recognize how creativity changes at different levels of development. Most people have ideas about what creativity is in adulthood, but what might we look for in a seventh grader or a kindergarten child? It is important for early childhood teachers to see this whole picture." (Tegano, Moran & Sawyers, 1991, p. 65)

There has not been too much research about creativity developmental trends in the life-span period. Furthermore, the emergence of creativity and creative thinking across the span of child development has, to some extent, been neglected (Munro, 2006,). Feldman (1999, p. 169) also noticed the scarce research conducted in this area "compared with other topics like reading acquisition or metacognition, relatively little research has been done on creativity regardless of the approach". This negligence is attributed by Munro (2006) to:

(a) the relevance given to intelligence, which holds the main focus; in this sense, Feldman also noticed that as consequence of comparing creativity with intelligence and trying to use similar methods to measure it, the creativity concept has been reduced to its four main dimensions (fluidity, flexibility, originality and elaboration), thus an improvised conception of creativity development across life span has emerged.

(b) the dominance of child development theories that had difficulty explaining how knowledge that was new or novel could be acquired (as is the case of Piaget's Epistemological development theory).

Perhaps another factor that has contributed to this negligence may be the fact that some authors believe that creative thinking is no different from ordinary thinking (i.e., Perkins, 2000). Authors such as Russ (1996) believe that the same process that predicts adults' creativity will do so with children's creativity, although children's creativity lacks the technical experience and mastery that provides the base knowledge. However, as Sternberg (Sternberg & Lubart, 1995) and others have pointed out, creativity is not limited to the thinking process, but it is also influenced by other variables such as personality-related factors and environmental factors, which make the study of creativity harder. Nevertheless, whether creativity in adults and in children is defined or not by the same dimensions, it is clear that some kind of evolution does occur during the life span; whether this difference between child and adult creativity is qualitative or quantitative has not been studied enough. Sak and Maker (2006) see this variation in the development of creativity as the result of age, acquired knowledge and school experience. In this sense, as Feldman (1999) says, a developmental point of view, should take into account the different dimensions of creativity, such as the cognitive process, b) the social/emotional process, c) the family aspects, and d) education and preparation: formal and informal.

Some authors have questioned whether creativity could be studied as a differentiated Skill/ability in young kindergarten children. For instance, Starkweather (as cited by Moran et al., 1983 and by Arasted & Aarasted, 1976) wonders whether some criteria of creativity found in older children and adults could also be differentiated in young children. Dudek (1973) refutes speaking of a 'creative ability' in young pre-school children, and instead it should be referred to as a 'creative attitude', according to this author creativity would emerge at 8-9 years old, as at this age creativity is stabilized when operational and causal thinking emerge. Gowan (1971) concedes an early age for creativity to emerge and states that it is during the period from 4 to 6 years old that it begins to develop, being very influenced by the parent-child relationship. In this line, Moran (1983) could differentiate between divergent thinking skills and IQ in children from 3 to 6 years old. On the contrary, Smith and Carlsson (1990, cited by Claxton et al., 2005) state that until the child is able to differentiate between external reality dimensions, creativity would not emerge and thus the beginning of creativity should be found at 10-11 years old. Furthermore there are those who maintain that it is not until adolescence that we become creative (i.e., Rothemberg, 1990, cited in Claxton, 2003)

This debate about the emerging age of creativity points to what Pickard (1990) noticed: as the transformative ability (creativity) means to explore different possibilities, it requires a jump from known to unknown alternatives, this means that in order to see the different alternatives the individual needs to be able to make hypotheses, imagine, and to understand the meaning of his/her own creative action, this means that in the Piagetian system the individual should reach the stage of formal operations, as this type of thinking gives the individual freedom to escape from the constraints of reality using the imagination. According to Tegano, Moran and Sawyers (1991), other necessary cognitive processes that are important for creativity are fantasy, divergent thinking, metaphoric thinking, conceptual tempo and curiosity.

In summary, what these authors are highlighting is the creative thinking dependency on other cognitive skills such as imagination, abstraction and logical thinking. Developmental stages regulate what kind of information children are able to incorporate (Runco 2006).

Even with the limitations of the formal thinking and cognitive process that the child needs to reach, there still exists creativity in children that even if it is not of relevance for society as a whole, it is for the child himself.

Runco (1999) says that children may not seem creative because they show a specific response to their experience and may not express their insights, or even when creating something new it only supposes a novelty at the personal level. Runco states that children can be creative even when they do not need to show this skill and it can be appreciated in their imaginative play and in their tendencies to lose themselves in play, even when this is just an enjoyable activity it represents a new understanding of their own experience.

As Russ (1996) states, even when children lack the knowledge and the experience of adults, they do have good and novel ideas and are able to produce creative products for their age group. Children do engage in creative acts and creative solutions to problems.


## Characteristics of child creativity

In this section the characteristics that define child and adult creativity are compared.

### Creativity as a general ability

Lubart (2006) supports the idea that creativity in children is more a general ability, not depending on the domain to which it is applied, whereas in adults creativity is highly related to the domain, and thus becomes a specific ability. A possible explanation is the previous knowledge required to create something that is new, as Sternberg and Lubart (1995) said, it is difficult to acquire knowledge in each domain of human activity; the "ten years rule of mastering" supports this statement. In addition, Dudek (1973) corroborated that at early ages when measuring creativity with divergent thinking tests, it appears strongly related to personality and mental health, and this relationship is much weaker from 10-11 years old. Researchers on cognitive abilities have shown that the structure of intelligence (cognitive skills) does change across lifespan. In this sense Cattell's (1987) investment theory postulates that at the first stages of life there is a single, general, relation-perceiving ability. Such general ability is viewed as "capital" to be invested in cognitive skills through learning, experience, and cultural opportunities. The result of this learning is a broad array of so-called crystallized abilities. As the individual grows up, there is an increase in the number of cognitive abilities. This process of structural change is commonly called differentiation. The age differentiation hypothesis states that from the childhood ages to early maturity, the structure of intelligence changes from a unified, general ability to a set of abilities (Garrett, 1946).

### Playfulness and spontaneity in children's creativity

During childhood, creativity is characterized by its link to play and enjoyment. From a humanist approach this playfulness and spontaneity is the core of creativity. Spontaneity excludes the rigid and the inflexible, and it is likely to ensure a kind of mindful awareness about the individual's own experience. Improvisation is necessarily spontaneous. Runco (1999) supports the idea of child creativity being based on self- expression and enjoyment rather than in the utility of the final products. Children do not create in order to solve problems or serve others but to express themselves. There are some authors like Saracho (1992) who have studied the links between creativity and type of play.

*Taking risks and non-conventional thinking in child creativity*

Children's production may sometimes look original to adult's eyes, on occasions the originality shown by children may look accidental (fortuitous). Sometimes, when a child says something that is considered to be insightful or witty to adults it is the result of a mere effort to find the right words to capture his/her idea, for example a misspelling of 'kinds' for 'kings', or when a child draws a picture using colours and represent forms in an unusual way. Some times children act creatively by accident, just because they do not know the usual way of doing something. The children's awareness of rules and usual ways of doing something has been discussed. Creativity as is said, is linked to a factor of mental openness, and to the wiliness to take risks and break with the usual ways of doing something. In the case of children, when they give original or unconventional answers, these are not the results of disconformities with conventions, but due to an ignorance of conventions. The lack of conventional thinking makes children free of certain assumptions, this facilitates more flexible thinking, nevertheless children are not conscientious enough about rules to appreciate the novelty in their own answers, thus their adventurousness is not significant as it is not intentional (Dudek, 1973; Pickard, 1990; Runco, 1999). As Sternberg and Lubart (1995) point out, "creativity is a [conscious] decision", and a young child has not yet the awareness of such decisions.

Intentionality of the child's creativity Due to the lack of purpose-orientation of children's creativity, some authors maintain that it is not accurate to speak of creativity as such. Since creativity is a conscious act, at some stage, the individual should be aware of the significance of his/her transforming activity and whether it is meant to develop new perspectives and insight that will be shared (communicated). Creativity is a conscious and deliberate act characterized by intentionality (Pickard, 1990; Runco, 1999; Sternberg & Lubart, 1995). In addition, Pickard (1990) noticed that the transforming activity (creativity) of the child reflects its understanding of the child as much as the limited context which this unfolds. The same idea is defended by Runco (1999, 2006) who says that the child's creativity does not have a purpose (a goal) and may be unintentional. This author states that creativity in young children is more characterized as a form of self-expression rather than for the usefulness of the final product.

*Relative originality*

Some authors have argued that childhood creativity often fails to make it into the real world (Albert, 1996) whereas others, as Pickard (1990), or Runco (1999) see the value of novelty as a relative one. Novelty can refer to what the child knows, to what a particular group know, or to what is new to the whole society. Therefore, a child can come with ideas or products that are novel to him.

Tegano, Moran and Sawyers (1991) do notice that in children, rather than looking and evaluating the originality of the product, it is more relevant to assess the process by which the child arrived at that product. These authors refers to the 'creative process' in which the child explores different possibilities and does not confine himself to a first solution.

As stated by Sawyers et al. (1990, p. 45) "creativity may be defined as the interpersonal and intrapersonal process by means of which original, high-quality and genuinely significant products are developed". This definition does consider three different developmental criteria for creativity: originality for young children, high quality for older children, and a genuine significance for adults and societal standards (Tegano, Moran & Sawyers, 1991).

*Strategies to find new ideas*

Cropley (1999) noticed that the production of novelty requires a large number of mental elements (pieces of information, memories, ideas, concepts). When these are combined randomly, a great deal of novelty is produced and, every now and then a configuration occurs (a happy combination that contains precisely what is needed, i.e., effective novelty). However, that information processing leading to effective novelty cannot proceed by "brute force" in a process of perceiving, blindly associating, and occasionally recognizing that a new combination is the required solution. This would lead to a "combinatorial explosion" involving huge numbers of empty trials and leading to cognitive strain. Thus, combinatorial processes must be guided in some systematic way if they are to produce effective novelty. In this sense Lubart (2006) argues that the mechanisms and strategies to find new ideas used by children and adults are different. Children base their search of new ideas in association of ideas, whereas adults have more logically-organized search strategies.

Low and Hollis (2003) conducted a study in which it was proved that young children appear to require more constraints and directions to exhibit generative thinking whereas older children appear to require fewer sets of constraints to engage in such thinking. Young children would have both concrete and generative strategies available to them, but they require more constraints to exhibit creativity. Given all the information processing requirements, young children may be more likely to fall back upon concrete responses when these are possible and may only consider more generative ones when constraints direct thinking in particular ways.

*Developmental stages of creativity*

Probably the best well-known peak of creativity during childhood is the so-called "fourth grade slum". This phenomenon has been found across different cultures and in different studies and have been fairly studied by authors since Torrance. Some authors remark this decrease in creativity as a result of and adaptation process during adolescence, at the age of 9-10 children feel more concern for the reality (i.e.. Rosenblatt And Winner, 1988, Gardner, Phelps & Wolf 1990, as cited in Guignard & Lubart, 2006). Other perspectives support the idea that this and other slumps - in adolescence and in adulthood - are indicators of the interaction between the development of standard logical-reasoning based thinking ability and creative-thinking ability (Georgsdottir & Lubart, 2003; Guignard & Lubbart, 2006; Runco 1999).

Some authors have tried to establish the developmental trends in creativity, and its stages.

In this regard, Taylor (1975) describes five levels of creativity, which help to clarify the relationship between cognitive development and creativity, these levels are: (1) 'expressive spontaneity' (involves unhindered productivity, without regard to reality. It can occur on the basis of concrete operations or even pre-operational or sensor-motor thinking. In this case, the novelty is produced in the form of observable behaviours or other concrete products, and is probably novel only for the producer and is based on concrete, physical properties of real objects. Nonetheless, novelty can be produced at this level); (2) 'technical creativity' (involves unusual mastery of knowledge, techniques or skills); (3) 'inventive creativity' (makes use of the already known in new ways. Both of these activities require at least concrete or formal operational thinking. However, they produce novelty based on direct application of what already exists, and are bound by the structures and rules of the existing); (4) 'innovative creativity' (extension of existing systems); and (5) 'emergent creativity' (development of new systems. This occurs when the novelty produced is at the level of classes or systems. There may, of course, be concrete products, but the crucial point is that these forms of production of variability extend or change existing ways of symbolizing an area of knowledge. The production of variability at this level seems likely to require systematic and met systematic operations).

Rosenblatt and Winner (as cited in Cropley 1999) described three phases of children's creativity:

(1) the pre-conventional phase (up to the age of about 6-8 years). Pre-conventional production of novelty derives from pre-operational thinking. It displays spontaneity and emotional involvement and may lead to aesthetically pleasing products, but it is dominated by perception (especially

visual) of the immediate concrete environment.

(2) the conventional phase (from age 6-8 to about 10-12), Conventional production of novelty involves operational thinking, but becomes increasingly rule-bound as critical and evaluative skills develop, with the result that the novelty produced is stilted and conforms to external standards (i.e., it is not effective).

3) the post-conventional phase (from about 12 years of age and extending into adulthood). Post-conventional novelty production involves formal operational thinking and, with increasing cognitive development, operations on classes and systems, while it is enriched by, for instance, increased experience with the external world. The crucial element in post-conventional production of novelty is that the individual takes account of external constraints and conventional values (necessary for effectiveness), but is able to produce novelty despite this. The difference between the pre-conventional phase and the post-conventional can be stated rather baldly by saying that, predominantly, children under about 10 produce novelty as a result of being ignorant of the constraints of the external world, a state of affairs that is not favourable to effectiveness. By contrast, people in the post-conventional phase are familiar with these constraints, but are able to transcend them. For some writers (e.g., Smith & Carlsson, 1983) this means that children under about 10 cannot be creative. According to Rosenblatt and Winner (1988), what is missing in the novelty production of children under about 10 is the regulatory element of (self-) evaluation. Their productions may be novel, spontaneous, uninhibited, and even aesthetically pleasing, but they often lack accuracy and adaptation to the constraints of reality (i.e., effectiveness).

## References

Albert, R.S. (1996). Some reasons why childhood creativity often fails to make it past puberty into the real world. New directions for child development, pp. 72, 43-56.

Arasteh, A. R. & Arassteh, J. D. (1976). Creativity in human development. An interpretive and annotated biography. New York: Schenkman Publishing company. Halsted Press Division.

Cattell, R. B. (1987). Intelligence: its structure, growth, and action. Amsterdam: North-Holland.

Claxton, A.F., & Pannells, T. C. (2005). Developmental trends in the creativity of school-age children. Creativity research Journal, 17(4), pp. 327-335.

Cropley, A. J. (1999). Creativity and cognition: producing effective novelty. Roeper review, 21.4. pp. 253-260.

Dudek, S.Z. (1973). Creativity in young children –attitude or ability. Paper presented at the Annual Meeting of the American Psychological Assn. (81st, Montreal, August 27-31, 1973).

Feldman, D.H. (1999). The development of creativity. In R. Sternberg (Ed.), The handbook of creativity (pp.169-186). New York: Cambridge University Press.

Gardner, H., Phelps, E., & Wolf,D. (1990).The roots of adult creativity in children's symbolic products. In C. N. Alexander & E. J. Langer (Eds.), Higher stages of human development (pp. 79-96). New York: Oxford University.

Garrett, H. E. (1946). A developmental theory of intelligence. American Psychologist, 1, pp. 278-372.

Georgsdottir, A., & Lubart, T.I. (2003). La flexibilicé cognitive et la créativité [Cognitive flexibility and creativity]. Psychologie Française [French Psychology], 48(3), pp. 29-40.

GOWAN, J.C. (1971) The development of the creative individual. Paper presented at 18th Annual Meetings of the national Asssociation for Gifted Children, May 3-5, 1971. Regency Hyatt House, Chicago, Illinois. Gifted Child Quartely, 15 (3) pp. 156-174.

Guignard, J., & Lubart, T. (2006). Is it reasonable to be creative? In J. Kaufman & J. Bare (Eds.), Creativity and reason in cognitive development (pp. 269–281). New York, CUP.

Low, J & Hollis, S. (2003). The eyes have it: Development of children's generative thinking. International Journal of Behavioral Development, 27 (2), pp. 97–108.

Lubart, T. I. (2006). Creativity from a cognitive developmental science perspective. International Journal, 1. Retrieved from http://www.google.co.uk/search?client=safari&rls=en-us&q=Creativity+from+a+Cognitive+Developmental+Science+Perspective&ie=UTF-8&oe=UTF-8&redir_esc=&ei=S8xnTMPRFcj64Aafq4WZBA

Moran, J.D.; Milgram, R,M., Sawyers, J.K., & Fu, V.R. (1983). Original thinking in pre-school children. Child Development, 54, 4 pp. 921-926.

Munro, J. (2006). Insights into the creativity process. Hawthorn, Australia : Ed Assist.

Perkins, D.N. (2000). Archimedes bathtub: The art and logic of breakthrough thinking. Norton, New York.

Pickard, E. (1990) Toward a theory of creative potential. The journal of creative behaviour, 24(1) pp. 1-9

Rosenblatt, E., & Winner, E. (1988). The art of children's drawing. Journal of Aesthetic Education, 22, pp. 3-15.

Rothenberg A. (1990). Creativity in adolescence. Psychiatric Clinic North Am. 1990 Sep; 13(3): 415-34.

Runco, M. (2006). The development of children's creativity. In B. Spodek, & O. Saracho (Eds.), Handbook of research on the education of young children, second edition (pp. 121-129). Mahwah, NJ: Erlbaum.

Runco. M.A. (1999). Developmental trends in creative abilities and potentials. In Runco, M.A. & Pritzker S.R. (1999), Encyclopedia of Creativity (pp. 537-540). San Diego, CA: Academic.

Russ, S. W. (1996). Development of creative processes in children. New directions for child development, 72, pp. 31-42.

Sak, U., & Maker, J.C. (2006 ) Developmental Variation in Children's Creative Mathematical Thinking as a Function of Schooling, Age, and Knowledge . Creativity research Journal, 18 (3), pp. 279-291

Saracho, O.N.(1992) Pre-school children's cognitive style and play and implications for creativity. Creativity Research Journal, 5: 1, pp. 35-47

Sawyers, J.K., Moran, J, D., III; & Tegano, D. (1990). A theoretical model of creative potential in young children. In C.W.,Taylor (Ed.), Expanding awareness of creative potentials worldwide Salt Lake City: Brain Talent-Powers Press, p. 65.

Smith, G. J., & Carlsson, I. M. (1990). The creative process: A functional model based on empirical studies from early childhood to middle age. Madison, CT: International Universities Press.

Smith, G.J., & Carlsson, I. (1983). Creativity in early and middle school years. International Journal of Behavioral Development, 6, pp. 167–195.

Starkweather, E. K. (1964). Problems in the measurement of creativity in pre-school children. Journal of Educational Measurement, 1, pp. 543-547.

Sternberg, R. J., & Lubart, T. I. (1995). Defying the crowd: Cultivating creativity in a culture of conformity. New York: Free Press.

Taylor, C. W., & Sacks, D. (1981). Facilitating lifetime creative processes – a think piece. Gifted Child Quarterly, 25, (3), pp. 116–118.

Taylor, I. A. (1975). An emerging view of creative actions. In I. A. Taylor, & J. W. Getzels (Eds.), Perspectives in creativity (pp. 297-325). Chicago: Aldine.

Tegano, D.W., Moran, D.J. III, & Sawyers, J.K. (1991). Creativity in early childhood classrooms. Washington, D.C.: National Education Association.

# 5 Creativity and technology – An early childhood education perspective

*Inka Kotsalainen and Tuula Nousiainen*

Taking part in creative activities, starting from an early age, is essential for acquiring the skills required in today's world. The role of creativity and the relationship between creativity and information and communication technology (ICT) have been increasingly emphasized as new technologies have enabled users to produce and share their own, very diverse content on an unprecedented scale and in numerous different ways (Binkley, Erstad, Herman, Raizen, Ripley, Miller-Ricci & Rumble, 2012). The significance of ICT for the fostering of creativity lies especially in its potential for supporting collaboration, sharing and co-reflection (Binkley et al., 2012; Loveless, 2007).

This article examines the use of technology in early childhood education through the lens of supporting creativity. First, we will take a look at how creativity and technology manifest in the frameworks of the 21st century skills. Next, we will address the role of technology in children's lives, the role of creativity and technology in early childhood education, and the role of teachers in using technology to foster creativity. Finally, we will look at the theme of creativity and technology from the point of view of involving children as designers and creators of technology.

Creativity and Technology in the Framework of the 21st Century Skills

Living in the modern technological world requires all citizens to have diverse technological literacy skills: people should know how to use different technologies and to make decisions between different kinds of alternative solutions. In addition, society increasingly needs people that have the preparedness and motivation to study and work in the field of technology. (Turja 2011, p. 197) The "Assessment and Teaching of 21st-Century Skills" (ATC21S) project has defined a framework for 21st century skills, consisting of ten skills which have been categorized into four groupings: Ways of Thinking, Ways of Working, Tools for Working, and Living in the World (Griffin, Care & McGaw, 2012). In this framework, both creativity and ICT skills have an important role. Creativity and innovation, the first of the ten essential skills, is grouped under Ways of Thinking whereas Information literacy and ICT literacy are the two skills forming the group Tools for Working (see Table 1).

The competences related to these skill areas are approached through a set of transversal elements (KSAVE framework): knowledge, skills, attitudes, values, and ethics (Griffin et al., 2012).

| *Table 1* | |
|---|---|
| **Group** | **Skills** |
| Ways of Thinking | 1. Creativity and innovation |
| | 2. Critical thinking, problem solving, decision making |
| | 3. Learning to learn, metacognition |
| Ways of Working | 4. Communication |
| | 5. Collaboration (teamwork) |
| Tools for Working | 6. Information literacy |
| | 7. ICT literacy |
| Living in the World | 8. Citizenship – local and global |
| | 9. Life and career |
| | 10. Personal and social responsibility, including cultural awareness and competence |

What the KSAVE framework means in the context of creativity is that an individual should have some background knowledge related to creativity (such as awareness of different idea creation techniques, knowledge of existing ideas and the effects of innovations, etc.), practical skills to use and apply this knowledge (e.g. to develop innovative and creative ideas, to evaluate and refine one's ideas, to communicate one's ideas to others, and to elaborate one's ideas into implementable form), and a certain attitude and stance (such as openness and responsiveness to new ideas and different perspectives, seeing failures and mistakes as learning opportunities, and persistence in developing and promoting one's ideas) (Binkley et al., 2012). Similarly, when it comes to information and ICT literacies, the competences are about knowing about the appropriate tools, being able to apply information and different tools creatively and efficiently, and being open to new information, ideas and tools (Binkley et al., 2012). Creativity and ICT skills are brought up also in the European Key Competences for Lifelong Learning (European Commission, 2007) which span different ages and educational levels starting from early childhood.

**Technology in children's lives**

This article focuses principally on ICT and its role in early childhood education but will also touch on such technology education where technology is defined in broader terms. Technology can be defined as the know-how and the creative process for using different kinds of tools, equipment, resources, environmental conditions and personal capabilities in order to observe targets and change them in order to make life easier and to solve problems in specific situations (Blandow, 1992, p. 4; Turja 2011, p. 195). Technology is seen to start from human needs and goals and from attempts to find solutions to them (Dugger, 1997).

Children gradually learn from the very first year how to use the diverse technology that is around them (Turja, 2011, p. 196). Even six-month-old babies learn how to use technical devices that suit them the best, and children of all ages are generally very enthusiastic users of ICT innovations. This is because when children are growing, they are very curious about the things that are around them and they have an urge to learn new things. (Tamminen, 2001, p. 235) The foundation of the meaningful usage of technology is created from these very early experiences (Sinko & Lehtinen, 1999).

Today's children and young people are often referred to as "digital natives" (Prensky, 2001): they have grown up surrounded by new technology so that it is an integral part of their world and their everyday lives. They have never lived in, nor can they imagine living in, a world where ICT has not penetrated their lives to the extent it presently does. This also means that ever younger children are immersed in the digital world. Pre-school-aged children are already used to new technologies to a completely different degree from previous generations both in terms of how extensively these technologies are present in their lives and how comfortable and confident they are with them (Centre for Educational Research and Innovation, 2008).

## Technology and creativity in early childhood education

The use of technology is a significant and inseparable part of people's everyday lives, and therefore it is also important to create possibilities for technology education in the early years (Järvinen, Lindh & Alamäki, 2001, pp. 7-8). The goals of technology education in the early years include many things. The main goal is that children learn to understand the man-made, technological world and that they learn to see technology as something that has the capacity to help people as well as nature. Children adopt information, knowledge and attitudes about technology that help them to act cooperatively, experimentally, creatively, innovatively, responsibly and confidently in the field of technology. While exploring and learning about technology, children also learn how to think critically, how to take other people and nature into consideration, and how to use technology safely. (Turja, 2009; Turja, 2011, p. 197) Technology is seen to be born from the need to create something meaningful and important, and therefore the children should also have a chance to act from the needs that arise from the children themselves and from their environment (Järvinen & Hiltunen, 2000).

Technology education can include computers and ICT, but just as well it can include design, creating things, constructing or getting to know mechanics, electronic devices, energy sources or different kinds of materials (Järvinen et al., 2001, pp. 20-22). The use of a camera, for example, is also an excellent tool for technology education and visual education (Pekkarinen, 2001). Järvinen et al. (2001) emphasize that technology education with young children is a subject that offers creative opportunities and experiences and gives chances for developing curiosity. Children should have a possibility to be active, create new experiences and try and explore new things that arise from their own interests. Technology education is seen to be child-centred and child-focused education, meaning that the educators should bring learning opportunities that stem from the children's interests into educational situations.

Technology education plays a role in fostering different thinking skills, including creativity. McCormick, Murphy, Hennessy and Davidson (1996) state that the basic essence of technology includes a certain kind of inventiveness, innovativeness and openness in problem solving. Järvinen et al. (2001, p. 11) agree with this and continue that technology education should not be conducted in accordance with a certain model; instead, ideally it is creative and divergent problem-solving thinking which leads to new kinds of inventions and solutions.

When it comes to fostering the expression and development of creativity, learning environments such as schools and kindergartens are have a key role. Sternberg and Lubart (1999) emphasize the significance of such an environment that encourages and rewards creativity: even though an individual has an innate capability for creative thinking, the support of the environment is required in order for one to be able to present and share his/her creative ideas and products.

Available materials and equipment are one aspect of educational settings affecting the possibilities to produce creative outcomes and share them (e.g., Sharp, 2004). Today, technological tools and environments play a substantial role in this process, making it possible for everyone to share and co-create. Digital technologies have the potential to create opportunities for "play, exploration, reflection and focused engagement with ideas" which, in turn, are conducive to creative activity (Loveless, 2007, p. 9).

Another role that ICT can play with regard to creativity and education is the facilitation of the assessment of creativity. Binkley et al. (2012), citing Ridgway et al. (2004), Sefton-Green and Sinker (2000) as well as Harlen and Deakin Crick (2003), discuss the potential of new digital media in assessing creative thinking as a separate skill from analytical thinking. They point out that ICT tools make it exceedingly easy to share and reflect on one's creations but despite this, ICT-based assessment of the creativity of such products has not been widely addressed so far, largely stemming from the difficulty of specifying the elements of which the skill of creativity consists.

**Teachers' role in fostering creativity with the aid of technology**

Despite the ever-increasing selection of technological tools and resources, they are rarely used to their full potential from the perspective of fostering creativity. The ways of using ICT are often very static and one-directional, disregarding the interactive possibilities of the technologies - despite the fact that their creative potential is seen to manifest especially in such situations where learners are allowed ample time and space to explore these tools themselves (Cachia, Ferrari, Ala-Mutka & Punie, 2010, p. 26; Sharp, 2004). The core of this challenge lies often in the mindset that the teacher must be more competent than the learners while in fact the greatest potential for creativity may emerge from exploring and learning things together (Cachia et al., 2010). According to Lucas (2001), in order to foster creativity, it is important to recognize multiple intelligences, different learning styles and individual interests as well as to provide possibilities for experimenting with different ways of doing things instead of giving one standardized model.

Exploration is in a key role also in the practices of using ICT with children. Children naturally explore things and learn about their environments through inquiry, and information technology can help children extend the domain and range of this inquiry. Over the past decade, there has been a growing number of different kinds of interactive games addressing, for example, science, reading and mathematics, but most software packages have yet to integrate technology into inquiry-based learning in early childhood. (Wang, Kinzie, McGuire & Pan, 2009) Kankaanranta (2001) points out that it should be made possible to create opportunities for children to learn from information technology and computers but also to learn new things through computers and information technology. While it is necessary to offer more computers and technical devices to children in order to reach this goal, it is also important to focus on the information technological skills and motivation of the teachers so that they are able to guide the children on how to use technical devices (Kankaanranta, 2001, p. 112).

Gimbert and Cristol (2004) emphasize that teachers should know how to teach with technology rather than about technology. Applying ICT in teaching is an interesting but also a difficult task which can never be learned completely, but it is something that constantly provides something new for everyone (Haugland & Wright, 1997). It has been discovered that innovative teaching happens more in environments where teachers collaborate to share practices and to support each other in improving them (Shear, Gallagher & Patel, 2011). A supportive overall culture is one of the prerequisites for achieving fruitful collaboration (Shear et al., 2011).

When the teacher experiences the use of computers as a resource rather than a burden, he/she knows how to use and how to take advantage of them in different fields of learning. The teacher knows how to plan such activities that create opportunities for children to reflect on things together, to discuss and to share solutions and techniques. When this happens, technology is no longer a subject of its own, but it can be integrated as a tool in other activities. This kind of integration can enhance children's enthusiasm and motivation related to learning and it can also help them invent and present their own ideas (Muhonen 2001, pp. 55–56).

Children as Designers and Creators of Technology

As pointed out above, the possibilities for children to be involved in the creative use, design, and evaluation of technology as part of their everyday life are essential for acquiring the skills needed in mastering various 21st century skills. In one definition of 21st century literacy, the skill of "media creativity" is highlighted as a skill that emphasizes the person as an active creator of content - as opposed to a mere user of ICT - and refers to the ability to produce and publish media content (Bertelsmann Foundation & AOL Time Warner Foundation, 2002).

When discussing children and technology, the focus is often on specific software and applications (such as games) and especially on their potential effects on children, be they positive or negative. However, where the issue of creativity particularly comes into play is when we turn this mindset around and think about how children can affect the use and creation of technology. The role of digital tools has been shifting "from role-playing and exploration of mediascapes authored by others, to opportunities for learners and teachers to create and author their own ideas" (Loveless, 2007, p. 8). Technology can help children make and share their own creations, and children can even have a creative input in the design of technology.

Certain types of applications, such as game authoring tools, aim to provide children with an easy way of creating technology of their own. By using these tools, children are able to both design and implement their creations. Such tools include both easy-to-use editors for making simple games (Nousiainen, 2009; Tikka, Kankaanranta, Nousiainen & Hankala, 2009) and tools that require some more technical skills, such as programming tools for children. There is an increasing amount of research on children as game creators. For example, Neverwinter Nights, a toolset for creating 3D adventure games, has been popular in the creation of games with children and in studies related to these activities (e.g., Robertson &

Nicholson, 2007; Steiner, Kaplan & Moulthrop, 2006). Tools such as these are often principally aimed for school-aged children but some can be applied with pre-school children as well, with the support of an adult.

A different dimension to creating technology is children's participation in the creation and elaboration of ideas for new technologies and in the evaluation of prototypes. Participatory technology development has been carried out even with pre-school-aged children (e.g. Guha, Druin, Chipman, Fails, Simms & Farber, 2004; 2005). Methods that have been used in involving children in technology design processes have included, for example, such techniques as drawings (Bilal, 2003; Nousiainen, 2008), collages (Verhaegh, Soute, Kessels & Markopoulos, 2006), photography and documentation (Bekker, Beusmans, Keyson & Lloyd, 2003; Oosterholt, Kusano & de Vries, 1996), comic strips or storyboards (Hall, Woods, Dautenhahn & Sobreperez, 2004; Jones, McIver, Gibson & Gregor, 2003), low-technology prototypes out of art and craft materials (Druin 2002; Druin, Bederson, Boltman, Miura, Knotts-Callahan & Platt, 1999), and narrative and story-based activities (Dindler, Eriksson, Iversen, Lykke-Olesen & Ludvigsen, 2005; Verhaegh, Soute, Kessels & Markopoulos, 2006). Especially when working with very young children, the process of merging individual ideas into collective ones is an important step in these activities (Guha et al., 2004; 2005). At its best, technology design tasks have the capacity to foster creativity by aiming to produce outputs that are both innovative and meaningful, thereby responding to both of these essential elements of creativity (see e.g., Sternberg & Lubart, 1999).

When children participate in innovating and evaluating technology, they acquire new skills and perspectives. Druin and Fast (2002) suggest that during their participation in a design project, the children's roles can evolve from learners through critics and inventors to design partners. Firstly, the children learn to understand the process of invention. After some time, their role can expand to that of a critic, providing feedback on the good and bad aspects of different technologies, and an inventor, suggesting new ideas for technology applications. Finally, the children can adopt the role of a design partner where they begin to understand the meaning of collaboration in the invention process and to build onto other partners' ideas (Druin & Fast, 2002).

Naturally, chances for children to participate in real technology development projects from the very beginning are very limited, but the aforementioned points also translate to the everyday contexts of schools and pre-schools. The same underlying principles are addressed, for instance, by giving children a say in the process of choosing technological tools to be used in the activities of the kindergarten or by enabling them to creatively explore different technologies and ways of using them (e.g. Nousiainen 2008). Such an approach where collaborative exploration is encouraged and where children and adults learn and discover together is conducive to creativity, as pointed out above (Cachia et al., 2010; Sharp, 2004).

## Conclusions

As seen above, the educational use of technology with children is not merely playing with computers or other technical devices; it is about developing children's curiosity and letting them be creative as well as offering them creative opportunities and experiences. It can entail playing, exploring, trying out new things, using electronic devices or just imagining using them. It can also be about design, problem solving, creating new things, constructing and getting to know different kinds of materials, mechanics and energy sources.

One of the main strengths of ICT in fostering creativity, compared to traditional materials, lies especially in how it provides the users with different and flexible ways of creating, mixing and manipulating contents. At present, most ICT tools associated with producing creative outputs focus on visual and auditory contents, but as the technological landscape is continuously changing and evolving at a rapid speed, new forms of expression - such as tactile and motion-based activities - can be expected to become increasingly important.

Another aspect with regard to which ICT has the capacity to facilitate creativity on a completely new level is the extent to which it enables sharing, collaborating and getting an audience for one's creations. Children can create products together with others, as well as share their own creations with others, regardless of whether these other children are close by or on the other side of the world. As discussed above, creativity is not only about developing ideas but also about evaluating them, communicating them to others and elaborating them (Binkley et al., 2012). With the aid of ICT, the aspects related to the value and meaningfulness of the creative products can be addressed by taking advantage of various different tools of interaction, discussion and reflection.

It seems that the use of technology is still quite scarce in many kindergartens despite the fact that we live in a world full of technologies. Some of the potential reasons can include the lack of knowledge on different possibilities as well as adults' attitudes and preconceptions regarding technology. There is a need to address educators' attitudes towards technology and to support them in learning more about technologies and how to use them. When the educators have the knowledge, skills and especially a positive attitude towards technology and technology education, then they have the readiness to learn more and also to educate the children. An essential aspect is the willingness to learn and explore together with the children; educators don't have to know everything about technology, but rather, they should allow themselves to learn with, and from, the children. After all, children are digital natives in whose world ICT is present from the very beginning and it is just as commonplace as any other tools and materials with which children learn and create.

## References

Bekker, M., Beusmans, J., Keyson, D., & Lloyd, P. (2003). KidReporter: a user requirements gathering technique for designing with children. Interacting with Computers 15 (2), 187–202.

Bertelsmann Foundation & AOL Time Warner Foundation (2002). White Paper: 21st Century Literacy in a Convergent Media World. Berlin, Germany. Retrieved from http://sueculig.com/digital/web_design/21century/white/WhitePaperEnglish.pdf

Bilal, D. (2003). Draw and tell: children as designers of web interfaces. In R.J. Todd (Ed.), Proceedings of the 66th annual meeting of the American Society for Information Science & Technology (ASIST 2003), Long Beach, CA, USA: Medford, NJ: Information Today, pp.135–141.

Binkley, M., Erstad, O., Herman, J., Raizen, S., Ripley, M., Miller-Ricci, M., & Rumble, M. (2012). Defining twenty-first century skills. In P. Griffin, B. McGaw & E. Care (Eds.), Assessment and teaching of 21st century skills, Dordrecht: Springer, pp.17-66.

Blandow, D. (1992). The elements of Technology for Education. Inaugural lecture presented at the Technical University of Eindhoven (Eindhoven, The Netherlands, December 11, 1992). ERIC Document Number ED360517.

Cachia, R., Ferrari, A., Ala-Mutka, K., & Punie, Y. (2010). Creative learning and innovative teaching. Final report on the study on creativity and innovation in education in the EU member states. JRC Scientific and Technical Reports EUR 24675 EN. Retrieved from http://ftp.jrc.es/EURdoc/JRC62370.pdf

Centre for Educational Research and Innovation (2008). New Millennium Learners: Initial findings on the effects of digital technologies on school-age learners. OECD/CERI International Conference on Learning in the 21st Century: Research, Innovation and Policy. Retrieved from http://www.oecd.org/site/educeri21st/40554230.pdf

Dindler, C., Eriksson, E., Iversen, O.S., Lykke-Olesen, A., & Ludvigssen, M. (2005). Mission from Mars – a method for exploring user requirements from children in narrative space. In Proceedings of the 2005 conference on Interaction design and children, Boulder, Colorado, USA. New York: ACM, pp. 40–47.

Druin, A. (2002). The role of children in the design of new technology.

Behaviour & Information Technology 21 (1), 1–25.

Druin, A., Bederson, B., Boltman, A., Miura, A., Knotts-Callahan, D., & Platt, M. (1999). Children as our technology design partners. In A. Druin (Ed.) The design of children's technology, San Francisco: Morgan Kaufmann, pp. 51–72.

Druin, A. & Fast, C. (2002). The child as learner, critic, inventor, and technology design partner: an analysis of three years of Swedish student journals. International Journal of Technology and Design Education 12 (3), 189–213.

Dugger, W. E., Jr. (1997). Next step: Developing standards for technology education. The Technology Teacher, 56 (6), 10−18.

European Commission (2007). Key Competences for Lifelong Learning. European Reference Framework. Luxembourg: Office for Official Publications of the European Communities. Retrieved from http://ec.europa.eu/dgs/education_culture/publ/pdf/ll-learning/keycomp_en.pdf

Gimbert, B. & Cristol, D. (2004). Teaching curriculum with technology: Enhancing children's technological competence during early childhood. Early Childhood Education Journal 31 (3), 207–216.

Griffin, P., Care, E., & McGaw, B. (2012). The changing role of education and schools. In P. Griffin, B. McGaw & E. Care (Eds.) Assessment and teaching of 21st century skills (pp. 1-15). Dordrecht: Springer.

Guha, M.L., Druin, A., Chipman, G., Fails, J.A., Simms, S., & Farber, A. (2004). Mixing ideas: a new technique for working with young children as design partners. In Proceedings of the 2004 conference on Interaction design and children, College Park, Maryland, USA. New York: ACM, pp. 35-42.

Guha, M.L., Druin, A., Chipman, G., Fails, J.A., Simms, S., & Farber, A. (2005). Working with young children as technology design partners. Communications of the ACM 48 (1), 39-42.

Hall, L., Woods, S., Dautenhahn, K., & Sobreperez, P. (2004). Using storyboards to guide virtual world design. In Proceedings of the 2004 conference on Interaction design and children, College Park, Maryland, USA. New York: ACM, pp. 125-126.

Harlen, W., & Deakin Crick, R. (2003). Testing and motivation for learning. Assessment in Education: Principles, Policy & Practice 10, 169-208.

Haugland, S. & Wright, J. (1997). Young children and technology: A world of discovery. New York: Allyn & Bacon.

Jones, C., McIver, L., Gibson, L., & Gregor, P. (2003). Experiences obtained from designing with children. In S. MacFarlane, T. Nicol, J. Read & L. Snape (Eds.) Proceedings of the 2003 conference on Interaction design and children . Preston, UK. New York: ACM, pp. 69-74.

Järvinen, E.-M., & Hiltunen, J. (2000). Automation technology in elementary technology education. Journal of Industrial Teacher education, 37 (4), pp. 51-76.

Järvinen, E-M., Lindh, M., & Alamäki, A. (2001). Yleissivistävästä teknologiakasvatuksesta. In M. Kangassalo (Ed.), Tietotekniikan mahdollisuuksia varhaiskasvatuksessa, Helsinki: Edita, pp. 7–26.

Kankaanranta, M. (2001). Digitaaliset portfoliot varhaiskasvatusympäristöjen avaamis- ja arviontimenetelmänä. In M. Kangassalo (Ed.), Tietotekniikan mahdollisuuksia varhaiskasvatuksessa, Helsinki: Edita, pp. 93-113.

Liikanen, H-L. (2010). Taiteesta ja kulttuurista hyvinvointia. Ehdotus toimintaohjelmaksi 2010-2014. Opetusministeriön julkaisuja 2010:1.

Loveless, A. M. (2007). Creativity, technology and learning – a review of recent literature. Report 4 update. Futurelab Series. Retrieved from http://archive.futurelab.org.uk/resources/documents/ lit_reviews/Creativity_Review_update.pdf

Lucas, B. (2001). Creative teaching, teaching creativity and creative learning. In A. Craft, B. Jeffrey, & M. Leibling (Eds.), Creativity in education, London: Continuum.

McCormick, R., Murphy, P., Hennessy, S., & Davidson, M. (1996). Research on student learning of designing and problem solving in technology activity in schools in England. American research association annual meeting (). New York: Springer, pp.8-11.

Muhonen, H. (2001). Lasten yhteistoiminnallisuus avoimessa tietokoneympäristössä. In M. Kangassalo (Ed.), Tietotekniikan mahdollisuuksia varhaiskasvatuksessa, Helsinki: Edita, pp. 43-61.

Nousiainen, T. (2008). Children's Involvement in the Design of Game-Based Learning Environments. Doctoral dissertation. Jyväskylä Studies in Computing 95, Jyväskylä: University of Jyväskylä.

Nousiainen, T. (2009). Children's Involvement in the Design of Game-Based Learning Environments: Cases Talarius and Virtual Peatland. In M. Kankaanranta & P. Neittaanmäki (Eds.), Design and Use of Serious Games. Intelligent Systems, Control and Automation: Science and Engineering 37, Dordrecht: Springer, pp. 49-66.

Oosterholt, R., Kusano, M., & de Vries, G. (1996). Interaction design and human factors support in the development of personal communicator for children. In M. J. Tauber (Ed.) Proceedings of the SIGCHI conference on Human factors in computing systems, Vancouver, Canada. New York: ACM, pp. 450-457.

Pekkarinen, A. (2001). Tieto- ja viestintätekniikka lasten ja aikuisten viestinnässä varhaiskasvatuksen alueella. Teoksessa M. Kangassalo (Ed.), Tietotekniikan mahdollisuuksia varhaiskasvatuksessa, Helsinki:Edita, pp.78-92.

Prensky, M. (2001). Digital natives, digital immigrants. On the horizon 9

(5), MCB University Press, pp. 1-6.

Ridgway, J., McCusker, S., & Pead, D. (2004). Literature review of e-assessment (report 10). Bristol: Futurelab.

Robertson, J., & Nicholson, K. (2007). Adventure Author: a learning environment to support creative design. In T. Bekker, J. Robertson & M. B. Skov (Eds.) Proceedings of the 6th international Conference on Interaction Design and Children (pp. 37-44). Aalborg, Denmark. New York: ACM.

Sefton-Green, J., & Sinker, R. (Eds.) (2000). Evaluating creativity: Making and learning by young people. London: Routledge.

Sharp, C. (2004). Developing young children's creativity: what can we learn from research? Topic, 32, pp. 5-12.

Shear, L., Gallagher, L. & Patel, D. (2011). ITL Research 2011 Findings: Evolving Educational Ecosystems. SRI International. Menlo Park, CA: SRI International. Retrieved from http://www.itlresearch.com/images/stories/reports/ITL%20Research%20 2011%20Findings%20and%20Implications%20-%20Final.pdf

Steiner, B., Kaplan, N. & Moulthrop, S. (2006). When play works: turning game-playing into learning. In Proceedings of the 2006 Conference on Interaction Design and Children, Tampere, Finland. New York: ACM, pp. 137-140.

Sternberg, J. R. & Lubart, I. T. (1999). The concept of creativity: prospects and paradigms. In J. Sternberg (Ed.) Handbook of creativity, Cambridge: Cambridge University Press, pp. 3-16.

Tamminen, T. (2001). Lapset tietoyhteiskunnassa. In M. Kangassalo & J. Suoraranta (Eds.) Lasten tietoyhteiskunta, Tampere: Tampere University Press, pp. 234-240.

Tikka, S.-M., Kankaanranta, M., Nousiainen, T. & Hankala, M. (2009). Telling Stories with Digital Board Games: Narrative Game Worlds in Literacies Learning. In T. Connolly, M. Stansfield & L. Boyle (Eds.) Games-Based Learning Advancements for Multi-Sensory Human Computer Interfaces: Techniques and Effective Practices, Hershey: Information Science Reference, pp.174-190.

Turja, L., Endepohls-Ulpe, M. & Chatoney, M. (2009). A Conceptual Framework for Developing the Curriculum and Delivery of Technology Education in Early Childhood. International Journal of Technology and Design Education 19 (4), pp. 353-365.

Turja, L. (2011). Teknologiakasvatus varhaisvuosina. In E. Hujala & L. Turja (Eds.) Varhaiskasvatuksen käsikirja, Juva: Bookwell pp. 195-207.

Verhaegh, J., Soute, I., Kessels, A. & Markopoulos, P. (2006). On the design of Camelot, an outdoor game for children. In Proceedings of the 2006 conference on Interaction design and children, Tampere, Finland. New York: ACM, pp. 9-16.

# 6 Creativity and expressive languages
*Henriette Vognsgaard*


The Italian educational thinker Loris Malaguzzi once said: " The child has a hundred languages (and a hundred hundred hundred more) but they steal ninety-nine." A question which arose from this is; how is it possible to identify and get a better understanding of children´s expressive languages in their everyday lives - and give back the ninety-nine languages to the children?

Expressive languages can be supported by art and artistic processes, but it is not the only way. Children express themselves in everyday lives as a way of communicating and participating in their peer culture. Children play, sing, rhyme, dance, draw and paint. Children explore and experiment with materials in their interaction and relationship with the world. Aesthetic expression is a way to tell stories, to express what is important, to identify who you are as a person and as a part of the community.

As the aesthetic learning process is always relational and developed in interaction with the surrounding culture, the participants in the aesthetic activities can develop cultural identity and social skills. Add to this that the individual can share its inner world with others through aesthetic activities in the potential space and in this way create balance between its inner and outer world, realize itself and develop individual and collective identity (Austring and Sørensen, 2006).

All human beings express themselves in different ways. This is about communication and about communicating in different languages. Every language has its own grammar, its own specific nature, but it also has a structure disposed towards communication and relationships. We all need to express ourselves; what we think, how we feel, what we hope and we express ourselves in different languages – different ways of expression in our everyday lives. Expressive languages can then be understood as a way of communicating, a way of expressing one self, a way of interacting.

When Reggio pedagogy declared that a child possesses and "speak a hundred languages" (Malaguzzi, 2006) – by which they stress many communicative possibilities with which our species is generally equipped. Learning processes take place in several languages (or disciplines) and interact together (Vecchi, 2010). This is a matter of extending the term language beyond the verbal and consider languages as the different ways used by human beings to express themselves; visual language, bodily language, verbal language, mathematical language, scientific languages etc. So when speaking of languages we refer to the different ways children (and human beings in general) represent, communicate and express their thinking in different media and symbolic systems – that is forms of expressions strongly characterized by expressive or aesthetic aspects (see also Vecchi, 2010).

The concept of expressive languages and aesthetic languages is somewhat coherent and is defined by a number of profound international thinkers. Most thinkers also correspond to the concepts of play and creativity. According to Hohr, a special significant feature of the aesthetic activity is that you can use it to express the unspeakable. The unspeakable can be thoughts and knowledge that you are not capable of putting into words and thus capture in discursive language. This primarily includes the subjective, emotions and sensory experiences that to the subject it self appear silent, unclear and fragmented, and topics such as hate or love, whose complexity and emotional meaning can only be captured roughly and insufficiently in discursive phrasing. Through the aesthetic mediation of the unspeakable, we thus become able to reflect on and communicate about the things we would not otherwise be able to speak of.

The relationship between aesthetic creative activities and children's development and learning, based on among other theories of Malcolm Ross, Hansjörg Hohr and Bjørn Rasmussen. Aesthetic activities strengthen the joy of life, and they are an arena for development of imagination and creativity - maybe society's most important resources.

Expressive and aesthetic languages seems to grow within informal mentorships among children. Henry Jenkins defines participation like this:

"Where members believe that their contributions matter, with some type of informal mentorship, relatively low barriers for engagement, care about others´ options of self and work, strong support for sharing creations with others" (Jenkins, 2009).

Therefore the pedagogue or teacher must act to support these informal mentorships. Of course formal mentorships can support expressive languages – and then the role of the pedagogue or teacher is crucial in order to understand the importance of these informal mentorships. Expressive languages are part of children's social interaction and play and grow within social interaction and play.

Play is vital for children and for creative processes. Johan Huizinga stresses the playing human (Homo Ludens) and argues that play is a vital way of the human expression.

"Play as a voluntary activity or occupation executed within certain fixed limits of time and place, according to the rules freely accepted but absolutely binding having its aim in itself and accompanied by a feeling of tension, joy and consciousness that it is different from ordinary life" (Huizinga, 1938).

Roger Caillois adds the following to Huizinga´s definition of play: play as an activity which is essentially: 1. Free: in which playing is not obligatory;

if I were, it would at once lose its attractive and joyous quality as diversion, 2. Separate: circumscribed within limits of space and time, defined and fixed in advance, 3. Uncertain: the course of which cannot be determined, nor the result attained beforehand, and some latitude for innovations being left to the player´s initiative, 4. Unproductive: creating neither goods, nor wealth, nor new elements of any kind; and except for the exchange of property among the players, ending in a situation identical to that prevailing at the beginning of the game (Caillois, 2001).

Play then is stressed to be crucial element in creative processes. Malcolm Ross argues that the playing approach is vital in order to work express oneself in symbolic languages and that playful processes are prerequisite for creativity. Ross argues that playful processes with different materials in different environment, space and time.

Children thus at the beginning of their lives are governed by cognitive opportunities that they use and that makes their gaze on the world intentionally: They try to shape everything in their everyday lives so it makes sense here and now - for themselves at least. The claims patterns, styles and expressions that enables children to copy, to transform, to transcend materials in their everyday lives. In that sense children have their own culture, they act actively within their own peer culture (Juncker, 2004). Children's culture is characterized by aesthetic interaction, e.g. the doctrine of recognition using observation, humor and emotion. The aesthetic patterns in children's free togetherness is expressed through sounds, facial expressions and gestures, and repetition (Juncker, 2004).

Some conclusive remarks on children´s expressive language. Children has a hundred languages but they are taken away the 99 so it seems to be a matter on focusing on the quality of the expressions and expressive languages children express and perform in their everyday life. They express them and communicate in creative ways in their play and in their peer culture and communities. A pre assumption on creative expressions and expressive languages are the importance of play. Play is a vital for human expression and interaction – and children´s play seem to make sense and meaning in their everyday life. So play is fundamental to creative processes and expressive languages which means that play must be regarded and a fundamental way to support creativity.

## References

Austring & Sørensen (2006) Aesthetics and Learning, Hans Reitzels Forlag, Copenhagen

Caillois, Roger (2001) Man, Play and Games, University of Illios Press

Hansjörg Hohr (2004) Et dannelsesteoretisk perspektiv på det estetiske, http://www.ucn.dk/Files/Filer/Om%20UCN/Udgivelser/Paedagogiske%20udgivelser/SocialXPress/Socialxpress_2_2004.pdf

Huizinga, Johan (1950) Homo Ludens - a Study of play element in culture, Beacon Press

Jenkins, H (2009), Confronting the Challenges of Participatory Culture: Media Education for the 21st Culture http://digitallearning.macfound.org/atf/cf/%7B7E45C7E0-A3E0-4B89-AC9C-E807E1B0AE4E%7D/JENKINS_WHITE_PAPER.PDF

Juncker, Beth (2004), Gakkede gangarter, vilde vitser, rallende râb! Børns kulturelle udtryksformer og værdier, http://www.uvm.dk/Uddannelser-og-dagtilbud/Dagtilbudsomraadet/Fakta-om-dagtilbud/~/media/UVM/Filer/Udd/Dagtilbud/111018%20Gakkede%20gangarter,%20vilde%20vitser,%20rallende%20råb.ashx

Malaguzzi, Loris (2006) Everything has a Shadow, except ants, Reggio Children

Ross, Malcolm (1980) The Arts and personal growth, Pergamon Press

Vecchi, Vea (2010) Art and Creativity in Reggio Emilia – Exploring the role and potential of ateliers in early childhood education, Routledge

# 7 Creativity in pre-school teachers' education
*Maria Teresa dos Santos and Maria do Céu André*

## Introduction

When addressing the issue of creativity in pre-school education it is of utmost importance to consider the role of the professionals and their own education.

Studies on the lives of many creative people in different areas of expression point out that school (even high school) had little effect on their creative potential and in many cases the academic failure was evident (e.g., Einstein, Picasso) (Csikszentmihalyi, 1996).

This raises the question of the possibility to educate for creativity at the formal systems of education and represent a challenge for those dedicated to teachers' training.

Initial training courses are the first step to socialize within the profession, therefore to develop a theoretical and practical body of knowledge that makes it possible to start building a personal repertoire which needs to be permanently reconfigured throughout one's career.

In many of the educational systems, the courses' curricula (from elementary to high education) are built within a linear and disciplinary logic presenting knowledge trimmed in shelves where the contents of one area seldom has contact with another and where some are given a top position, like language, mathematics, science, while for others, mainly arts, the consideration is usually minor.

Delors (as cited in Martins 2004, p. 300) expressed: "Educational systems are formal, often accused, rightly, of limited personal development, imposing on all students the same cultural and intellectual model, without taking into account the diversity of individual talents. Increasingly tend, for example, to prioritize development of abstract knowledge, to the detriment of other human qualities like imagination, (...) the sense of the beautiful (...)".

The educational reforms of the 80s and 90s in most European countries brought some hope to the development of creativity due to the emphasis put on the constructivist perspective of learning processes, either in children or adults that would require a different approach to teaching and learning, centred essentially on the learners' active role in the process and not so much on the contents. As stated by Santos, Nuñez and Tavares (2010) this focus on content overloads students with information and therefore does not allow them to reflect on relevant issues and to think creatively.

The conclusions of the European Council meeting (2008/C - 141/10) on the subject of promoting creativity and innovation through education and training, state:

(..) beyond their essential tasks of ensuring the acquisition of key competences and providing the knowledge triangle with a solid skills base, education and training systems can play a fundamental role in the development of creative and innovative capacities as key factors in enhancing future economic competitiveness and promoting social cohesion and individual well-being;

(...) starting at school level, education systems need to combine the development of specific knowledge and skills together with that of generic capacities linked to creativity, such as curiosity, intuition, critical and lateral thinking, problem solving, experimentation, risk taking and the ability to learn from failure, use of the imagination and hypothetical reasoning, and a sense of entrepreneurship; (p.17).

Europe established 2009 as the year for creativity, inspiring many educational documents with reflexes in the goals of European school curricula. In spite of this movement, nowadays, in many of those countries the political guidelines seem to go in the direction of back to basics. From top administration to the level of classroom, the raising measures of control and bureaucracy in the obsessive pursuit of school ratings, academic success, and evaluation procedures are strong constraints to the development of creativity. The key words are results and efficiency with the least resources and cost, which most of the time are attained by imposing the same rhythm of learning, a model of thought, passivity and uniformity.

The type of thinking, often encouraged in school, is especially linear and convergent while more affective and social personality dimensions are underestimated. Other components of cognition, like creativity, intuition or imagination, are less valued in terms of content and process (Martins, n.d., p. 302, quoting Almeida & Mettrau, 1994).

Sæbø, McCammon and O'Farrell (2006, p. 4) argue that "Despite the fact that educational documents make claims for creativity in education and give several reasons for implementing creative teaching and creative learning in schools, most schools retain too many features which are fundamentally uncreative (Lucas, 2001; Sæbø, 2003). Most current practice appears to reflect outmoded traditional practices emphasizing positivist views of learning driven by standardized testing".

In the opinion of Ferrari, Cachia and Punie (2009) the recognized benefits of creativity to society and individuals, the growing educational interest for the subject, the efforts to bring it to a more central position, have been "overshadowed by other demands on teachers' and students' schedules".

Therefore, some tensions and hidden agendas on the issue of creativity and teaching-learning processes can easily be found. Nevertheless, reflection must be done on pre-school teachers' training and their essential role on the development of creativity in childhood education.

## The complexity of teaching-learning processes

The pedagogical act is a complex one which requires a great number of skills from the professional who needs to be prepared for a practice that is not characterized by certainty. The improvisation is also part of teachers' activity and like a jazz musician he must be attentive and be able to read the different "instruments" and "tunes" played by children in order to have a dialogue with them at a profound level.

To develop the ability to learn with experience, to question and reflect, to discover other paths, to come up with new solutions is something which training activities should pursue.

Contributing to building professional projects that are rooted in personal development - contextualized meaning and personal significance - is a main goal of teacher training models which have, during the last 20 years, stressed the relevance of preparing reflective practitioners, who are able to understand, relate, organize, and give meaning to what they do, adjust to multiple demands of modernity and especially overcome the challenges of learning to think and learning to learn (Gómez,1992; Perrenoud, 1993; Schön,1992; Silva, 2008; Woods, 1991; Zeichner, 1992).

Usually, creativity has been a peripheral area of study in teacher training curricula, either in initial or in-service courses and when it is considered, the content-centred perspective and the methodological strategies used, lead frequently student teachers to receive information passively, mechanically and de-contextualized from the realities of their future practice (Oliveira, 2011; Santos, Nuñez & Tavares, 2010; Silva, 2008).

The fact that teachers have a long socialization in schools (first as students and then as teachers) is also seen as a constraint to creativity development and has contributed quite often to the "weakening of intellect" and consequently to alienation and lack of reflection from teachers on their professional field (Woods, 1991).

In such a scenery, how can we ask a teacher to be able to open the disciplinary boundaries of school knowledge, and transform it making the integration, the (re) connection or to show openness, flexibility to the multiple problems he/she will be facing during his/her practice.

The conclusions of the European Council meeting (2008/C 141/10, p. 17) stress the relevance of the teacher's role "in nurturing and supporting each child's creative potential (...) by exemplifying creativity in their own teaching" and exerting teacher education institutions to contribute to the development of the knowledge and skills seen as crucial.

It seems evident for many researchers that if, in their training, teachers were encouraged to be creative and aware of the importance of creativity in the formation of the person as well as having known pedagogical practices that stimulate creativity, the more easily they can apply those competences to their class and school environment (Castro & Fleith, 2008; Cramond, 2008; Fryer, 1996, 2008; Oliveira, 2011; Prado, 1987, 1999; Romo, 1997, 2008).

Oliveira (2011) supports the view that the engagement of creativity in the learning process of teacher training will form not only someone with a creative vision and an agent of change, but also a person of ethical sensitivity and political consciousness.

However, as Silva (2008) reminds us the transfer of knowledge acquired in training to the practical context of performance constitutes one of the most difficult problems to overcome in the training of teachers in general and though it is believed that such an achievement is possible, there are limitations.

The pedagogical arena is a complex field of work where most of the problems of the political, economic, social and cultural contexts are reflected and many aspects of the different levels - from the educational system to the class - can interfere in the teachers' desire to create.

In a fast developing world which demands many different skills from teachers, there is a special need to create conditions for their personal self-improvement linked with their professional development. This requires time for inner reflection, psychological maturity that makes it possible to look at others in a more open, intuitive, free way, especially the young children they are going to work with.

In this perspective, Alencar (1996) cit. in Martins (n.d.) states that there is a need to rethink the system of education and build a platform for creativity, in which the skills related to creative thinking and strengthening of personality attributes that foster creative expression must be developed, as well as to immunize students against diseases that can undermine their creative energy, like fear of failure or apathy.


**Developing creativity in pre-school teachers' education**

Several authors refer to the influential document of the British National Advisory Committee on Creative and Cultural Education (NACCCE, 1999), which fed into the review of the United Kingdom National Curriculum (Jeffrey & Craft, 2004; Sæbø, McCammon & O'Farrell, 2006; Tracey, 2011)

The NACCCE report (1999) makes a distinction between teaching creatively and teaching for creativity. Teaching creatively is related to teachers' use of imaginative strategies to make the learning process more interesting and appealing, while teaching for creativity focuses on intentional forms of developing young people's own creative thinking.

Jeffrey and Craft (2004) question such distinctions, since they support the view that teaching for creativity can occur spontaneously, and suggest that the focus should be on creative learning rather than on creative teaching. Accordingly, the assumption that the two processes of teaching creatively and teaching for creativity are closely related, needs further explanations focused not only on the studies which examined some established features of creative teaching such as those developed by Woods (1990, cit by Jeffrey & Craft, 2004) like innovation, ownership and control and relevance, but also a focus has to be put on the effects of creative teaching on learners as most recent research emphasizes.

The authors present a case study of an early years' school they have followed and where both concepts were evident: "The approach highlights and prioritises the 'agency' of the learner in the teaching and learning process and might be contrasted with a 'child considerate' approach (Jeffrey 2001a) that views the child as an organism that needs nurturing rather than being democratically included. We suggest that teaching for creativity could involve generating a 'learner inclusive' pedagogy, where the learner is encouraged to engage in identifying and exploring knowledge." (Jeffrey & Craft, 2004, p. 14).

As stated by Sæbø, McCammon and O'Farrell (2006, p. 5) quoting Craft (2005, p. 131) "Creative teaching is regarded as a key component in all good teaching, but it does not guarantee that the children are developing their own creative potential nor does it guarantee that a teacher's own creativity is applied with clear ethical guidance; creative teachers may, in fact, diminish the creativity of others around them, or possibly do great harm, either to students or to other teachers".

In order to avoid the dangers figured by the authors there is a need to provide opportunities to engage teachers in creative learning themselves so that they might understand the processes involved.

Lucas (2001), cit. by Sæbø, McCammon and O'Farrell (2006) sustains that in order to foster creativity in schools two areas need to be developed: teacher's understanding of learning how to learn, respecting the unique individuality of the learner and a more structured intervention by creative mentors and teachers.

As expressed by Fisher (2004, pp. 14-16) cit. by Sæbø, McCammon and O'Farrell (2006, p. 6) "to transform education to foster creativity, it is necessary to build creative capacity both in students and in teachers as individual learners. The most important keys to individual creativity are:

• Motivation – which is the key to creativity. The things we want to do, we feel passionate about; they engage us and are fed by internal encouragement.

• Inspiration – which means being inspired by oneself or by others, getting fresh input and lots of knowledge and stimulating curiosity by being more observant and asking more questions.

• Gestation – that is allowing time for creative ideas to emerge. We need time to think things through on conscious and unconscious levels. Creative insights often result from processes that are unconscious and lie below the level of awareness.

• Collaboration – because we normally are more creative when we have others to support us. The learning environment in school needs to open up for ideas to be created, examined, shared and tried out, and for this we need creative partners."

A common feature to most of these authors is the relevance they put on the person as a learner (either teacher or child) in a context that allows for the relation with others in a stress-free, inspiring environment where creativity is reflected in everyday life as a way of thinking and acting, which brings joy from every individual and collective achievement and celebrates diversity.

Learning processes are a result of personal appropriation and re-construction where mind and body (as taught by ancient Greek philosophers) have to work together. If this is recognized easily in young children, the same is not the case for adults, thus teacher training courses tend to underestimate such relationships for the education of a sensitive aesthetic and ethic being, overvaluing the technical aspects of the profession.

Kleiman's research (2008, p. 216) emphasizes that the experience of creativity in learning and teaching among lecturers of higher education courses, show a perspective essentially linked to the importance of creativity - "creativity-as-transformation" and in relation to "personal and/or professional fulfilment" and adds: "Another potentially significant finding is that whilst for the institution (and even the government) creativity is the means to an essentially productive (and profitable) end, for those engaged at the whiteboard, engaging in creative processes and producing creative outcomes is very much about personal and professional fulfilment, and escaping from or at least resisting the constraints and frustrations of daily academic life."

Providing rich environments for the improvement of pre-school teachers' creativity during initial and in-service training is a challenge for those responsible for curricula organization and development. Having as a source the knowledge and understanding of universal and national cultures' heritage, as well as the knowledge of development and learning and the different means of expression will make possible the emergence of original activities and products, where processes should play a central role.

Promoting a sense of community is also of undeniable value for the pleasure of creating together where risk taking can be shared and therefore reducing the anxiety connected with the fear of failure and that of academic and social comparison, so much cheered in our societies.

Such an approach will require adults and children that feel free to express in a variety of languages and feel confident about their own potential to uncover, transform reality and bring to light new possibilities of interpretation.

All these principles do not happen in a void but in physical spaces which should be taken into account and Tracey's study (2011, p. 6) based on the experiential module Creativity in Practice for Educators shows the relevance of the spaces in which creativity occurs and where participants are offered opportunities to engage in arts-based activities to develop the understanding of their own creativity, as well as that of their practice.

Inspired by Boden's framework (2004) of creativity as a process of engaging with conceptual spaces, Tracey (2011, p. 6) presents the referred author differentiation between "three types of creativity: combinational, which involves the juxtaposition of dissimilar concepts; exploratory, which refers to conceptual explorations of the thinking styles and frameworks of fields of knowledge and enquiry; and transformative, which results when the process of exploration generates new ways of thinking and ideas".

The activities promoted within this training module revealed that teachers gained in confidence, in awareness to plan and organize creative activities in relation to the physical learning environment (real or imaginary) and expanded their reflection, through a variety of arts-based resources like collage, creative writing, three-dimensional artwork such as self-boxes (in which images are gathered to represent aspects of teacher identity, Leitch, 2008, cit. by Tracey, 2011). Tracey suggests also that for initial teacher education opportunities for the exploration of digital spaces should be offered.

The data collected from this research has shown an increasing sense of self-control among those involved as expressed by Tracey (2011, p. 15) "(…) it appears that the teachers are coming to see themselves as quilt makers, responsible for constructing and managing spaces for creativity in their practice".

It is this kind of self-confidence that teacher training proposals have to be able to promote, thus generating an educational culture for creativity which can overtake the traditional way of pedagogical work still pervasive in most schools where processes and products of creativity are less valued compared with the results of reproduction of knowledge (Ferrari, Cachia & Punie, 2009).

Among researchers there is a great unanimity regarding the fundamental role of teachers towards the aimed changes in formal education contexts, usually more conservative and rigid than non-formal settings.

In spite of the increasing knowledge and understanding of creativity in education, both theoretical and practical, the multidimensionality of the concept, the specificities of individuals and social and cultural contexts where it occurs, the diversity of languages and media through which it is expressed, there are common traits and convergent ideas about the features that are essential for the promotion of creativity.

Personal characteristics, knowledge, media and contexts have to be taken into account in educational settings and the main goal, either for adults or young children's education will be to develop positive attitudes to learn in unconventional ways and keep an inquiring mind towards what happens around them.

Burnard et al. (2006) reveal the importance of an adult-child co-participative approach that illuminates what they define as "possibility thinking" - a type of thought that answers the question "what if" and generate a great number and diversity of ideas. "Possibility thinking" guides action and leads to a strong engagement of children and adults through questioning, play, making connections, being imaginative and self-determined.

It is then put into evidence that a content approach to teachers' training curricula is a very limited one and a move is needed towards a more global and integral perspective centred on pre-school teachers learning and reflective processes to promote student teachers' and professionals' personal development while developing a wide range of pedagogical knowledge and skills.

Cremin, Burnard and Craft's (2006, p. 11) study case on pedagogical approaches to possibility thinking in young children has shown a kind of "invisible" pedagogy where "the teachers positioned themselves off-centre stage and promoted learning through the children's self-chosen activities and interests within broadly conceived subject domains. Whilst not afraid to use direct instruction and teacher-led work where necessary, they sought to balance teacher and child-led initiatives, explicitly fostering a sense of possibility and agency in their young learners. In addition, they created the time and space for children to explore their environment and the materials provided, encouraging both actual and mental play (Joubert, 2001). The features of this distinct pedagogic practice appeared to promote and foster the children's full engagement in problem solving - problem finding activities and thus supported their development as young possibility thinkers."

Such a pedagogical model should also be adopted in most higher education contexts that aim to form and educate pre-school teachers, given the role they are called to perform in young children's development.

## Final reflections

In his book "Out of our minds: learning to be creative", Ken Robinson (2011) identifies three related tasks in teaching for creativity: encouraging, identifying and fostering.

The first step in teaching for creativity in any field is to encourage students to believe in their creative potential and to promote their confidence to try.

The second task is to support students in identifying their own creative strengths, in other words to discover their creative capacities.

The third role for the teacher is to foster: this means to help students in developing skills (like self- confidence, independence, etc.) that enable them to be more effective in dealing with problems and objectives.

The overwhelmed load of information and high pace of modern societies can be strong constraints to creativity development.

Time and space need to gain other dimensions if the desire is to form educators who are able to relate and connect with others and with different domains of knowledge – theory and practice; educators who can think in a divergent way, who are not afraid to experiment and improvise, who can visualize their profession not only as science and technique but as art, where many pedagogical situations can be lived with elegance, beauty and enthusiasm which are characteristics of all creative processes.

Creativity calls for holistic thinking that mobilizes what is inside and what is outside both of the individual and the formal educational institutions, thus there is a need to promote a rich cultural learning environment that provides the field for the learner's potential development.

## References

Burnard, P., Craft, A., Cremin, T., Duffy, B., Hanson, R., Keene, J., Haynes, L., & Burns, D. (2006). Documenting 'possibility thinking': a journey of collaborative enquiry. International Journal of Early Years Education, 14(3), pp. 243–262. Retrieved from http://oro.open.ac.uk/6546/1/6546.pdf

Castro, J.S.R., & Fleith, D. S. (2008). Criatividade escolar: relação entre tempo de experiência docente e tipo de escola. Revista Semestral da Associação Brasileira de Psicologia Escolar e Educacional (ABRAPEE), Volume 12, Nº 1, 101-118. Retrieved from http://www.scielo.br/pdf/pee/v12n1/v12n1a08.pdf

Cramond, B. (2008). Creativity: An international imperative for society and the individual. In S. Bahia, & M.F. Morais (Coord.), Criatividade: Conceito, necessidades e intervenção (pp.14-40). Braga: Psiquilíbrios Edições.

Cremin, T., Burnard, P. & Craft, A. (2006). Pedagogy and Possibility Thinking in the Early Years. Thinking Skills and Creativity, 1(2), 108–119. Retrieved from http://oro.open.ac.uk/12952/2/6F6D71D8.pdf

Csikszentmihalyi, M. (1996). Creativity: Flow and the psychology of discovery and invention. N.Y.: Harper Collins Publishers.

Ferrari, A., Cachia,R., & Punie, Y. (2009). Innovation and Creativity in Education and Training in the EU Member States: Fostering Creative Learning and Supporting Innovative Teaching. Retrieved from ftp://ftp.jrc.es/users/publications/public/EURdoc/EURdoc/JRC52374_TN.pdf

Fryer, M. (1996). Creative teaching and learning. London: Paul Chapman Publishing Ltd.

Fryer, M. (2008). Creative teaching and learning in the UK: Early research and some subsequent developments. In S. Bahia, & M.F. Morais (Coord.), Criatividade: Conceito, necessidades e intervenção, Braga: Psiquilíbrios Edições, pp.136-156.

Gómez, A. P. (1992). O pensamento prático do professor – a formação do professor como profissional reflexivo. In A. Nóvoa (Coord.), Os professores e a sua formação (pp. 93-114). Lisboa: Pub. D. Quixote.

Jeffrey, B., & Craft, A. (2004). Teaching creatively and teaching for creativity: distinctions and relationships. Educational Studies, 30 (1), pp. 77-87. Retrieved from http://oro.open.ac.uk/425/2/CT-TFC-Final-Ed_Studies.pdf

Kleiman, P. (2008). Towards transformation: conceptions of creativity in higher education. Creativity Special Edition: Innovations in Education and Teaching International (IETI), 45:3, 209-217. Retrieved from http://dx.doi.org/10.1080/14703290802175966

Martins, V.M.T. (2004). A qualidade da criatividade como mais valia para a educação. Retrieved from http://www.ipv.pt/millenium/Millenium29/37.pdf

Official Journal of the European Union (Ed.) (2008). Conclusions of the Council and of the Representatives of the Governments of the Member States, meeting within the Council of 22 May 2008 on promoting creativity and innovation through education and training (2008/C 141/10). Retrieved fromhttp://eurlex.europa.eu/LexUriServ/LexUriServ.do?uri=OJ:C:2008:141:0017:0020:en:PDF.

Oliveira, Z.M.F. (2011). 'Criativar' a formação e a atuação do professor: uma necessidade no século XXI. Retrieved from http://educere.bruc.com.br/CD2011/pdf/4437_2330.pdf

Prado, D. (1987). Manual de activación creativa. Santiago: Universidade de Santiago de Compostela.

Prado, D. (1999). EDUCREA: la creatividad, motor de la renovación esencial de la educacion. Santiago: Universidade de Santiago de Compostela

Perrenoud, P. (1993). Práticas pedagógicas, profissão docente e formação – perspectivas sociológicas. Lisboa: Pub. D. Quixote.

Robinson, K. (2011). Out of our minds: learning to be creative. Chichester,

UK: Capstone Publishing.

Romo, M. (1997). Psicología de la creatividad. Barcelona: Ediciones Paidós Ibérica, S. A.

Romo, M. (2008). Creatividad en los dominios artistic y científico y sus correlatos educativos. In S. Bahia, & M.F. Morais (Coord.), Criatividade: Conceito, necessidades e intervenção, Braga: Psiquilíbrios Edições, pp.66-90.

Sæbø, A.B., McCammon L.A., & O'Farrel, L. (2006). Exploring Teaching Creativity and Creative Teaching: The First Step in an International Research Project. Retrieved from http://www.dramanett.no/Creativity%20in%20Education%20Research.pd f

Santos, F.A.A., Nuñez, I.B., & Tavares, A.M.B.N. (2010). Criatividade e formação docente: as histórias de vidas e os percursos escolares e acadêmicos como possíveis entraves na compreensão do ensino na perspectiva da criatividade. Retrieved from http://www.senept.cefetmg.br/galerias/Anais_2010/Artigos/GT8/CRIAT IVIDADE_E_FORMACAO.pdf

Schön, D. A. (1992). Formar professores como profissionais reflexivos. In A. Nóvoa (Coord.). Os professores e a sua formação, Lisboa: Pub. D. Quixote, pp. 77-91.

Silva, K.R.X. (2008). Criatividade e inclusão na formação de professores: representações e práticas sociais. PhD thesis presented to the Faculty of Education of Universidade Federal do Rio de Janeiro (Brasil). Retrieved from http://www.educacao.ufrj.br/ppge/teses/tese_katia_regina_xavier_da_silv a.pdf

Tracey, S. (2011). Containers, Creativity and Quilt-making: an exploration of teachers' conceptualisations of creative spaces for teaching and learning. Tean Journal, 2 (1). Retrieved from http://194.81.189.19/ojs/index.php/TEAN/article/viewFile/67/81

Woods, P. (1991). Aspectos sociais da criatividade do professor. In A. Nóvoa (Coord.), Profissão professor, Porto: Porto Editora, pp. 125-153.

Zeichner, K. (1992). Novos caminhos para o practicum: uma perspectiva para os anos 90. In A. Nóvoa (Coord.), Os professores e a sua formação, Lisboa: Pub. D. Quixote, pp. 115-138.

# 8 Teachers' implicit theories of creativity
*Antonella Pugnaghi*

"The creative filter between us and the world is always" Bateson, 1979

## Creativity between definitions and representations

There are concepts that seem to convey many meanings, full of a cultural tradition that provides them with a plurivocity of sense, thus making it difficult to grasp a full understanding and definition of them. Among these concepts, marked by a high semantic complexity, the multidimensional construct of creativity today occupies a prominent place, because it concerns many aspects of human life. In fact, because of the highly complex and multi-faceted nature of this phenomenon, in literature there is not yet a full  agreement about what it is and how it develops and multiple perspectives of study exist: clinical theories, cognitive, developmental, economic, educational, historical, organizational and social (Kozbelt, Beghetto & Runco, 2010; Runco, 2007; 2008; Sternberg & Kaufman, 2010).

In order to examine and compare the theories related to creativity in a systematic way, a good starting point is to consider the framework presented by Rhodes (1961) and taken up by Sharp (2004), in which the different types of perspectives of study are reduced to four broad categories:

- person: the traits, abilities, motivational, and affective states, and behaviours that appear to be correlated with creativity (Amabile, 1990; Barron & Harrington, 1981)

- process: the cognitive and social dynamics governing the generation, expression, and acceptance or adaptation of new ideas (Csikszentmihalyi, 1990; Runco, 1991);

- press: pressures in the social and material environment that enhance or inhibit creativity (Murray, 1938), such as access to resources, family or organizational structure, support for and valuing of originality, or the need to find solutions to urgent problems (Albert & Runco, 1989; Amabile & Gryskiewick, 1989);

- product: studies of creative outputs such as publications, patents or art works.

Within this functional segmentation, however continually at risk of oversimplification, many possible readings of creativity are hidden, which describe a very rich heritage of meanings and interpretations. Despite all the possible definitions that can be given to the terms "creative" and "creativity", there is a consensus about the fact that creative products must be new and "accepted as plausible or useful or satisfying by a group at some point of time" (Stein, 1953, p. 311). This dual criteria of originality and appropriateness to the task forms the nucleus of a scientific approach to creativity, but it is important not to forget that, behind its relative simplicity, unfolds a complex history of thoughts and theories (Sternberg & Lubart, 1999). In this regard the analysis performed by Glăveanu (2011) appears to be particularly interesting, in which the author faces the controversy about the creativity of children, bringing out the different conceptualizations and readings which have been given to this complex phenomenon over time. Specifically, the author arrives to describe three general paradigms of creativity, which still continue to pervade and influence both explicit and implied theories tacitly. The most important of these, which has gone through several historic times up to the present day, derives from a romantic association between creativity and figure of genius. The romantic model of genius, with its nuances of individuality, intuition and exceptional ability (Mason, 2003 cit. in Glăveanu, 2011) has largely contributed to the break between creation and living, for this figure is recognized by the task of detaching him or herself from society so as to revolutionize it, and radically change the perspective of the world. Embracing this paradigm, founded on the outstanding abilities of the genius (Mason, 2003, cit. in Glăveanu, 2011), an elitist and essentialist vision of creativity is shared (Pickard, 1990) and the role of co-creation or collaboration in the creation process (Barron, 1995) is excluded, because creativity becomes the domain reserved for a limited number of selected individuals or talented people that create important masterpieces in the arts and carry out relevant scientific discoveries. However, the paradigm of genius has not remained unchallenged. Since 1950, psychology has contributed greatly to impose a new perspective on creativity, according to which every individual is creative (although to varying degrees) and this ability can and should be educated. Under this vision children earn their "right" to creativity, however modest its expression may be (Glăveanu, 2011). In line with this perspective, Gardner says that "our romantic tradition, remodeled in terms of modern ethics, has made us sensitive to the notion of the child as an artist, and the child in every artist" (Gardner, 1982, p. 92). This paradigm shift has led to a real "democratization" of creativity (Bateson, 1999) and to significant methodological advances in the study of this phenomenon, but also this perspective doesn't recognize the cultural and social roots of the creative process. "Creativity is not born from nothing (as in the case of genius), or from the individual alone (as proposed by some cognitive models), but exists between self and other, creator and public, individual and community" (Glăveanu, 2011, p. 125). In contrast, therefore, with the atomistic and positivist conceptions of creativity, during the recent decades, a new conceptual paradigm has spread, a We-paradigm, which, adopting holistic and systemic perspectives, considers creativity as a complex collaborative and intersubjective endeavour. In fact, according to this interpretative framework, creativity is not just influenced by immediate social and contextual factors, but it is the very nature of this process to be relational and as such it cannot exist outside of certain cultural resources and dialogic relations. The recent spread of such a conceptualization has led many scholars to investigate implicit theories of creativity in non-Western cultures, focusing mainly on the profiles of creative individuals identified within different cultural groups (Andiliou & Murphy, 2010; Chan & Chan, 1999; Dinka, 1999; Fryer & Collings, 1991; Lim & Plucker, 2001; Raina, Kumar & Raina, 1980; Rudowicz & Hui, 1997; Rudowicz & Yue, 2000; 2002).

The adoption of such implicit or explicit conceptual paradigms has marked the evolution of representations and definitions of creativity, as a general construct and of its various aspects, provided both by researchers and common people, especially by those who carry out a key role in social and educational contexts. In this perspective, a particularly interesting area of research, although not yet much developed, concerns the study of teachers' implicit theories about creativity, connections and differences that the latter exhibits with the explicit theories formulated with regards to the study of this phenomenon.

Specifically, the concept of implicit theory indicates "the set of beliefs, opinions and attitudes that individuals develop about a certain phenomenon and on the basis of it they supply the explanations" (Pizzigrilli & Antonietti, 2009, p. 62). Consequently, the implicit beliefs about creativity describe a collection of thoughts and ideas about a specific paradigm that individuals possess and use in order to interpret the nature of this phenomenon. Particularly, Runco (2007) argues that implicit theories are a process to rationalize the subjectivity of the individual perception of creativity and these idiosyncratic and groundwater conceptualizations are real reference systems that condense a set of meanings, through which individuals rewrite and interpret the creativity and the reality in general. Therefore, the study of such beliefs becomes of primary importance, especially in education, in order to identify the stereotypes and prejudices that teachers develop about this phenomenon (Sternberg, 1999), which tend to hinder the real advancement of it within different educational contexts.

**Thoughts and ideas about creativity: the point of view of teachers**

There is no doubt that innovation and initiative are essential for survival and social progress (Craft, 2003; 2006), however, creativity, while almost universally regarded as important for society, it is often not recognized and valued within educational contexts (Craft, 2006; Danescu, 2009;

Zimmerman, 2009). To recognize the creativity within school settings it is necessary to adopt a broad and democratic definition (Sharp, 2004), according to which each child has a creative potential that must be promoted, focusing more on the process rather than on the assessment quality of its products. Given the important role assigned to education in the promotion of creative thinking and, not being teachers, immune from myths or misconceptions, many scholars have highlighted the importance of investigating in-depth the implicit theories of who plays an important educational role by obtaining information about their decision procedures and the educational behaviours adopted at school (Beghetto, 2007). According to Aljughaiman and Mowrer-Reynolds (2005, p.17) "the challenge to promote creativity for teachers is to identify the characteristics of the creative personality, recognize creative products, understand the cognitive processes used by creative students, and eventually create an environment that promotes the interests of children." For this reason, implicit theories and conceptions of teachers about creativity have gained the interest of researchers since the mid-eighties (Sternberg, 1985; Runco & Bahleda, 1986, cit. in Rudowicz, 2003).

What does the term creativity mean? Who is the creative child? And what social and cultural factors influence the development of creative potential in school?

These questions form the cornerstones of the research which, in the psychological and pedagogical sphere, have investigated and still continue to explore the implicit theories related to creativity, with particular attention to those unspoken and tacit that guide the educational activities of teachers.

The main aim of this work is therefore to explore, summarize and systematize the investigations that, in the international arena, have examined the naive conceptions of teachers about creativity in order to understand which interpretative frameworks often unconsciously guide the educational practices.


## What ideas of creativity?

A first important research strand deals with implicit theories about creativity by taking into consideraton representations and conceptualizations of its multifaceted nature.

However, before considering the studies that have focused mainly on teachers, the analysis carried out by Andiliou and Murphy (2010) is particularly interesting; in their review of studies, as well as outlining a conceptual framework overall, they examine also the conceptualizations of creativity proposed by the researchers in their investigations. This analysis shows that in the different studies the researchers embrace different conceptualizations of the construct, they rarely give explicit definitions of the latter and sometimes appear to be contrary to the contemporary theoretical writings on the nature of creativity. Such a multitude of meanings and vagueness of interpretations is in line with the findings of the different studies related to the representations of teachers and students on the creativity.

In this regard, Diakidoy and Kanari (1999), administering a questionnaire, asked a group of college students at the end of their training to define creativity, creative commodities and the factors related to this phenomenon. The results of this research indicate that creativity as conceptualized by the students, involved mainly a general ability and a source of individual differences. Furthermore, most of them define it on the basis of its products, which are considered as new elements, thus drawing on the assumptions of traditional approaches. Nevertheless, students do not perceive individual differences in creativity as extensive and impressive and they reject the concept of exceptionality of the phenomenon, showing an agreement with the point of view of ordinary creativity. In addition, according to these future teachers it is evident that the major differences in creativity are largely attributable to environmental factors. Students of the sample firmly believe that it is possible to facilitate creativity in everyone, and, more specifically, that it is duty and responsibility of the teacher.

Even Kampylis, Berki and Saariluoma (2009) have examined the naive conceptions on creativity by administering a questionnaire (Questionnaire on conceptualizations of teachers around the Creativity - TCCQ) in a sample of 70 in-service teachers who work in government primary schools and 62 Greek students enrolled at the Faculty of Primary Education of the University of Athens. The results of this study have shown that Greek teachers, both in service and future, conceptualize creativity as a key factor in the personal and social progress influenced by socio-cultural and environmental contexts. In addition, the overwhelming majority of participants supports a democratic approach to creativity, as it is recognized that the creative potential, present in every child, can be promoted and developed. However, with regard to education, the teachers involved have appeared less secure and more skeptical towards the school, emphasizing the lack of opportunities and resources offered to students for expressing and developing their creative potential.

From these early studies, it clearly emerges that the idiosyncrasy which characterizes the implicit theories formulated by teachers, who do not present themselves as faithful reproductions of explicit theories formulated by researchers and theorists, tend to be eclectic aggregations of cause and effect propositions, assembled by various sources: generalizations based on personal experience, beliefs, values and prejudices.

## Who is the creative child? Which characteristics identify him/her?

Many authors have identified specific factors or traits so as to accurately describe the characteristics of creative subjects (Dawson et al., 1999). In 1950, Guilford identified a set of exclusive characteristics of creative individuals, including continuous involvement in activities such as inventing, planning, contriving, composing and scheduling (Guilford, 1950). Dawson et al. (1999) have identified as traits of creative individuals, which cut across the different descriptions given by scholars, such as being impulsive, individualistic, unconventional and free spirits. Furthermore, Runco et al. (1998), by conducting a survey on a sample of 143 researchers in the area of creativity, discovered that for the majority of the scholars involved, creative individuals are:

- open to new experiences;
- competent in their performance in different tasks;
- able to perceive the concepts from a variety of perspectives.

Finally, many authors consider creative individuals as people with considerable self-confidence, less concerned with the opinions of other people, able to concentrate, to accept the conflict and to have the courage to be different (Clark, 2008).

These descriptions appear to be consistent with what has emerged from research conducted by Runco and co-workers (1993) regarding the implicit theories of teachers and parents about the representative characteristics of the creative personality. In this investigation the authors used the Adjective Check List (Gough & Heilbrun, 1980, cit. in Runco et al., 1993), asking participants to select adjectives to describe creative and non-creative children. The results of this first survey have shown that about half of the sample of teachers and parents selected the same adjectives to describe the creative child, indicating him as adventurous, enthusiastic, artistic, imaginative and curious. However, some differences were noted between the two groups of subjects involved because while teachers focused their attention on some temperamental and social characteristics (cheerful, friendly and quiet), parents indicated intrapersonal characteristics of the child (enterprising, impulsive, full resources and self-confidence) (Runco, 2011). Both groups, however, tend to negatively identify the characteristics of the creative personality, selecting adjectives such as pessimistic, self-centered, shallow and unambitious (Saracho, 2012a).

Towards creativity and, in particular, in relation to creative children, the teachers, nevertheless, do not seem to keep taking a general positive attitude. In fact, if the explicit descriptions of the scholars appear to be coherent and favourable to the different traits highlighted in them, it does not seem to be confirmed by the conceptualizations expressed by teachers, which in most cases negatively characterize the student who demonstrates some features of the creative personality (Lim & Plucker, 2001).

Specifically, Torrance (1963) revealed that the personality of the creative students is in contrast with the features appreciated by the majority of teachers. The behaviours of creative pupils, as well as being emotional, open, critical of others and tenacious, are not encouraged and are seen as harmful to the organization and order of each class. Creativity in the classroom seems to be regarded as a form of deviance, potentially destructive, so that teachers often come to reject unexpected and new ideas from the students (Saracho, 2012a). Furthermore, Oral and Güncer (1993) found a negative correlation between creativity and conformity to school discipline as indicated by the assessments provided for teachers. Based on these assessments, the children identified as very creative are also considered as the most provocative towards the order of the school and therefore unappreciated. Teachers therefore seem to prefer students who get high scores on standardized tests, with less creativity and high conformism.

Another important study that fits into this area of investigation was conducted by Scott (1999), which explored the potential representations and prejudices of teachers towards creative children, using a set of behavioural criteria and comparing the answers provided by a sample of primary school teachers with those given by a sample of college students. The results showed that it is significantly more likely that teachers evaluate creative children as more disruptive than students. The author interprets this result underlining the fact that creativity is often associated with children who ask many questions and the teachers seem inclined to regard it as a source of interference in the teaching schedule thought up by them.

In general, these results are in line with those obtained previously from Westby and Dawson (1995), with the study of which it has been attempted to identify the actual preferences of teachers towards the different characteristics associated with creativity. In order to achieve this research purpose, scholars have developed a creative prototype (a list of characteristics and personality traits deducted from the scientific literature concerning the topic of creativity) and they asked teachers to assess their pupils using such a device. From the analysis of the collected data, high correlations have emerged between the characteristics of the prototype and the student profile underappreciated, traced by teachers, thus confirming the preference for non-creative behaviours in school. The teachers have been subsequently asked to identify the traits that they think to be indicative of a creative child. The latter have also confirmed a significant correlation between the profile of the underappreciated student indicated previously by teachers and the profile of the creative child. To sum up, if on the one hand the teachers recognize the importance of creativity as an educational goal, from the other, literature emphasizes the negative meaning attributed by the same teachers to certain traits of the creative personality.

Aljughaiman and Mowrer-Reynolds (2005) have tried to identify the reasons for this conflict by examining the definitions of creativity and creative students supplied by a sample of primary school teachers. The analyses show an adoption of a democratic interpretation of creativity on the part of the participants, according to which every child has got a creative potential at different levels. However, in spite of showing positive attitudes towards the teaching of creativity in the classroom, the teachers involved did not perceive it as their responsibility. The authors noted three important aspects associated with such reluctance in assuming certain educational responsibilities. Firstly, the relative importance attached by teachers to creativity in school achievement. In fact, none of the participating educators has shown suitability to the task or the utility as a criterion for evaluating and as a distinguishing feature of the creative process/product. Thus, education for creativity is to emerge as something additional, optional and separate from traditional curricula. In support of this first interpretation, the authors reported that some teachers have associated creative activities with moments of fun rather than as real learning opportunities. The second explanation given by scholars relates the definitions of creativity provided by the teachers and their resistance to bear the consequent responsibility. In particular, in the descriptions given by the teachers, one can see a limitation of the creative expression to the scope of art and literature, consequently the promotion of creativity is considered by educators to be reserved to specific educational figures within each school. Finally, the authors have speculated as one of the reasons for this reluctant attitude is the lack of knowledge about the phenomenon in question and, therefore, the consequent inability to recognize the creative students and/or to teach different educational approaches to promote the creative potential of all students. However, the conceptualizations that teachers involved in this investigation have provided about the creative students, deviate from what has emerged from previous research and seem to be in part related to social desirability. In their descriptions, the teachers have emphasized those positive traits, usually appreciated by adults at school, but despite this fact they have neglected other aspects that experts attribute constantly to the creative personality, such as the autonomy in thinking and independence in judging. The perceptions of teachers towards creative pupils turn out to be complex and, therefore, it can become difficult to recognize the students' creative abilities adequately.

In this regard, Morais and Azevedo (2011) have administered a questionnaire to a sample of teachers at different school levels in order to investigate their representations of creativity, focusing in particular on the profile of the creative child and the role of the teacher. The analyses show that the teachers involved perceive themselves as creative, but do not recognize the school in general as a positive context and influential in promoting creativity. The concept of creative teacher in this case is essentially associated with the enthusiasm shown by the teacher in the classroom, the promotion of the autonomy of the students, in being able to establish genuine relationships with students and to possess a deep knowledge and skills in their subject of teaching. However, even more interesting is the complex profile and conflictual child's creative expression outlined by teachers. In fact, the descriptions provided show a significant ambiguity with regard to school discipline. So all in all, if on the one hand these teachers seem to have an accurate perception of the creative child with regard to certain important dimensions of personality, on the other hand the same teachers show a significant negative association between creativity and acceptance of school rules. As well as reproposing a recurring theme in literature, that is the adversarial relationship between creativity and discipline, from the analyses of the data the need clearly emerges to consider the ambiguities and tensions that daily cross the figure of the teacher, tacitly influencing attitudes, decisions and educational practices.To analyze the naive conceptions of teachers towards creativity, creative pupils and the factors that affect their development means providing teachers with opportunities to question their educational views that are implicit in practice so as to give them back greater awareness and also the possibility to make a rational restructuring of their daily acting.

## What factors influence the development of creativity in school?

The overcoming of an elitist and subjectivist conception of creativity has polarized the attention on environmental and social factors which are involved in the creative process. The recognition of the contextual and generative nature of creativity (Csikszentmihalyi, 1999) resulting from the adoption of systemic and ecological perspectives for the study of this phenomenon, has led many scholars to investigate the environmental conditions that most influence the thoughts and creative actions, the latter more and more released from the characteristics and personality traits of each individual (Amabile, 1990). Therefore, another area of research has been focused on the study of creativity in the educational context, particularly on the perceptions of the factors that stimulate and/or hinder the development of creative potential in the classroom.

In this section of study the survey conducted by Fleith de Souza (2000), which aimed to investigate the points of view of a group of teachers, students and experts with regards to the conditions that characterize school environments which are considered favourable to the development of potential creative children, is of great importance . The specific profile of the way of perceiving contextual features that are benevolent to the creative process described by teachers is based on three main components: the attitudes, teaching strategies of teachers and activities. Specifically, the attitudes considered relevant for the development of creativity on the part of teachers are: not to impose too many rules and predetermined positions on the students; offering them the opportunity to choose and decide for themselves; and finally, strengthen their self-esteem. While among the teaching strategies which are deemed favourable for the development of creative thinking, teachers indicate the predisposition of the situations of cooperative learning in small groups, thus providing pupils with opportunities to explore and investigate a problem from different points of view. To let the students have some free and unstructured time, is also considered by teachers as an important chance to give them the opportunity to experiment themselves in mutable and evolving situations. Finally, the teachers focus attention on those environmental factors considered inhibitors for the evolution of the creative process within educational contexts. When students believe that they can't share their ideas, because the latter are often ignored; when errors are not tolerated, because the activities predict one possible solution; when the expected contents in the curriculum is too large and the time is limited so, according to the teachers, it is not possible to realize a favourable environment for the development of the creative process. While the students involved show a positive attitude towards school and creativity and on numerous occasions, they conclude by confining the latter in the specific domain of artistic disciplines. Without taking into account the specific subject, pupils recognize that the situations in which they could express their creativity in school are those characterized by a certain degree of flexibility and the possibility to express their ideas and thoughts freely, having also more time to think, experiment and reflect. Similar elements are indicated by the group of experts involved in the research, which also emphasize the importance of ensuring children a certain psychological security and providing them with opportunities to reflect on their achievements and learning. Finally, in order to expose the elements which hinder the creative skills, the experts describe a rigid school environment, centred on the teacher and based on high levels of competition and extrinsic rewards (Souza Fleith, 2000).

The perceptions of teachers towards the influence of certain environmental factors on the development of creativity have been taken into consideration in research projects more complex and articulated, in part already discussed within the above review of studies.

Specifically, the survey conducted by Kampylis, Berki and Saariluoma (2009), apart from examining the conceptualizations of teachers towards the creativity as a general construct, investigates the points of views of participants about the influence of the school on the creative thought of pupils, paying particular attention to the role of the teacher. In general, the teachers involved believe that the primary school does not offer sufficient opportunities and means for students to express and develop their creative potential, mainly because of inadequate teaching materials and rigid and urgent educational programming. Finally, another obstacle appears to be the inadequate training of teachers, which, while recognizing creativity as a crucial factor for the personal well-being and social development of pupils, teachers do not perceive themselves adequately trained to play an important role in the promotion of creative thought.

Similar considerations have emerged from the study conducted by Diakidoy and Kanari (1999) aimed at exploring beliefs of a group of college students about creativity and the environmental factors connected to it. Among the favourable contextual elements for the development of creativity in educational contexts, the authors focus their attention on the relational dimensions related to the figure of the teacher. Particularly, they emphasize the importance of offering situations in which the teacher proves him/herself creative, able to accommodate and accept the children's ideas, flexible in his/her plans and able to establish the genuine relationships of mutual trust and respect with pupils. Finally, with regard to teaching strategies, great importance must be given, according to the students, to learning through discovery and the autonomy of the students, offering them open tasks that require continuous explorations and connections between areas of reality and aspects of experience first isolated and far between.

As a result, leaving out the organizational elements, in educational contexts the research related to the representations of teachers about the contexts of experience favourable to creativity, have focused on the relational dimensions of the latter and, specifically, on attitudes and strategies implemented by teachers (Andiliou & Murphy, 2010). So the teacher becomes a learning expert who is flexible, tolerant and confident, willing to accept the contributions and uncommon opinions of children, assuming a fully open position against them. The creative teachers are then those who take risks and communicate their creativity freely in the classroom (Bonds & Bonds, 1990). In addition to providing an educational environment which is emotionally safe, many theorists and researchers argue that teachers can promote the thinking and creative expression of children, using different approaches and strategies. In this regard, an analysis provided by Jeffrey (2006) in which some types of instructional strategies which are important in order to show the creative learning experiences that are meaningful to the children are identified, turns out to be particularly interesting.

• Creative use of space. "The important events frequently require that space where teachers and children work needs be modified to develop creative learning" (Jeffrey, 2006, pp. 405-406).

• Modeling creativity. "[...], Teachers can motivate children to generate ideas and support them, work cooperatively with children, model learning to them, and show pleasure in teaching and learning. They can also model creative learning by being spontaneous and modifying their plans based on classroom situations" (Jeffrey, 2006, pp. 406-407).

• Intellectual inquiry. "Creative learning includes being innovative, experimental, and inventive. In addition, young children can participate in facets of knowledge enquiry such as intellectual enquiry around the possibility, thinking and involvement with problems "( Jeffrey, 2006, pp. 408-409).

• Engaged productivity. "In creative learning, young children participate in productivity in their activities such as generating new ideas and discoveries, driven by a continuous display of the high levels of concentration and interest" (Jeffrey, 2006, pp. 409-410).

• Review process and product. "The creative learning process includes reflecting and analyzing the stages of production to determine whether to continue or modify the process in view of more creative actions" (Jeffrey, 2006, pp. 410).

• Meaningful experiences. "Children engage in and respond to creative learning based on the experiences that are meaningful to them; how they feel about the learning experience; the degree of importance to their self-identity; and their feeling of inclusion. The experiences for creative learning need to be important to their "self", as such children need to enjoy the experience and the quality of the trusting relationships needs to be assessed"( Jeffrey, 2006, pp. 410-411).

Therefore the study of teachers' implicit theories about creativity is outlined as a strategic area of research to understand the effects that these naive conceptualizations may have on attitudes and approaches adopted by the teachers themselves (Saracho, 2012a). In order to ensure that this knowledge not expressed, contained in professional jargon and sometimes independent of scientific observation, explains itself and becomes the object of reflection, it is necessary to propose to these teachers educational training courses on the topic of creativity, the latter intended as privileged opportunities to promote an increase in awareness about those silent and invisible interpretative frameworks that continually affect their work (Andilou & Murphy, 2010).

In this sense, education to creativity, as a priority objective of each school system, will not be a rhetorical appeal to a world of fantastic evasion, but it will become a real challenge to go beyond the usual solutions, travelling along unexplored paths and creating unpublished connections between knowledge and experiences distant between them, not only directed to children but also to teachers, aware that: "how electricity is not only present in a magnificent thunderstorm and dazzling lightning, but also in a lamp; so also, creativity exists not only where it creates great historical works, but also everywhere human imagination combines, changes, and creates anything new" (Vygotskij, 1930-1972, cit. in Smolucha, 1992, p. 54).

## References

Albert, R. S., & Runco, M. A. (1989). Indipendence and cognitive ability in gifted and exceptionally gifted boys. Journal of Youth and Adolescence, n. 18. pp. 221-230.

Aljughaiman, A., & Mowrer-Reynolds M. (2005). Teachers' conceptions of creativity and creative students. The Journal of Creative Behavior, vol. 39, n. 1, pp. 17-34.

Amabile, T. M. (1990). Within you, without you: The social psychology of creativity and beyond. In M. A. Runco, & R. S. Albert (Eds), Theories of creativity (pp. 61-91). Newbury Park: Sage publications.

Andiliou, A., & Murphy P. K. (2010). Examining variations among researchers' and teachers' conceptualizations of creativity: A review and synthesis of contemporary research. Educational Research Review, 5, pp. 201-219.

Barron, F., & Harrington D. (1981). Creativity intelligence and personality. Annual Review of Psychology, vol. 32, n. 1, pp. 439 - 476.

Barron, F. (1995). No rootless flower: An ecology of creativity, New York:Hampton Press, .

Bateson, M.C. (1999). Ordinary creativity. In A. Montuori & R. Purser (Eds.), Social Creativity (vol. 1, pp. 153-171). New York:Hampton Press, Hampton Press,

Beghetto, R. A. (2007). Ideational code-switching: Walking the talk about supportino student creativity in the classroom. Roeper Review, vol. 29, n. 4, pp. 265-270.

Bonds, C., & Bonds L. G. (1990). Adding creativity to reading instruction. Reading Improvement, n. 27, pp. 106-110.

Chan, D. W., & Chan L. K. (1999). Implicit theories of creativity: Teachers' perception of student characteristics in Hong Kong. Creativity Research Journal, v. 12, n. 3, pp. 185-195.

Clark, B. (2008). Growing up gite: Developing the potential of children at home and at school. Columbus: Merrill.

Craft, A. (2003). The limits to creativity in education: Dilemmas for the educator. British Journal of Educational Studies, vol. 51, n. 2, pp. 113-127.

Craft, A. (2006). Fostering creativity with wisdom. Cambridge Journal of Education, vol. 36, n. 3, pp. 337-350.

Cskszentmihàlyi, M. (1990). The domain of creativity. In M. A. Runco & R. S. Albert (Eds), Theories of creativity (pp. 190-212). Newbury Park: Sage pubblications.

Cskszentmihàlyi, M. (1999). Implications of a systems perspective for the study of creativity. In R. J. Sternberg (Ed.), Handbook of creativity (pp. 313-335). New York: Cambridge University Press.

Danescu, E. (2009). Supporting creativity in society. Petroleum-Gas of Ploiesti Bulletin, Educational Sciences Series, vol. 61, n. 1, pp. 75-78.

Dawson, V. L., D'Andrea T., Affinito R., & Westby, E. L. (1999). Predicting creative behavior: A reexamination of the divergence between traditional and teacher-defined concepts of creativity. Creativity Research Journal, v. 12, n. 1, pp. 66-78.

Diakidoy, I. A., & Kanari, E. (1999). Student Teachers' Beliefs about Creativity. British Educational Research Journal, n. 25, pp. 225-243.

Dinca, M. (1999). Creative children in Romanian society. Childhood Education, v. 75, n. 6, pp. 355-358.

Fryer, M., & Collings, J. A. (1991). Teachers view about creativity. British Journal of Educational Psychology, n. 61, pp. 207-219.

Gardner, H. (1982). Art, mind, and brain: A cognitive approach to creativity. New York: Basic Books.

Glãveanu, V. P. (2010). Paradigms in the study of creativity: Introducing the perspective of cultural psychology. New Ideas in Psychology, v. 28, n. 1, pp. 79–93.

Glãveanu, V. P. (2011). Children and creativity: A most (un)likely pair? Thinking Skills and Creativity, vol. 6, n. 2, pp. 122-131.

Guilford, J. P. (1950). Creativity. American Psychologist, vol. 5, n. 9, pp. 444-454.

Jeffrey, B. (2006). Creative teaching and learning: Towards a common discourse and practice. Cambridge Journal of Education, v. 36, n. 3, pp. 399-414.

Kampylis, P., Berki, E., & Saariluoma, P. (2009). In-service and prospective teachers' conceptions of creativity. Thinking Skills and Creativity, n. 4, pp. 15-29.

Lim, W., & Plucker, J. A. (2001). Creativity through a lens of social responsability: implicit theory of creativity with Korean samples. Journal of Creative Behavior, n. 35, pp. 115-130.

Morais, M. F., & Azevedo, I. (2011). What is a creative teacher and what is a creative pupil? Perceptions of teachers. Procedia Social and Behavioral Sciences, n. 12, pp. 330-339.

Oral, G., & Günçer, B. (1993). Relationship between creativity and nonconformity to school discipline as perceived by teachers of Turkish elementary school children, by controlling for their grade and sex. Journal of Instructional Psychology, vol. 20, n. 3, pp. 208-214.

Pickard, E. (1990). Toward a theory of creative potential. The Journal of Creative Behavior, n. 24, pp. 1-9.

Pizzigrilli, P., & Antonietti, A. (2009). La rappresentazione della creatività. In M. Cesa-Bianchi, C. Cristini, E. Giusti (a cura di), La creatività scientifica: il processo che cambia il mondo (pp. 60-88). Roma: Sovera edizioni.

Raina, M. K., Kumar, G., & Raina, V. K. (1980). A cross-cultural study of parental perception of the ideal child. Creative Child and Adult Quarterly, v. 5, n. 4, pp. 234-241.

Rhodes, M. (1961). An analysis of creativity. Phi Delta Kappa, n. 42, pp. 305-310.

Rudowicz, E., & Hui, A. (1997). The creative personality: Hong Kong perspective. The Journal of Creative Behavior, n. 34, pp. 175-192.

Rudowicz, E., &Yue, X. D. (2000). Concepts of creativity: Similarities and differences among Mainland, Hong Kong, and Taiwanese Chinese. The Journal of Creative Behavior, v. 34, n. 3, pp. 175-192.

Rudowicz, E., & Yue, X. D. (2002). Perception of the most creative Chinese by undergraduates in Beijing, Guangzhou, Hong Kong, and Taipei. The Journal of Creative Behavior, v. 36, n. 2, pp. 88-104.

Runco, M. A. (1990). The divergent thinking of young children: Implications of the research. Gifted Child Today, v. 13, n. 4, pp. 37-39.

Runco, M. A. (1991). Divergent thinking. Norwood: Ablex.

Runco, M. A., Johnson, D. J, & Bear, P. K. (1993). Parents' and Teachers' implicit theories on children's creativity. Child Study Journal, n. 23, pp. 91-113.

Runco, M. A., Nemiro, J., & Walberg, H. J. (1998). Personal explicit theories of creativity. Journal of Creative Behavior, v. 32, n. 1, pp. 1-17.

Runco, M.A. (1999). Implicit theories. In S.R. Pritzker & M.A. Runco (Eds.), Encyclopedia of Creativity (vol. 2, pp. 27-30). San Diego: Academic Press.

Runco, M. A., & Johnson, D. J. (2002). Parents' and Teachers' Implicit Theories of Children's Creativity: A cross.cultural perspective. Creativity Journal Research, n. 14, pp. 427-438.

Runco, M.A. (2007). A hierarchical framework for the study of creativity. New Horizons in Education, vol. 55, n. 3, pp. 1-9.

Runco, M.A. (2008). Creativity and Education. New Horizons in Education, vol. 56, n. 1, pp. 107-115.

Saracho, O. N. (2012a). Teachers' perceptions and behaviors on creativity. In O. N. Saracho (Ed.), Contemporary Perspectives on Research in Creativity in Early Childhood Education (pp. 355-375). Charlotte: IAP.

Saracho, O. N. (2012b). The creative process in early childhood education. In O. N. Saracho (Ed.), Contemporary Perspectives on Research in Creativity in Early Childhood Education (pp. 109-133). Charlotte: IAP.

Scott, C. L. (1999), "Teachers' Biases toward Creative Children", in Creativity Research Journal, v. 12, n. 4, pp. 321-328.

Sharp, C. (2004). Developing young children's creativity: What can we learn from research? Topic, n. 32, pp. 5-12.

Smolucha, F. (1992). A reconstruction of Vygotsky's theory of creativity. Creativity Research Journal, v. 5, n. 1, pp. 49–67.

Sousa Fleith, D.(2000). Teacher and Student Perceptions of Creativity in the Classroom Environment. Roeper Review, v. 22, n. 3, pp. 148-153.

Stein, G., & Poole, P. (1997). Meeting the interests and needs of gite children: A strategy for teaching and learning. Early Child Development and Care, n. 130, pp. 13-19.

Sternberg, R. J. (1985). Implict Theories of Intelligence, Creativity and Wisdom. Journal of Personality and Social Psychology, n. 49, pp. 607-627.

Sternberg, R. J. (Ed.) (1999). Handbook of creativity. New York: Cambridge University Press.

Sternberg, R. J., & Lubart, T. I. (1999). The concept of creativity: Prospects and paradigms. In R. J. Sternberg (Ed.), Handbook of creativity (pp. 3-15). New York: Cambridge University Press.

Sternberg, R. J., & Kaufman, J. C. (2010). Constraints on creativity: Obvious and not so obvious. In J. C. Kaufaman & R. J. Sternberg (Eds.), The Cambridge handbook of creativity (pp. 467-482). Leiden: Cambridge University Press.

Torrance, E. P. (1963). Adventuring in creativity. Childhood Education, n. 40, pp. 79-87.

Westby, E. L., & Dawson, V. L. (1995). Creativity: Asset or burden in the classroom? Creativity Journal Research, n. 8, pp. 1-10.

Zimmerman, E. (2009). Reconceptualizing the role of creativity in art education and practice. Studies in Art Education: A Journal of Issues and Research, vol. 50, n. 4, pp. 382-399.

# Part 3

## The teachers' perspective on creativity

# 9 About the methodology
*Tuula Nousiainen*

The aim of the research work conducted in CREANET was, firstly, to understand pre-school teachers' perceptions on creativity; secondly, to characterize the nature of the activities, methodologies and attitudes contributing to the promotion or inhibition of creativity in pre-school settings; and thirdly, to reflect upon the processes and products of children's creations.

The research work employed a mixed methods approach combining both quantitative and qualitative elements (e.g., Creswell & Plano Clark, 2007; Johnson, Onwuegbuzie & Turner, 2007). The approach used in this project included data gathering with the aid of surveys, focus groups, interviews and field work. On the level of individual partner countries, some used a combination of different methods while others focused on employing one method extensively. The main benefit that is aimed for by using mixed methods is a better understanding of the research problems in terms of breadth and depth, as well as improved corroboration of the findings (Creswell & Plano Clark, 2007, p. 10; Johnson, Onwuegbuzie & Turner, 2007).

**The survey**

The principal instrument for gathering data was a survey administered to pre-school teachers in order to explore their views on creativity. Surveys for pre-school staff were conducted in Finland, Germany, Latvia, Lithuania, Portugal, Spain and Sweden. Altogether, there were 425 respondents in the survey. The numbers of respondents per country were as follows:

- Croatia: 42 respondents
- Finland: 57 respondents
- Germany: 24 respondents
- Latvia: 51 respondents
- Lithuania: 75 respondents
- Portugal: 45 respondents
- Spain: 29 respondents
- Sweden: 102 respondents

The questionnaire followed the same general structure in every country, consisting of three main themes: 1) educational practices, 2) the nature of creativity and 3) training in the field of creativity. The design of the questionnaire was based on the general goals of the CREANET project and on instruments used in previous research with equivalent aims (e.g., Diakidoy & Kanari, 1999). In addition to these main sections, the questionnaires could include country-specific additions and modifications, such as questions addressing the special focus areas of each country (e.g. in Finland, the role of technology and creativity in the pre-school context). In each country, the questionnaire was translated into the native language of the country before it was sent out.

The questionnaires included both multiple-choice and open-ended questions. The quantitative data was analysed with statistical software, using descriptive statistical procedures in order to provide a summary of the findings. In the analysis of the qualitative data, a data-driven approach was employed in order to be able to describe the teachers' perceptions without imposing strict, pre-set structures on them. The categorization grid was built from the meaning units emerging from the content (e.g., Bardin, 1991; Ghiglione & Matalon, 1992; Lieblich, Tuval-Mashiach & Zilber, 1998).

In some countries, the survey was complemented with additional, qualitatively oriented data gathering methods such as focus group interviews (Portugal) and e-mail interviews to selected respondents (Finland). The e-mail interview in Finland was sent to everyone who had earlier answered to all of the questions in the CREANET survey and also to the ones that had participated in the CREANET conference. Altogether, the e-mail interview reached 12 people, out of whom six people responded. The e-mail interview included eight questions, and the main purpose of this interview was to understand kindergarten teachers' conceptions of a creative child, the creative process and a creative product. The purpose was also to get a better understanding of how teachers can foster children's creativity. Focus group interviews are described in more detail in the next section.

## The focus groups

The use of focus groups was another method for gathering data in the CREANET project, aiming to obtain a more qualitative perspective to pre-school teachers' representations and ideas of creativity to complement the survey data. A focus group is a form of qualitative research in which a group of people are asked about their perceptions, opinions, beliefs, and attitudes towards a product, service, concept, advertisement, idea, or packaging (Hastrup, 1995). Questions are asked in an interactive group setting where participants are free to talk with other group members. Focus groups are especially useful in exploring people's experiences, views and concerns. Whereas polls can provide indicators of opinions and measure the frequency of certain behaviours or views, focus groups are more appropriate when exploring how people understand their social and natural environment. In particular, they can be helpful in investigating people's perspectives and experiences concerning specific issues. Focus groups allow the participants to bring forth their own concepts and frames and express themselves in their own vocabulary (Kitzinger & Barbour, 1999).

The advantage of the focus group (or group interview) approach over individual interviews is that it allows for more spontaneity and interaction between the participants: they can build onto each other's ideas and comments, and the role of the facilitator does not become so strong (Madriz, 2000, p. 836). Participating in focus groups can also give the participants incentives to change their own environment based on the experiences shared in the group (Madriz, 2000, p. 848).

Focus groups were carried out in Portugal, Italy and Denmark. In Portugal, the focus group consisted of eight pre-school teachers and it met every two months for a three-hour session. In Italy, there was a series of ten focus group sessions involving a total of 75 teachers. Six of the groups consisted of kindergarten teachers only, two consisted of nursery educators, one was composed of atelier teachers, and one included both nursery educators and kindergarten teachers. In Denmark, the focus group interview was conducted in two steps. The first one involved nine pedagogues from one nursery and the second one consisted of pedagogues from nine other day-care centres in the municipality; in both cases, day-care m nagers, pedagogues and pedagogue-assistants were represented.

In each of these countries, the general framework for the focus group work was similar in terms of the main scope and objectives. The main rationale for carrying out qualitative investigation was that it was considered important to explore the theme of creativity without proposing predefined categories for analysis and thereby leaving open the possibility for teachers to express themselves freely. By encouraging dialogue in focus groups, the aim was that even the most implicit aspects relative to how teachers consider creative processes and the relationship between creativity and education could emerge. One more objective of a more strictly professional development nature was the creation of an opportunity, in the initial stage of the process, for stimulating debate and reflection in a systematic way between the teachers participating in the project.

The aims for the focus groups included, for example, identifying the teachers' perceptions of creativity, characterizing strategies to promote creativity, analysing children's involvement and relationships regarding the stimuli at their disposal, and reflecting upon the processes and products of children's and adults' creativity. The practical implementation of the focus groups and the concrete activities included in them were defined by each country in ways that were the most feasible for them.

In Portugal, the focus group activities were based on the cycle of action research, with a special focus on situational aspects, collaborative practices, participatory activities and self-evaluative methods. The teachers shared experiences resulting from their projects and their observations on children's creative activities (either spontaneous or induced by adults). The issues that were presented were analysed by the group, enriched by the reflection on other possible ideas for promoting creativity in young children and in professionals. The focus group work employed different instruments for discussion and data collection: brainstorming, group reflections and a very open-structure questionnaire for describing and reflecting upon practices.

In Italy, the main themes of discussion in the group interviews included definitions of creativity, examples of a creative child, examples of good or bad educational practices in relation to creativity, as well as the space and organization of activities that can foster creativity. These themes were defined in such a way that they were analogous with questions posed in the questionnaires administered in different countries.

In Denmark, the first focus group interview focused on a broad understanding and elaboration on the question "what is creativity?" while the second focus group interview focused on a reflection on creativity inspired by activities in the nursery (presented by one of the pedagogues connected to the project). Both interviews took a broad focus on creativity from both a professional and institutional perspective. They were conducted with a number of open-ended questions in order to let different points of view emerge from the dialogue and from listening to one another in the group.

## Fieldwork

In addition to questionnaires and focus group interviews, fieldwork was also employed as a method in this study. Fieldwork is a qualitative approach, aiming at identifying internal significant matters in everyday life and putting them into non-metric categories. A key word in field work is participant observation: the researcher takes part of people's everyday lives in order to achieve an inside understanding of significant qualities in these lives, and withdraws in order to acquire a matter-of-fact description of the daily incidents. Both of these efforts are embedded in certain theoretical understandings, such as the views of e.g. Baumann, Bourdieu, Foucault and Sigsgaard with regard to their understanding of everyday lives, experiences, and institutions.

Out of the CREANET partner countries, fieldwork was carried out in Denmark. The field work was conducted in four institutions: one classical kindergarten/nursery in a bigger town, one outdoor kindergarten with indoor facilities in an old farmhouse, one kindergarten in a small provincial town, and one kindergarten in a bigger town in a somewhat deprived area.

Eight pedagogues were directly participating and several others participated indirectly. The fieldwork was partially conducted by researchers, and partially the pedagogues made observations for this purpose.

Thematically, the fieldwork focused on the conditions for creativity, i.e. whether the pedagogues managed to be appreciative and inclusive. Another point of view was to look for children's creative contributions to daily life, such as using things for other purposes than for which they were originally meant, giving original suggestions to problem solving, and fantasizing.

## References

Bardin, L. (1991). Análise de conteúdo. Lisboa: Edições 70.

Creswell, J.W., & Plano Clark, V.L. (2007). Designing and conducting mixed methods research. Thousand Oaks: Sage Publications.

Diakidoy, I-N., & Kanari, E. (1999). Student teachers' beliefs about creativity. British Educational Journal 25 (2), 225-243.

Ghiglione, R., & Matalon, B. (1992). O Inquérito: Teoria e prática. Oeiras: Celta Editora.

Hastrup, K. (1995). A passage to anthropology: Between experience and theory. London & New York: Routledge.

Johnson, R.B., Onwuegbuzie, A.J., & Turner, L.A. (2007). Toward a definition of mixed methods research. Journal of Mixed Methods Research 1 (2), 112-133.

Kitzinger, J, & Barbour, R.S. (1999). Introduction: the challenge and promise of focus groups. In R.S. Barbour & J. Kitzinger (Eds.), Developing focus group research. Politics, theory and practice (pp 1-20). London: Sage Publications.

Lieblich, A., Tuval-Mashiach, R., & Zilber, T. (1998). Narrative research: Reading, analysis and interpretation. Thousand Oaks: Sage Publications.

Madriz, E. (2000). Focus groups in feminist research. In N.K. Denzin & Y.S. Lincoln (Eds.), Handbook of qualitative research (2nd ed., pp. 835-850). Thousand Oaks: Sage Publications.

# 10 Results of the European survey
*Tuula Nousiainen, Ilaria Mussini, Nelson Santa Eufemia*

This chapter presents the results from the survey which was administered to pre-school teachers in Croatia, Finland, Germany, Latvia, Lithuania, Portugal, Spain and Sweden in order to examine their views on creativity. Altogether, 425 pre-school teachers from eight countries responded to the survey. An overwhelming majority (95.5%) of the respondents were female, and almost half (47%) of them had more than 20 years of work experience.

All respondents stated that they had participated in some form of training in the field of creativity. For 62% of the teachers, training on creativity has been an integral part of their pre-school teacher education. The most common way of learning about creativity, however, was studying or reading about the theme independently, in a self-directed way (71%). Almost as frequent was participation in in-service training courses or workshops where creativity was addressed (68%). More than half of the respondents (55%) also reported taking part in seminars or congresses related to the topic. The teachers felt that the most rewarding formative experiences related to training on creativity had been creative workshops where it has been possible to test new materials and approaches, aesthetic in-service training related to arts (drama, music, painting), and pedagogical seminars that have encouraged going outside the box.

In the following sections, we will examine three principal questions in light of the qualitative answers provided by the respondents. These questions are as follows:

1. What is creativity? The question aims to uncover the pre-school teachers' conceptions of the nature of creativity in general: what the concept of creativity entails and how it manifests in pre-school activities, in children, and in children's creations.
2. What fosters creativity? Here, the goal is to find out the teachers' views on such practices, materials, attitudes and other resources and ways of working that are conducive to creativity in pre-school settings.
3. What hinders creativity? In contrast with the previous question, this question examines the teachers' views on such practices and conditions that inhibit the display of creativity in the pre-school.

We will first examine these issues by country and then proceed to provide a summary of the most prominent issues at the end of this section.

## Results from Croatia

In the Croatian area of Verteneglio, the questionnaire was presented to 42 education workers, mainly women, with at least 10 years of experience in the sector.

*What is creativity?*

According to the Croatian respondents, the main factors that support creativity included personality, intelligence, and knowledge. The survey indicated that creativity was deemed significant in areas such as dramatization, self-expression, symbolic games, imagination, but not as significant when it comes to science or logical challenges.

*What fosters or hinders creativity?*

Strategies and techniques reported to enhance creativity included presenting children with open-ended questions or with problems that may have different solutions, as well as issues that were not well-defined. There were some practices on the effects of which on creativity the teachers disagreed. These included situations where children are presented with problems with which they were not familiar or, on the contrary, children facing issues on which they already had extensive knowledge.

## Results from Finland

The Finnish survey was responded to by 57 pre-school teachers whose average age was 43. Their professional experience varied from less than a year to 36 years, the average being 17 years. All of the respondents were female. In addition to the survey, more detailed e-mail interviews were conducted with six kindergarten teachers, aiming to obtain a more in-depth understanding on the teachers' insights about fostering creativity. The results presented in this section are based on both of these methods.

*What is creativity?*

When the teachers were asked to describe what they meant by creativity in the context of early childhood education, many of the teachers approached the question through concrete examples of different creative activities and forms of play. Such examples included e.g. mentions of arts, problem solving, creative efforts and outputs initiated by the children themselves, and the discovery of new ways of using familiar objects in play. A frequent characterization of creativity was related to the diversity of the ways of doing things, meaning that the children are not provided with exact patterns or models to be followed, that there is no one, right answer, that the children have the freedom to try things in many different ways, and that a child's personal way of doing things should be valued. Two themes closely related to this were those that emphasized allowing children to explore and those that focused on the relationship between creativity and child-centredness. These depictions entail the willingness and ability of the teacher to draw ideas from the children's world, listening to the children, allowing the children to share their ideas and co-developing these ideas with them, and giving the children chances to express themselves according to their own interests and in their preferred ways. A frequent aspect brought up in the teachers' views was also the concept of ability - which was mostly used in reference to the adults' ability to support children's creativity and to recognize their creative potential but some answers also pointed out children's ability to innovate and to become enthusiastic about something.

The teachers were also asked to mention an example of a situation where they have observed something particularly creative about a child's action or behaviour. The most commonly mentioned situations included child-initiated creations (situations where a child has come up with e.g. a poem, song, performance or story of their own), doing things in unconventional ways, imaginative play, problem solving, and assigning new purposes for things.

*If a certain thing/object is not available, the child comes up with a way of substituting it with something else.*

*The child makes his/her creation completely according to his/her own ideas, taking no notice of others' creations or instructions.*

*One child came up with the idea of using a snow sled as part of a machine, constructing it together with a jump rope and shovels, and managed to make it work like a steam engine.*

Furthermore, the teachers were asked to characterize a creative output or idea of a child. The most frequent characteristic, mentioned by almost every respondent, was originality (a creation that is unconventional, unique, personal, novel and different). The teachers also brought up other characteristics that were closely related to originality, such as open-mindedness and courage to be different, as well as imagination and innovativeness. Many teachers also highlighted the enthusiasm going into producing such an output as one aspect that characterizes creativity - indicating that they considered the process as significant as the outcome. The process-related comments included issues such as pleasure, feelings of achievement, immersion and flow.

*What fosters creativity?*

When the teachers were asked about their views regarding such conditions that would be conducive to the development of creativity in the children, the answers covered both tangible and intangible resources. One aspect that entails both tangible and intangible dimensions is the role of the environment, entailing aspects related to the physical, psychological and social environment. The teachers referred to an environment that is e.g. stimulating, aesthetic and flexible as well as accepting and positive.

In terms of the physical environment, the teachers highlighted the significance of sufficient materials and equipment as well as spaces. They emphasized allowing children to freely explore and experiment with different materials, ensuring the availability of a variety of materials at all times, and having adequate space to allow continuous, long-term activities without having to pack the materials used in the activity immediately away.

*I use a lot of recycled materials [and they] make you wonder, by default, what a certain item might have originally been and what else it could possibly become!*

*[The learning environment] should be versatile and offer interesting objects, pictures, fabrics and toys, etc.*

*There should be plenty of equipment related to exploration and experimenting available for the children, and [they should be able to use it] freely.*

The teachers' views on aspects that are part of such a psychological environment that fosters creativity referred to the feelings and reactions stimulated by the environment. Especially the significance of a supportive and encouraging atmosphere was strongly emphasized. The teachers highlighted also the need for allowing adequate time and keeping schedules as flexible as possible in order to allow for the development of ideas and activities.

*The psychological environment should be safe, positive, supportive and inspiring.*

*I mean that the atmosphere is warm, accepting and open. The children are encouraged to spontaneous and self-directed activity.*

*Schedules should adjust to the rhythm of doing things.*

*There should be time, and a lack of haste, and even a little bit of boredom.*

Aspects related to the social environment were not as prominent in the teachers' views as the physical and psychological issues. Several respondents pointed out, however, that increased time for activities carried out in small groups would have a positive effect on creativity.

Moreover, worth highlighting as a theme of its own is the adoption of a child-centred approach which overlaps both the physical and the psychological aspects of the environment, encompassing the role of the teachers and the role of the spaces and materials alike. The teachers emphasized the need to listen to the children and to allow them to initiate activities, some of them mentioning concrete examples such as a "Child of the Week" theme when one child at a time actively participates in planning the activities of the pre-school. A key factor in the child-centred perspective is recognizing the individuality of the child. Many of the respondents also pointed out the adults' role in general: their attitude, willingness to improvise, ability to stimulate the children's imaginations, and a genuine interest in recognizing and addressing the creative potential that exists in children.

*It is important to address the child as an individual so that you are able to recognize the strengths of the child, and in this way the adult is able to support the child in his/her own processes.*

*An easily modifiable environment that adapts according to the children's needs, wishes, and ideas.*

*It's good to pose creative questions to the children often and thereby tune up the children's creative thinking: how could we do this, how could we make that, could that be true and what if it were, should we invent that, etc.*

The teachers also provided examples of practices or activities that they considered to support and foster the development of creativity. A clear overlapping theme across the different practices was children's ability to freely explore different materials and resources and to initiate activities according to their own interests.

*What hinders creativity?*

The teachers' responses to the question about factors that inhibit creativity entailed mainly the polar opposites of the issues they had brought up as main contributors in fostering creativity. While child-centred approaches and free exploration were seen as crucial in fostering creativity, an adult-directed approach and narrow and restricted rules and limitations were the main issues that were seen to hinder the manifestation and development of creativity.

*It inhibits the development of the child's creativity if the adult always has strict plans that are not flexible at all, and the children are never asked for ideas or suggestions before planning the activity, or during the activity.*

*The child is told, for example, that he/she can't bring toy cars into doll play "because they don't belong there".*

Another, closely related theme mentioned by the teachers was requiring the children to follow a certain pattern and to produce the "right" kind of outcome.

*An adult-directed activity session where the children make crafts according to a model made by the adult, and all of them end up being identical.*

*Children are given a ready-made model and everyone has to make a similar one, as similar as possible. As a student, I was in a school class where the children had made bunnies in crafts. The teacher said to me, 'look how similar they all are'. I had steam coming out of my ears and I said, 'oh, that's too bad, they are indeed'.*

*I think the experiences of "wrong", "not done right", etc. extinguish creativity.*

It is also a threat to creativity if the daily routines and activities are organized in an overly structured way.

## Results from Germany

In Germany, the survey involved 28 councils in the area of Pforzheim and in particular 24 education services dedicated to 0-to-6-year-olds, plus one dedicated to 6-to-12-year-olds. Altogether, there were 24 respondents to the survey. The teachers were all female with many years' experience in the education sector.

*What is creativity?*

The teachers believe that children are creative when they produce something that expresses their individuality and that is both unique and inimitable. The contexts in which children express their creativity the most are those that involve symbolic games, invention, building of various objects and music.

Creativity is most affected by the learning context and the children's personality, while intelligence and knowledge seem to be less significant factors. According to the teachers, a creative child is full of ideas, self-assured and curious. Other characteristics associated with creativity seem to be imagination, the ability to define goals, as well as independence.

*What fosters or hinders creativity?*

When the teachers were asked about good practices that promote creativity in children, they mentioned several issues related to space, material, and freedom of expression. The teachers considered a wide range of learning materials as well as the availability of open spaces important for creativity. Moreover, they emphasized such expression of creativity that is not limited by predefined objectives. Finally, the teachers pointed out that it is conducive to creativity when children are allowed to work on their own.

Teachers may stimulate creativity by asking children open-ended questions or by presenting them with problems that may have different solutions. It is interesting to note how the respondents were split between those who believed that presenting children with problems they are not familiar with enhances creativity and those who believed that this practice hinders it.

Key areas that the teachers deemed to be detrimental to creativity included closed-ended questions, presenting children with problems that admitted only one possible solution, or presenting issues which were not well defined.

## Results from Latvia

The Latvian survey was answered by 51 respondents. More than half

(51%) of the respondents were between 20 and 30 years of age, and only 19% were over 40 years old. In terms of work experience, 24% of the respondents had less than five years' experience, 31% had 5 to 9 years and 29% had 10 to 19 years of experience. Only 12% of the teachers had more than 20 years of experience, out of whom one respondent had been working in the field for more than 30 years.

*What is creativity?*
The teachers' descriptions of their understanding of the concept of creativity reveal that most of them link creativity with expressive languages that result in self-expression. They also point out the importance of space and the availability of materials. The following list illustrates some of the characterizations.
- Use of expressive languages and self-expression
    - Children are allowed to express their creativity in arts and other spheres
    - Creative self-expression in implementing one's own idea – very important
    - Developing a creative personality
    - Creativity in all tasks and activities – finding new solutions, inventing something new on the basis of existing knowledge
- Space and availability of materials
    - Creating an environment where the children are given opportunities for choice, improvising, seeking solutions, playing problem-solving games, and enjoying the process
    - Not putting the children into a "frame" but letting them act on their own.

The understanding of creativity is connected with the activities and methods that pre-school teachers are already using – there is a lack of searching for new activities and understanding about that. Teachers have a more theoretical understanding but they do not dare to try it practically. Children's expressions of creativity have been evaluated and recognized more in planned activities (e.g. music and art), not in independent activities. Most teachers encourage children to be creative and independent in planned activities.
- Taking care that children are innovative and learn something new in every activity (lesson)
- The importance of using untraditional methods
- Respecting the uniqueness of a child's personality in different activities, especially in organized ones.
- Giving children a free choice to create a dance in the music lesson
- Need for the pedagogue to be creative – then he/she will promote it in children and be able to implement a creative approach to the learning process

Creativity is seen more as a particular activity, not in connection with personality traits that have to be developed (such as fantasy or motivation). Only a few of the teachers pointed out the importance of developing creative thinking skills – the flexibility of thinking. Personality is understood more as a holistic phenomenon. When the teachers were asked to describe a creative child, the following traits were mentioned.

- Active, communicative, curious, interested
- Goal-oriented, self-confident, responsive, helpful
- Open to new ideas, optimistic
- Expressive, able to surprise, does unconventional things, takes initiative
- Flexible – reacts quickly in different situations, notices different solutions
- Independent in thinking (outside the standard way), choosing materials, playing role plays, setting rules, etc.
- Possesses developed thinking, intellectual abilities, fantasy, imagination, a variety of ideas, leadership and risk-taking abilities;
- Can make decisions and is characterized by unconformity;
- Not afraid of failure.

A creative product has been characterized as original, unique, artistic, different, and having its own approach and attitude.

*What fosters creativity?*

The teachers were asked what kinds of tasks, activities, resources or organization they promote in the pre-school in order to develop children's creativity. The most frequent issues brought up in the answers were related to different kinds of activities such as playing, art and music activities, role play, didactic games, folklore, or developmental tasks. Another point heavily emphasized by the teachers was focused on the freedom of choice and exploration, including aspects such as finding new solutions, composing, creating opportunities for self-expression, independent activities not pressed by adults, and offering different types of materials or allowing the child to choose them. Also, the teachers' role was seen to be important in differentiating tasks and promoting imagination and self-expression. Some teachers also mentioned different forms of collaboration as a measure that would help teachers nurture the children's creativity: they considered it important to cooperate with parents, to consult pre-school teachers on creativity development, and to organize courses for teachers, offering them possibilities to share experiences with colleagues. Among the responses, there was also one discordant opinion where the respondent felt that young children, overall, were not creative but instead merely imitated adults. Most of the activities mentioned by the respondents had been implemented during learning activities but some respondents also brought up situations from free-time activities and doing different chores within the frames of the topic of the week.

When the teachers were asked to give an example of good practice aimed at developing creativity, most of the examples they mentioned were on a rather general level. They mentioned particular types of activities and methods of work that promote creativity. For example, activities such as constructing, role play, drama and performances, and creating fairy tales were seen to promote creativity. The teachers also highlighted certain ways of working, such as doing things without patterns, encouraging the children to express their thoughts and to feel satisfaction from creative self-expression, avoiding teaching by stereotypes, allowing opportunities for choice and supporting different approaches in solving tasks without focusing too heavily on what is "correct".

Some teachers gave more concrete examples of activities or practices they considered conducive to creativity. These are described in the following list.

- A work sheet for maths: a child is given a definite number of three kinds of shapes that have to be grouped in three different groups (one figure of every shape in each group)
- Painting in the snow using gouache paint
- Lying in the snow and watching the clouds: imagining things, animals, etc.
- Creating a picture of natural materials outdoors, then telling the group about it
- Activities with drama elements where children reflect on different situations and express moods through movements, gestures and intonations. It is exciting and allows them to express themselves creatively.
- Musical play develops creativity and music perception: listening to different sound bites (musical excerpts) children move in accordance with rhythm in a space. When the music stops, the children try to reflect it "on paper". Then follows another fragment, and when it stops, the children continue their drawings by expressing another mood. At the end of the game, the children look at each other's drawings and share their feelings.
- During sports activities, the children have the possibility to choose their equipment. The children get prizes if they invent something innovative. The invention is offered also to other children.
- Children work with glue, scissors, paper and other materials according to their own interests. During their free time, they make different "art work" out of their chosen materials. The pre-school teacher matches the activities with the children's choices.

*What hinders creativity?*

As regards the aspects that inhibit creativity, the issues related to authoritarian teachers and uniformity were the two issues that clearly rose above others. When discussing the qualities of the teachers that hinder creativity, the respondents referred to authoritarian teachers who believe that everything needs to be done according to a pattern, without giving the child possibilities to choose and to express creativity; teachers who are uninterested and not creative; and teachers who do not appreciate children's creativity. By uniformity, the teachers referred to following patterns, static and stereotypical teaching, not allowing any room for choice, and teachers' interruptions to the creative process by helping and "improving" the children's creations or the way in which they do things (e.g. the correct way of holding a pencil or a paintbrush).

In addition to these two aspects, some teachers pointed out issues pertaining to resources: the lack of materials and resources was seen as a challenge from the perspective of creativity, similarly as the fact that there is often a very limited amount of time for a particular activity, which can cause tension. Attitude-related issues were another point that could possibly hinder creativity, referring e.g. to parents' - or other children's - unwillingness to do activities together with the children.

## Results from Lithuania

In Lithuania, the study included 75 pre-school teachers, out of whom 78% were over 40 years old and 73% had more than 20 years of work experience. All of the respondents were female.

### What is creativity?

The majority of the pedagogues answered the question what child the pedagogues consider to be creative and that, in their opinion, a creative child is characterized by a lively imagination, is self-confident, has one's own opinion, is curious, inventive, brave, emotional, proactive, has a sense of humour and is not afraid to make mistakes.

A frequent notion was also that a creative child is distinguished by original expression and unconventional ways of solving problems such as managing to find a way out of various situations, and that a creative child is also characterized by quick reaction and finds an original and usually not the easiest way, to solve a problem. Such children are able to see certain opportunities where other children cannot see them.

Some respondents distinguished certain specific skills of creative children. In their opinion, creative children must be able to introduce themselves, talk about themselves, and create stories and small poems in an original and figurative manner. In their opinion, creative children are distinguished by their creations and thoughts which sometimes only they can understand.

The communication skills of creative children were mentioned as well. In the respondents' opinion, creative children are characterized by coherent and content-rich speech with an interesting and rich vocabulary. Children are able to express their thoughts and ideas freely and to communicate with their classmates about various topics. Creative children tell about and describe various phenomena smoothly and emotionally.

Most of the respondents believe that imagination (75 respondents) and self-confidence (74) are the most necessary characteristics for being a creative personality. Also, in the respondents' opinion, other important characteristics include inborn talent (67), independence (65) and inclination towards artistry (63).

*What fosters creativity?*

The surveyed pedagogues named a large number of different and innovative ways for stimulating children's creativity. The respondents consider the development of a safe environment stimulating children's creativity to be the most significant factor. It is only in a safe environment that the children have the possibility to fantasize freely, express their thoughts and ideas as well as to express them in their activities. Most respondents stimulate children's creativity by organizing project and artistic activities as well. The respondents prepare various projects, organize artistic expression hours, and use unconventional means and technologies of artistic expression. The products of children's creative processes are displayed in exhibitions of creative works. The respondents also stimulate children's creativity via cognition of the environment and nature by investigating various natural materials and invoking one's senses. They organize educational trips to the country-side, etc. Another way to stimulate children's creativity is the development of language and communication skills. For example, the respondents organize open discussions and conversations, read stories, and create rhymed fairy tales.

Some of the pedagogues stimulate children's creativity via theatrical, musical and playing activities enabling children to express themselves and to empathize in others' roles. Other ways in which they aim to foster children's creativity include unconventional work methods as well as presenting them with problematic issues where children are asked open-ended questions inducing them to think and analyse. In this way, it is aimed to involve children in the process of solving problems when children are looking for the answers by themselves. The pedagogues stimulate children's creativity by co-operating with parents and other pedagogues as well. They organize open days when the pre-schools may be visited not only by parents but also by other pedagogues who share their good practices. They also organize festivals together with parents.

In the respondents' opinion, taking children's individual needs and differences into account is important as well. Also, children's creativity is stimulated by compliments and incentives not only for the work done or a task solved but also for the efforts. The interaction between the pedagogue and the child is important. One respondent described it as follows:

*Education is based on the interaction between the child and the adult; one is communicated and co-operated with as if with a peer; the child is supported in case of a failure or in difficult times; one is helped if one asks or waits for help; new ideas and thoughts for exploration and activities are suggested; the child's self-confidence is stimulated, competences and feeling are developed and creative self-expression is aroused in this way.*

The examples of good practice presented by the pedagogues demonstrate that the pedagogue's example and interaction, i.e. positive and warm communication with pupils and their parents by involving them in joint activities of the group, is highly significant for developing children's creativity. Also, in the opinion of most of them, it is only in the favourable environment provided by the pedagogue that children's creativity and creative abilities may be developed. The importance of providing the conditions - such as the material base, methods, and the ways and means - for the child's self-expression is emphasized. Also, in the opinion of most respondents, various artistic activities must be organized in order to develop children's creativity: creative role plays, theatrical, musical, arts and crafts activities, writing fairy tales. In artistic activities, children not only develop their artistic abilities but also express themselves as well as get to know new phenomena and the surrounding world. In the opinion of the pedagogues, organizing various projects, contests, festivals and trips as well as journalistic activities (children create books, issue the newspaper of the group, or make an album of the group containing the children's photographs, thoughts and stories) develops creative abilities as well.

The pedagogues mentioned several types of questions or problems that, according to them, stimulated children's creativity the most. These included questions that are not defined (meaning that they are not precise and they force one to think), questions to which there are several correct answers, and open-ended questions without pre-defined answer choices. They also felt that children's creativity is stimulated when they have to solve problems related to which they do not have much previous knowledge and when they are presented with issues that are not known to them.

It is noteworthy that all pedagogues understand that the freedom to choose the activities in which one is interested is very important for the development of children's creativity. To summarize the examples of the respondents' good practices, it can be maintained that the surveyed people aim to develop children's creativity through various educational activities by invoking various educational methods, means, ways and material base. They perceive the importance and significance of the development of children's creativity at pre-school age. Most respondents engage in highly diverse and content-rich creative activities themselves and together with children. They organize and participate not only in local but also in international projects, organize various creative-artistic activities, conduct projects and sessions not only with children but also with their parents, and use a great deal of varying and innovative methods for stimulating children's creativity.

*What hinders creativity?*

The pedagogues also stated a variety of mistakes suppressing children's creativity which have occurred in educational practice. In their opinion, the main mistake is excessive leadership, i.e. authoritarian control when the child is constantly ordered what to do and how to do it, and when his/her activities are often interfered.

The majority of respondents also note that children's creativity is suppressed by the restriction of the freedom of choice. This refers to situations where the child is forbidden to choose games and other means independently and when the pedagogue imposes his or her activities on the child. Children's creativity is also inhibited by pre-prepared patterns and templates such as colouring books, and by the suppression of the child's initiative when the pedagogue controls the pupils too much and forbids them to express themselves freely. Another major mistake is the pedagogue's criticism, especially public negative assessment. The pedagogues' lack of patience and haste is seen as a factor that hinders creativity as well.

Traditional stereotyped education that does not stimulate children's originality and flexibility as well as poor educational environments also hinder the development of children's creativity. In the respondents' opinion, another big mistake of the pedagogues is focusing on the result, not on the process. It is likely to reduce the children's enjoyment in the activities taking place here and now, and the children may feel pressure to achieve a good final result. It is also likely to cause another mistake stated by the pedagogues – haste. The pedagogues also note that children's creativity is suppressed by too much care for the child. Children that are patronized too much are not able to choose and act independently anymore, as they get used to everything being done for them.

Most respondents attributed such questions that have a clearly predictable answer to the ones suppressing children's creativity the most. They felt that children's creativity was suppressed by such questions to which there is only one correct answer as well as by closed-ended questions which have a predictable answer.

## Results from Portugal

The sample was constituted by 45 professionals, and the group of respondents is mainly female (44, one did not answer). The age range varied from 26 to 54, the mean age being 39 years. Their professional experience varied from 1 to 30 years, the mean being approximately 14 years.

*What is creativity?*

To understand the participants' concept of creativity in education, they were asked about what creativity meant to them related to their practice in class. The most frequent issues mentioned by the respondents were related to the professionals' attitudes and practices. These were explained either by providing a diversity of opportunities and resources or paying attention to children's ideas/work. A special focus is put on the need for the educator to be original in the proposals presented and experiences promoted, as stressed below:

*All the work which stimulates the creative intelligence and the education of artistic sensibility.*

*We can stimulate behaviours, ways of interaction with the world that make the development of new cognitive patterns possible.*

*The originality of the proposals will be reflected on children's products.*

Another important factor is the reference to the children's ability for free expression, their spontaneity and ability to create.

*Creativity is a boom of ideas that can emerge through a word a child says and brings out various ideas.*

*It is the ability to express ideas, emotions, and feelings through aesthetic expressions.*

*A child found alternative ways to express herself and feels good with that. Creativity is a way to communicate what we are and feel.*

*It is the moment the child gets involved in an activity with imagination and is respected in his/her individuality.*

The respondents also emphasized the characteristics of the creative work as something that goes beyond the "normal" and shows novelty. Hence, references to originality and going beyond the basics were made by the teachers.

*Innovative work, in a unique and original way.*

*It is something different, something that expresses an idea, but is represented by different techniques, formats and materials.*

*The ability to create, to do more than was given to us, to go further.*

*Creativity is to overcome barriers, innovate, explore and learn.*

These results show consistency with previous answers and a fair and accurate awareness of the concept of creativity related to self-expression of either the adult or the child. The pre-school teachers are responsible for creating a physical and emotional climate where children and adults feel secure to discover without fear of failure.

*What fosters creativity?*

The examples of good practices aimed at developing creativity in children given by the respondents were mainly related to professionals' attitudes towards providing children with new experiences to facilitate their own expression, but above all a supportive attitude that values what the child has to communicate.

*Promoting self-esteem in a way that the child feels safe, therefore, free to 'fly'.*

*We should value children's ideas, so when they feel safe, their creativity emerges.*

*Questioning and encouraging the child to produce her/his creations in a way that she/he can discover their creative abilities.*

*Children are naturally creative, we only need to fight against 'normalization'.*

In order to reach such aims, the organization of the educational environment is considered essential, especially when it refers to space and materials, thereby facilitating curiosity and experimentation.

*The availability of multiple materials which can give 'wings to imagination'.*

*What helps most is free exploration of different materials.*

A rich environment is seen by some respondents as the ideal setting for the child's freedom of self-expression.

*Exploring freely whatever the child finds around.*

*The opportunity for the children to suggest, idealize and build in any circumstances of the school life.*

However, the teachers felt that in order to develop such creative potential, one must go beyond the limits, and further knowledge must be added, particularly in the field of aesthetic and artistic expressions.

*Inviting plastic artists to participate in the activities at the class, in order to show their knowledge.*

*All the work based on education through the arts.*

*Working on famous authors/artists in a playful way and crossing all areas which can promote creation and appreciation.*

*Creation of poems/stories.*

Our sample gives a particular importance to professionals' supportive attitudes towards children's ideas, processes and products, but also to the organization of the educational environment to facilitate children's free self-expression. These results show a good understanding of what is fundamental in order to foster creativity and a belief that creativity can be developed and is not something rare and only dependent on individual characteristics.

*What hinders creativity?*

The examples of educational practices that do not help or even inhibit children's creativity show a great unanimity among the participants. The majority of references appear in relation to professionals' attitudes, especially the restraints they put on children's free exploration and expression and the lack of supportive communication.

*Activities where children cannot be spontaneous.*

*Not letting the child explore, observe, discover and experiment.*

*The lack of dialogue.*

*Devaluating everything the child does, not listening to what she/he says, ignoring.*

*Limiting the creative ability [...] using expressions such as: 'the sun is not blue, it's yellow'.*

*All the activities that bring unsafety and do not contribute to the child's self-esteem.*

Almost the same number of respondents referred to issues related to the structure of tasks. These issues were described as extremely directive practices and ready-made tasks. The lack of space for children to express themselves and to make their own choices also played a role in this, according to the teachers.

*Forcing the child to do what the adult wants.*

*Where all children do the same activity, getting to the same standardized product.*

*Excessive intrusion from the adult during the child's moment of creativity.*

Moreover, there are also some references to the poverty of educational experiences, referring to experiences that are of little or no interest to the children, from which they do not learn anything, and that are considered by one of the pre-school teachers as "an example of pedagogical negligence".

These opinions are totally coherent with those stressed for the promotion of creativity and also reveal a comprehensive knowledge of both professionals' attitudes and pedagogical proposals which can contribute greatly to inhibit the children's expression of creativity.


## Results from Spain

A total of 29 teachers from 21 to 50 years of age (the mean age being approximately 36) took part in the study. Out of the respondents, 69% were female and, on average, they had 11 years of experience.

*What is creativity?*

When the teachers were asked what they understood by creativity in their school practice, the most important factor that they attributed to creativity was the possibility to show it. This means that they felt that divergent thinking required freedom to express oneself and to use different materials.

References to the role of the teacher in developing children's divergent thinking were almost as frequent, entailing issues such as giving opportunities and resources, taking the children's opinions into account, flexibility, and the ability to motivate the children. There were also several references to originality, meaning the capability to create something new. Moreover, some respondents defined creativity as a capability that must be developed, involving factors such as intelligence, context and motivation. There were also references to going beyond the basics, spontaneity and an open mind.

When asked what kinds of characteristics or behaviours of a child would lead the teachers to consider the child particularly creative, the most frequent answer was that the child exhibited originality in his/her behaviour. Another quality that was mentioned by several respondents was intrinsic motivation displayed by the child.

*Giving different and original solutions that are unexpected, also providing a variety of possible answers for the same situation.*

*When a child is able to achieve every task in an original way different from their peers.*

*Enjoying the activity.*

*Not resigning oneself to a result that is more or less expected.*

In addition to the aforementioned issues, the teachers also mentioned going beyond the basics, unexpectedness, being elaborate, clarity, fluidity, expression of imagination and sensitivity.

*What fosters creativity?*

With respect to the practices that the teachers considered to foster creativity in children, the most frequently mentioned issues were related to aesthetic, artistic and expressive languages, revealing that in the teachers' opinion, creativity is mainly developed through such domains. References were made also to problem-solving, stories, creating something new, providing new learning experiences, symbolic play and classroom distribution.

*What hinders creativity?*

The results concerning such educational practices that inhibit children's creativity showed a great degree of unanimity among the participants. The majority of the responses referred to the structure of the tasks.

*Structured works, the famous handwriting exercises.*

*Spoon-feeding children, meaning that you tell them, 'first you must do so, then so'. Sequencing everything, without leaving anything open.*

*Closed-ended tasks where there is only one solution.*

The rest of the answers referred to attitudes ("not giving value to children's ideas"), resources that do not facilitate creativity, and not allowing enough time for play.

**Results from Sweden**

The questionnaire in Sweden (Norrköping area) involved 102 pre-school teachers, 95% of whom were female. The average age of the respondents was 44 years, and their average professional experience was 17 years.

*What is creativity?*

In the context of children's education, the teachers involved in the research linked creativity to the following key concepts: imagination and the ability to be constructive, teachers' skills, acceptance of diversity, and the pre-school curriculum. The teachers reported that imagination and curiosity were essential prerequisites for anyone attempting to be creative.

*What fosters or hinders creativity?*

Many factors were deemed to affect creativity, the chief issues among them being stimulating learning contexts (both indoor and outdoor) and the teacher's approach and professional style.

Hence, in order to apply theories on creativity to the actual learning context, it is critical to support teachers with adequate training.

The teachers were asked to mention examples of good practices that stimulate children's creativity. Issues brought up in their answers included offering learning material that stimulates curiosity and interest, the introduction of experiments that lead to the development of logical and mathematical skills, and the use of story-telling as a starting point for other activities such as dramatization.

Creative thinking is supported by activities such as asking children open-ended questions that are connected to their experiences or familiar situations, as well as by asking questions on specific matters, or by presenting problems which allow multiple possible answers.

Examples of practices that hinder creativity are those which do not allow children's own creative thoughts, but are directed by the teacher's preconceived ideas. Another example is constituted by activities which are too limited in space and time to carry any real impact and significance for the children.

Once again, this study highlights the teacher's central role, either positive or profoundly negative, in the context of children's education; teachers have therefore the potential to either support or greatly hinder children's creativity.

**Summary and discussion**

In addition to examining the results on a country-specific level, we also made an aggregated analysis summarizing the teachers' views on the circumstances affecting creativity on the level of the whole consortium. Figure 1 presents the respondents' views on the circumstances they considered the most crucial in affecting creativity.

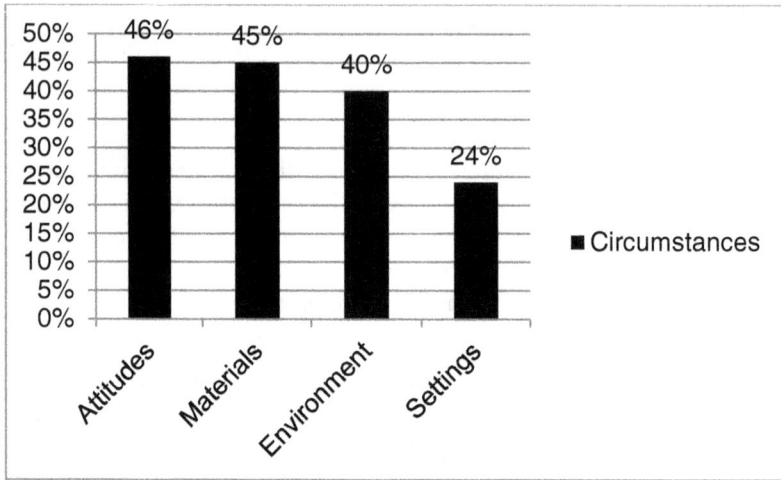

Figure 1. Circumstances that affect creativity

The most predominant circumstances affecting creativity were seen to be appropriate pedagogical attitudes amongst the teaching staff (46%), access to materials (45%), stimulating indoor and outdoor environments (40%), and a reliable ambience and attractive organizational settings (24%).

Practitioners mention teachers' attitudes and approaches as the conscious re-enforcement of the ability to see solutions to problems from divergent viewpoints. They see non-directive and non-judgemental behaviour amongst adults, granting children their freedom of expression, as an approach that favours the creative process. Also, a reassuring and non-invasive attitude that gives space to activities that are sufficiently open-ended and in which preferred individual expression is allowed seems to be conducive to creativity.

Materials are attributed great relevance. Flexible and unstructured or recycled materials seem to offer almost infinite opportunities that favour both transformation and invention, and promote exploration and self-expression. Appropriate environments shaped in flexible manners and outstretched time so as to respect children's rhythm also appear to be very significant variables that promote the thinking process and allow actions to be re-elaborated. They also facilitate children's autonomy, discovery, exploration and verbal expression, thus effectively favouring creativity. Other circumstances referred to by many teachers are divergent thinking ability, knowledge, intelligence, personality and self-confidence.

An overwhelming majority of the respondents have engaged in activities that promote children's creativity. Most activities refer to constructivism, drama, song and music and others to outdoor education, science, maths and technology. A great majority of these practices are run as projects spanning a whole term or school year.

When asked about the methods that the teachers believe to foster creativity, some approaches gather a consensus of opinion regardless of cultural and educational belongings. The teachers were particularly unanimous regarding open-ended questions and problems offering multiple answers (95%). Questions and problems that are well defined (86%) as well as questions and problems that children recognize and associate with previous knowledge (79%) were seen to be conducive to creativity as well.

When approaching the practices through which the teachers aim to promote creativity from the perspective of their content, certain types of activities and circumstances are highlighted. Aesthetic work, visual arts and joyful play are examples of the practices mentioned. The practices are very often referred to and connected with specific work circumstances of the practitioners. Though living and working in differing realities, the teachers mention the work environment as the best component to foster child creativity. Consistent and adequate approaches and professional attitudes towards the task are very often referred to as other fostering elements. Experiments related to science and technology both indoors and outdoors, reading and dramatizing fairy tales and cognitive projects on language learning that help develop children's imaginary skills, are practices that a great majority of the practitioners seem to be familiar with. Logical challenges are also looked upon as fostering practices.

Other approaches mentioned by many of the respondents are educational activities related to storytelling that involve children in symbolic play, drama and corporal expression. Artistic-figurative productions that are a complement to storytelling/symbolic play seem also to open creative doors. Finally, science experiments that aim at seeking explanations to the unknown and are logical challenges to the children are examples of other approaches that are believed to promote and foster creativity.

Many of the results presented in this section are consistent with those obtained by other empirical studies aiming to understand teachers' views on creativity (Diakidoy & Kanari, 1999; Fryer, 1996, 2008; Morais & Azevedo, 2008; Pequito, 1999). The results of our study reflect earlier research highlighting that the development of creative thinking requires flexible tasks and an environment conducive to freedom of choice (Amabile, 1983; Csikszentmihalyi, 1990; Prieto, López & Ferrándiz, 2003; Sternberg & Lubart, 1995). Furthermore, when reflecting on their practices of fostering creativity, the teachers emphasize artistic and expressive languages, revealing that in their views, creativity is mainly developed through such domains. This is a common finding in previous literature as well (Bahia, 2002, 2009; Diakidoy & Kanari, 1999; Fryer, 1996; Morais & Azevedo, 2008).

Some important findings in our study are the relevance given to adults' supportive attitudes towards children's ideas, processes and products, as well as the emphasis put on the organization of the educational environment to facilitate children's free self-expression and deep involvement, seen as essential features to promote creativity. Such views show the recognition of their own role in the education for creativity in young children and pre-school contexts but it does not mean they find themselves totally prepared for that and the needs for the training in the field of creativity appear to be evident.

## References

Amabile, T.M. (1983). The social psychology of creativity: a componential conceptualization. Journal of Personality and Social Psychology, 45(2), 357-376.

Bahia, S. (2002). Da educação à arte e à criatividade. Sobredotação, 3 (2), pp 101-126. Pdf: http://hdl.handle.net/10451/2730

Bahia, S. (2009). Constrangimentos à expressão artística. Revista Ibero-Americana de Pesquisa em Educação, Cultura e Artes, 0 - Dezembro, 137-148. Retrieved from http://hdl.handle.net/10451/2698.

Csikszentmihalyi, M. (1990). Flow: The Psychology of Optimal Experience. New York: Harper & Row.

Diakidoy, I-N., & Kanari, E. (1999). Student teachers' beliefs about creativity. British Educational Journal, Vol.25, n°2, pp. 225-243.

Fryer, M. (1996). Creative teaching and learning. London: Paul Chapman Publishing Ltd.

Fryer, M. (2008). Creative teaching and learning in the UK: Early research and some subsequent developments. In S. Bahia, & M.F. Morais (Coord.), Criatividade: Conceito, necessidades e intervenção (pp.136-156). Braga: Psiquilíbrios Edições.

Morais, M. F., & Azevedo, I. (2008). Criatividade em contexto escolar: representações de professores dos Ensinos Básico e Secundário. In S. Bahia & M. F. Morais (Coord.), Criatividade: Conceito, necessidades e intervenção (pp.157-196). Braga: Psiquilíbrios Edições.

Pequito, P. (1999). Representações de criatividade dos Educadores de Infância. Saber (e) Educar, 4, pp. 61-77.

Prieto, M. D., Parra, J., Ferrando, M., Ferrándiz, C., Bermejo, M. R., & Sánchez, C. (2006). Creative abilities in early childhood. Journal of Early Childhood Research, 4 (3), pp. 277-290.

Sternberg, R. J., & Lubart, T. I. (1995). Defying the crowd: Cultivating creativity in a culture of conformity. New York: Free Press.

# 11 Results of the focus groups conducted in Italy
*Antonio Gariboldi*

The explorative research on educators' and teachers' opinions and ideas of creativity was carried out in Italy through 10 focus groups which involved a total of 75 teachers (nursery educators and kindergarten teachers). The choice to give precedence to a qualitative investigation methodology was dictated by the fact that it was considered important to explore the theme of creativity without proposing predefined categories for analysis and therefore leaving open the possibility for teachers to express themselves freely. In this way, it was thought that, by encouraging confrontation within the working group and by the ways of speaking and discussing creativity in a context of dialogue, even the most implicit aspects relative to how teachers consider creative processes and the relationship between creativity and education could emerge.

One more objective of a more strictly professional development nature of the focus group was the creation of an opportunity, in the initial stage of the process, for stimulating debate and reflection in a systematic way between the teachers participating in the project. The main arguments that were the object of group interviews, and analogous with questions posed on questionnaires given out in different countries, regarded:
- Definitions of creativity
- Examples of the creative child
- Examples of good/bad educational practices in relation to creativity
- Space and organization of activities that can foster creativity.

**Different ideas of creativity**
The analysis of the focus groups, which is reported briefly and only with reference to the most significant results that emerged, showed in the first place that there is a very wide and pervasive concept of creativity spread between many teachers. Creativity is intended as being, in a general sense, a positive quality of being a child and of infantile action, a sort of colouring of the entire behaviour of the child towards external reality. Creativity seems to imply everything the child does spontaneously, without having a specific or peculiar significance:

The child is creative from when they enter the nursery, their whole being is creative at a daily level.

The child is always creative, it is up to us to welcome their creativity, it is up to us to welcome their creativity and make the creative process visible.

Creativity is innate in children, it is always there and it is their right to bring it out.

[Creativity is there in the sense that] the children give to things or to situations.

I believe that creativity is a free expression of the child from which they are able to extract feelings, emotions; it is something which they hold inside and which by leaving them free, by letting them touch different material, manipulate particular objects, they are able to express themselves through various fields.

In my opinion there is creativity even without knowledge [...] because a new born is already creative even only by sucking, they find their way, with what they know, to express themselves.

If on the one hand we underline the way in which creativity is an aspect that characterizes all children and not an element that belongs only to particular personalities, on the other hand it is considered to be an innate quality and it is identified as a free expression of the child. Spontaneous childhood activity and freedom of expression seem to be seen not only as conditions of creativity but as a definition of creativity.

In this sense the association made by many teachers between creativity and imagination appears significant:

This morning in the woods: a child approached a tree with his ear and I asked him: what is the tree telling you? In my opinion that showed [creativity], I noticed that he followed me in that direction.

We noticed a picture showing a wood and I asked them what they saw. One child answered that there were wolves, but that they were hidden. They thought about something that could not be seen.

For example, when it snows there are children who have an almost scientific explanation (perhaps given by their parents), others follow the train of their thought, and so a logical thread, their own completely imaginative explanation, but it is wonderful, really creative, really out of the scheme of things and this is really creative. It really surprises me a great deal.

There can be just imagination without it being put into practice.

Creativity is letting fantasy flow freely.

Creativity means entering into an unreal world.

As underlined by Vygotsky, only if we see imagination as a construction of unreal elements and wanting in concrete significance, can we attribute a rich creativity to the child. The expression "imaginative explanation, really wonderful, really creative, really out the scheme of things. It really surprises me" gives us an acceptance of creativity which coincides with imagination and with being "unconventional", "out of the scheme" - but which conventions, which schemes does the child have that enables the adult to say that their assertion (a theory which is defined as naïve) is unconventional? If the child is deemed to be outside the adult scheme, the prospective therefore becomes adult-centred. During childhood the child researches and interrogates what surrounds them so as to construct an image of the world which is as near as possible to reality, inside the scheme of things and, through this process, they also structure their own identity.

So what defines creativity? Being outside normal parameters? With respect to what? If I have not changed the scheme or the rule, can I venture into a creative process in these terms? Can creativity precede the rule? The teacher here seems to consider the childhood process/action of research outside the scheme to be thereby creative: they justify and exalt creativity a priori with respect to the rule.

In contrast, a minority of teachers offers a different definition of creativity, as an element of thinking more concretely operational, a combinatorial process that is based on knowledge and that involves the operations of processing of the stimuli that precede the creative act:

In my opinion, we mistake creativity with imagination. The discourse of creativity perhaps has its basis in the rule and in knowing the rules and the material. [Creativity] is therefore  the ability to construct from the known, according to the rules, that something new. In my opinion, creativity cannot exist without rules, because then we go back to the idea that everything is creative. The rule that says what you can and can't do and then unite the things and anyway it directs you in moving towards that something which allows you to move out the scheme of things. [...] first you need to know the rules, then you can see them in another way. So as to be creative you need to have understanding, a raw material to construct from: foundations. The child needs to be given experiences. After having tried things then they can make associations between them, play with them, use them, make them evolve [...] in creative behaviour I associate things with intention, it's guided by intention, by the desire to unite things which seem unlinked so as to arrive at new solutions. Because creativity is being able to bring together things so as to arrive at something new.

Creativity is certainly linked to freedom, but one must also feel completely part of a situation. [...] the more the codes in which the child can work and experiment are enlarged, the more they are given the possibility to affirm themselves. Procedures are therefore necessary so that the child can find their way within various contexts. They must find their way so as to be able express themselves in a creative way.

You must have understanding. If you do not know, you cannot construct something that you do not know.

In these teachers' view the possibility of being creative implies, therefore, the knowledge of rules and codes. In this sense the importance not only of giving stimulus but also of sustaining the ability to organize stimuli is underlined; the importance of sustaining the process of elaborating data and of knowledge and the intertwining between logical and analogical thought: "the possibility of giving space to divergent thinking and at the same time putting order into what you do."

## Good practices to promote creativity

The many conceptions of creativity translate, at least partially, into different ways of understanding the good or bad practices which can get in the way of or favour the creative process. Many teachers state how decisive it is that the adult assume a non-directive and non-judgmental style of behaviour, a behaviour which can instil feelings of safety in the child so that they can express themselves. The adult must guarantee the child the freedom to express themselves, avoiding guiding, intervening or conditioning.

When it comes to handing in their graphic work, I don't look at them. Teachers sometimes breathe down their neck.

Intrusion is, I think, bad practice. Always showing how to do something or directing the activity a lot or explaining always how something should or shouldn't be done, saying no a lot, not giving freedom of expression.

The teacher should follow the desires of the children. The teacher must make themselves available to the child, trying not to intervene too much.

Try to create a good relationship between them and with the adult so as to create the security needed to be able move beyond, to put them at ease and feel welcomed.

Other teachers, however, underline the importance of the adult not only assuming reassuring and non-invasive behaviour, but also adopting strategies which encourage and sustain the children's creative thoughts. In these teachers, there seems to emerge an idea with respect to the role of the adult which seems to recall that sustained by Munari ("don't tell children what to do but how to do it").

Good practice is us taking them beyond, perhaps saying to them: "yes, I see a castle, but what could we think about it together?" Perhaps because when exploring something you don't know, where creativity has no points of reference, you can feel lost, and if there is an adult who wants to get lost with you, it can help to develop creativity.

I think that creativity in education, even on behalf of the adult, is found in reinforcing the possibility of seeing the same problem from differing points of view, and in involving the different viewpoints.

Proposing a process which contains a quality, that is that there, in that context, there is a sense of direction.

Give space to activities which are sufficiently open-ended in which the preferred individual expression is allowed.

While they very often, through their examples, refer to the children's collective activities, few teachers explicitly declare that creativity can be promoted and enhanced by giving value to the social dimension of the processes:

Creativity is also linked to collaboration with peers, to verbal exchanges.

One could think that creativity is understood, most of all, as an individual cognitive process that is not transferable, rather than as an element which can be nurtured and developed by stimulating the interaction between children in specific contexts of experience. There is perhaps scarce understanding of how social processes can enhance creative processes and how others can help to see things and problems from different angles and perspectives, even proposing and soliciting situations and experiences which encourage exchange, therefore favouring the association and the recombination of different elements.

All the teachers agree, however, on attributing great relevance to the materials made available to the children. The agreement of teachers on the materials is wide and their centrality emerges from the rich description that they give: flexible or unstructured materials stand out, as do recycled and natural materials such as paper, foam rubber, pieces of wood, flour, sand, boxes, rope, etc. and the almost infinite combinations of such materials. They also give importance to the unconventional use of furniture or of food and their transformation by means of invention. The teachers seem more likely to see creativity in construction with such material than in artistic expression (or expression with standard tools) which is only mentioned rather than practiced.

Given the priority assigned to construction and invention with materials, it is not surprising that in the discussion of good and bad practice the availability of a variety of different material is cited as a condition for the creative exercise:

Different, varied material, which can be of all types, natural and artificial. Unstructured at least. A multiplicity of material, because even understanding the properties helps you understand how to use them.

There shouldn't only be a certain type of material, there should be a wide variety, so that they can put together different qualities and different material.

The argument is often upheld. In certain cases, the lack (or withdrawal) of material and objects as a stimulating condition is evaluated on the other hand:

Empty spaces are always very creative because here (the child) invents things more, everything and then some.

Put them in a context which is lacking in stimulus, few materials, so as to pull out their inventions. For example in the playground. Ours has nothing and they, if they go out, have to constantly invent games.

Time also appears to be a significant variable in implying that a context is effectively able to encourage creativity.

Create contexts in which they have the time to re-elaborate.

Perhaps overstimulation is a bad practice because it leaves no time to think. Does not allow the sedimentation of things, especially in children with difficulties.

So you need to allow children time to make their own experiences, to explore and experiment.

We are speaking then of outstretched time, in which it is possible to linger, to think and re-elaborate, and which must characterize experiences which favour childhood creativity. But it is also a time, as some teachers underline, which can be shaped in a flexible manner so as to respect the child's rhythm and guarantee continuity and the possibility to develop their actions.

Alongside aspects which refer to the organization of the context, such practices and project paths are highlighted in which the teacher directly proposes invention activities. In one particular case, reference is made to a project in which children are involved in observation, representation and invention activities regarding an art gallery. In another case they were involved in a game on the theme of "if we weren't here, if we were somewhere else, where would we be" which is an explicit invitation to imagine, prefigure and construct imaginary worlds in a collective manner. "Invented reading" is also mentioned. Using some white paper folded into book form: the teacher pretends to read a story, the children pretend to see the illustrations and they describe them, inventing in turn their own stories and pretending to read them. The game of distorting well known stories and fables is also mentioned (which uses a similar method to that proposed by Rodari), or else of the promotion of replies to a scientific enquiry (such as how was the world born?), in which all the children are invited, and they attempt to give answers, imaginative or not, that is, "turn the question around".

## Conclusions

In conclusion, one can underline how certain conditions brought up seem to be favourable to any educational activity: the teachers' approach in encouraging and supporting the child's expression, the variety of material for exploration, leaving time for autonomous discovery and exploration, favouring verbal exchange. All of these conditions appear favourable to learning, in exercising ability, in becoming sociable etc. One might reasonably agree that they also favour the demonstration of creativity and creative thinking. Of the elements pointed out, some seem particularly congruent with the activation of thinking and creative behaviour: the possibility of using unstructured material, the condition of  giving sufficiently open-ended stimuli so as to allow individual diversified expression, the proposal of different forms of expressive activity and invention, the action carried to reinforce the possibility of seeing the same problem from differing viewpoints or to support processes which weave together logical and analogical thinking.

It can be said that, from the teachers' words, beyond what their different ideas of what creativity is, or what are the most appropriate ways of stimulating its development, there emerges at least the importance and the educational value of creativity. The attention given to the conditions that promote and encourage the creative processes represents an aspect which must qualify a good educational context, as some teachers affirm, with reference to early childhood services.

# 12 Results from the danish focus groups and fieldwork

*Anne Lindegaard and Henriette Vognsgaard*

In Denmark, field work and a focus group interview were conducted in day-care centres related to the project. The questionnaire was not used in Denmark due to practical and scientific circumstances. This chapter presents a summary of the main issues discovered in the focus group and the field work.

**Background: definition of creativity**

Our definition of creativity is the ability and the will to imagine things different than they usually are – and to act according to that. In this understanding, creativity is not necessarily connected to arts. It might well be so, but it might as well be a sort of everyday creativity, an originality in the way life is lived.

We hold the following basic assumptions:

1. Creativity is a quality - not a skill. You cannot be creative on fixed times if the rest of the time the grown-ups always tell you what to do and how to do it.

From this follows:

2. It is of vital importance how daily life is organized. The grown-ups have institutionalized power over the children, both in regard to defining when, how, and why and in regard to their obligations to interpret the children's behaviour.

Thus it seems that:

3. Creativity is fostered best when the pedagogy is inclusive. That is, when every single child is a highly estimated member of the community, and when specific childlike behaviour is appreciated by the grown-ups - not only endured.

In summary, we assume that democratic inclusion and appreciation in day-care institutions is a necessary condition for children's creativity. Not in itself but as a part of daily practice. Still an absolutely vital condition is the relation between pedagogues and children.

Also, it appeared that the notion of transgression is vital in order to assure the possibilities of participating in creative processes. The transgression is about to break with existing practices and thinking in everyday life in day-care. In creative processes one connects thoughts, acts and materials not yet connected.

## Focus group interview

The focus group interview was conducted in two steps: 1) nine pedagogues in a nursery (related to the project) and 2) pedagogues from nine other day-cares in the municipality. The first focus group interview focused on a broad understanding and elaboration on "what is creativity?" The second focus group interview focused on a reflection on creativity inspired by presented activities in the nursery (presented by one of the pedagogues connected to the project). Both focus group interviews took a broad focus on creativity in both a professional and institutional perspective.

In both focus group interviews, the participants were all women, their ages ranging from 22 to 55 years. They had a various number of years of background in day-cares. In both interviews, managers of day-care centres, pedagogues and pedagogue-assistants were represented.

The focus group interview was conducted by using a number of open questions in order to let different points of view grow from the dialogue and from listening to one another in the group. It seemed that some questions generated new questions that seemed relevant in extension of the questions asked. We regarded this as a natural development and quality of the method focus group interview, so these supplementary questions are a part of the interview.

From the first question on the immediate understanding of "what is creativity?" (by each pedagogue individually), a long list occurs - for instance: painting, drawing, building, experimenting with materials, construction play, bodily interaction and activities, sensorial environment, creating an inclusive atmosphere and environment, creating space for challenges, problem solving and searching for "different" solutions, initiatives, immersion, spontaneity, exploration, playing with words and sounds. In other words, creativity and creative thinking lead to energy and engagement.

There are many descriptions and definitions on the concept of creativity. It is broadly defined, which makes sense as one of the pedagogues puts it: "Creativity is not only an act, it is a way of thinking. Creativity is not only a product, it is a way of thinking that makes sense in many contexts in everyday life and organizing."

On the question "from where does creativity origin?" some participants argue that children are born creative, that creativity has no age, and it is relevant to act creatively even with little children in nurseries. Also, creativity is seen as an ability to make everyday life meaningful.

On the question "what fosters creativity?" the staff have a general opinion that the professional staff "have more fun" and are inspired when they think and act creatively. That is, creativity generates positive energy and the joy of the staff imprints the children – and the other way around; the joy and energy of the children affect the pedagogues in positive ways. Some comments from two pedagogues on this:

Creativity is generating and creates a positive impact on the social environment in day care.

To dare to turn things upside down – indeed – and believe in the fact that things can be done differently. The world is not constant, that one can emphasize the world differently – the children will learn "the right way" anyway.

Another question arises from the question "what fosters creativity?" namely a question on "what is a material – and what are materials good for?" A vital point to the pedagogues is that a material changes. So how to interpret specific possibilities of the materials is a matter of being able to see possibilities upside down – and especially notice what the child does with the materials. One has to be aware of the possibilities of the material in different contexts, "get to know the material", and to experiment with "what is allowed and not allowed with different materials". This process fosters new recognition. A pedagogue puts it this way: "It is about creating freedom and possibilities of participation for the child, following the child and its 'imprints'." So there is a specific focus on the child/children and how children express themselves.

On the question "what hinders creativity?" various views are presented. Some argue that the children's environment and adults (pedagogues) are the main factors that prevent the creativity of children. That is why the pedagogues should notice the interests and the initiatives of the children and then encourage and care for this. Bans and rules are also mentioned as factors hindering the creativity of both children and pedagogues, and the inclusiveness disappears. Tests and measurements of the children in day-care centres are mentioned as preventing creativity from growing. Systems of testing and evaluation are not considered to promote creative thinking either.

Another hindering perspective is an understanding of correctness and control of the pedagogues – that the adult "dictates" what is right and wrong, what is creative or not. This is considered a problem as the adult pedagogue does not (always) know what is either right or best for the children.

A final hindering issue mentioned by the participants are "practical difficulties" in the daily organization of activities. The group mentions problems for "being creative" due to the extent of cleaning up from activities and also due to the lack of materials available. It is then discussed that creative activities do not need to have a result or a product, and the whole group of children does not necessarily have to participate either. It may be a matter of clarity, and by being aware of this it may be easier to facilitate creative processes.

On the question of "the role of the participants in creative processes?" the following arguments occur. Relations and communities are concepts that all pedagogues mention and agree on. They emphasise that creativity is something shared, something experienced. Togetherness is a driver in order to let creativity grow. That is to consider children as participants taking part in communities in a democratic way.

Some stress the importance of "following the child", paying special attention to the imprints of the children. It is also seen as important to focus on the process that is regarded as "additive joy" to the adult in the sense that it "adds further energy to the togetherness" with the children. This underlines the importance of the awareness on the children's reaction to the world. It is stressed that together with the children a creative atmosphere can grow. One pedagogue puts it this way: "Creativity is "colours", colours in a broad understanding. Colours that unite us all together. Otherwise it is worth nothing!"

Conclusive remarks so far

In general, the focus group interviews offer a deeper insight of the Danish pedagogues in Danish day-care centres (children aged from 1-6 years old). It seems that at least three perspectives are important to "a creative pedagogy":

1) An underlying understanding of democratic inclusion and appreciation in day-care institutions is a necessary condition for children's creativity; that is, to emphasize a democratic, participatory mind-set in our everyday lives with children.

2) A focus on "following the child/children". That is to focus on the significance of the "imprints" of the child/children or the expressive languages within their peer culture in order to let the inspiration, the additive joy and power arise from this.

3) To dare to focus on the world upside down in order to stress that creativity is (also) a matter of attitude.

**Field work**

The field work focused on the conditions for creativity, i.e. whether the pedagogues managed to be appreciative and inclusive (all pedagogues say they want to). We looked for children's creative contributions to daily life - these might be in the way of using things for new purposes, giving original suggestions to problem-solving or fantasizing.

In the following examples we do not distinguish between the institutions as it does not seem to be of any significant importance. The examples are chosen among a large amount of observations for which they are representative.

1. Using rooms in an unauthorized way

Two of the big boys hang around, clearly not quite knowing what to do. Sort of restlessly they start playing football in the hallway and they are absorbed in the game. The head of the institution comes around and soon she is enthusiastically involved in playing with the boys. They shout and laugh loudly - and the boys win the game.

The pedagogue might have stopped the boys, asking them to go outside with this kind of play. Instead she estimates that these two boys need no further reprimands - they need to be supported in their rather original and creative way of using a spacious and tempting indoor area to an activity that the grown-ups probably had not thought of.

2. What is proper behaviour - and who has the right to define it?

A child tells the pedagogue: Gustav belches beside me.

The pedagogue (wrongly assuming that the child wants her to interfere): Tell him that you do not want it.

The child: But I do.

There is more than one thing at play here: First the pedagogue supplies the child with means to cope for himself so that the children do not need to tell on each other. The child might then have given up, perhaps having tried too often to share something with the grown-ups. But luckily he goes on, thus teaching the pedagogue something important - while the child himself is confirmed that his experience is of value.

3. Playing with words

The children are getting ready to go on the playground, and Birgitte (the pedagogue) tells them to remember to put on their boots.

Later on one child asks another: What did Birgitte tell us to remember to put on our feet? After a little while the answer is: Nail polish.

This shows another very important daily event: Children's need (and capacity) to be creative with their imagination and their verbal language. If the grown-ups are keen to teach children what is reality then the children might lose this desire-driven ability.

Conclusive remarks

The above-mentioned examples from the fieldwork show small glimpses from life in kindergartens where pedagogues are highly conscious about the need of being appreciative and inclusive with the children, the wish being to provide conditions for children's creativity.

On purpose these examples are chosen from very small, banal daily incidents, taking place all the time in every kindergarten. And usually the outcome is exactly the opposite of that in the examples: the children are taught what halls are for, what proper behaviour is like, and what you are supposed to put on your feet - thus in the long run learning to keep their ideas to themselves, and finally losing them.

We do not doubt that the intentions of being appreciative inclusive are shared by the majority of Danish pedagogues. So a vital question seems to be: What are the impediments for making conditions for children's creativity in kindergartens?

## References

Hastrup, K. (1995). A passage to anthropology: Between experience and theory. London & New York: Routledge.

Kitzinger, J, & Barbour, R.S. (1999). Introduction: the challenge and promise of focus groups. In R.S. Barbour & J. Kitzinger (Eds.), Developing focus group research. Politics, theory and practice, London: Sage Publications, pp. 1-20.

# Part 4

# Creativity in pre-school education practices

# 13 Pre-conditions for creativity in pre-school education

*Henriette Vognsgaard*

The research presented in this book reflects theoretical contributions from the researchers from the participating countries. The reflections presented are - naturally - embodied in different approaches and traditions represented by the researchers´ cultural traditions and perspectives. This fact reflects that the research done through the project naturally is culturally contextualized and categorized according to this - theoretical as well as practical.

The research done shows that there are some fundamental understandings in conceptualizing creativity in the educational system. The diversity the research presents share some very crucial pre assumptions of creativity in pre-school education. In this project diversity is regarded as a qualifying aspect. The research activities therefore present and represent a manifold diversity in the educational systems as well as in practice. One basic assumption is the democratic humanistic approach and a basic humanity. Therefore some of the crucial pre assumptions and pre conditions are:

- Democracy
- Inclusion
- Appreciation
- Child centered perspective
- Participatory cultures
- Play

As creativity is considered to be present in all people (and not only gifted children) creativity can be defined as an ability and willingness to create more out of less with original ideas. Creativity can be encouraged by art and artistic expressions, but it is not the only way, more understandings are required.

Inclusion may be seen as when a child is included in a community when she or he feels truly accepted and appreciated - this gives ways to the development of creativity, though more is required.

A child centered approach is vital in a democratic perception stressing the importance of the child as the acting actor in everyday life. That is the child is both an individual person with the individual characteristic of the child but also a social person participating whit in communities. The child centered perspective is a crucial approach and is connected to the appreciation of the child as both an individual and a social person.

This underlines the child as an actor acting in everyday life. The child´s interacting attitude can therefore be considered as co exploration, co experimentation and co investigation. The child and children participate in participatory cultures with different media and ways of expressions and communication.

Play is another important aspect of creativity as playful elements are conditions for being creative; playfulness generates creativity. Play can be defined as a free and voluntary activity, a source of joy and amusement that can generate creative processes and thinking.

The attitude and ability of the professional adult is crucial in order to foster creativity in children, together with children. This implicates as well as requires a high level in the professional adult knowledge of children, society and its contradictions. The professional adult needs to focus on child centered activities, children´s social competences, children´s playfulness and focus on facilitation of the group process.

Also there may be pre assumptions concerning thematic issues of creativity – those are time, space, environment and materials. Those thematic issues seem to be fundamental and focal in order to qualify and develop creativity theoretically as well as practically.

In order to assure the above mentioned pre assumptions and pre conditions on creativity, different research methods were involved in the research activities in order to assure diverse knowledge on creativity in children´s pre-school education. Different scientific working methods were included due to a profound conviction that different methods of research should transcend the (im)material borders they usually work inside. E.g. national as well as international literature review and field work and focus group interviews were carried out in pre-schools and daycares.

# 14 Providing creative contexts

*Roberta Cardarello and Antonio Gariboldi* [1]

The analysis of existing literature on the subject and dialogue within the project research group (considering even the results of research carried out and the practices that were the object of discussion between teachers) allowed for the identification of  certain specific elements that can encourage childhood creativity within the early years setting. These are elements that appear relevant therefore for planning and organizing educational contexts that are functional in the promotion of creative processes, stimulating, giving value and supporting the free expression of children's original ideas within the different experiences and educational proposals.

## Exploring/experimenting with different spaces and materials.

The first point that is important to highlight is represented by the possibility of exploring and experimenting with different spaces and materials; an element that underlines the need to guarantee both an abundant choice of useful and interesting resources and material (Laslocky, Winefield; 2011), and a variety of experiential opportunities in which children are left free to act and interact with things, progressively discovering the potential of their use. The variety of spaces and material to explore and experiment with constitutes a useful condition for bringing out creative behaviour, in so far as creativity can be connected to all spaces and material: there exists not one exclusive one, and neither is creativity confined to one single area of experience.

The variety of spaces and material also implies the multiplicity and multiplication of possible experiences for the child and therefore for the development and consolidation of knowledge (of different material and environments) that each can draw from. Such experience/knowledge also represents potential that can be drawn on in the imaginative process (Vygotsky, 1932; Munari 1977) in so far as creativity is the result of a combinatory process that is founded on knowledge and which calls into question the operation of processing stimuli that precedes the creative act. In this sense the plurality of the experience with space and material represents a preparatory condition, or rather, a condition for the development and promotion of creative thinking.

This variety recalls then the debate on creativity as something general or domain specific

Baer, 1998). If , as sustained by various parties, creativity is not general and transversal but connected to a determinate area (H. Gardner's multiples intelligences go towards this direction), then the variety of experiences assured by the multiplicity of materials and spaces stimulates each individual to experiment in multiple environments, suited to finding the specific form of one's own creativity and therefore to multiply the possibilities that each one can find the occasion for experimenting with their own potential.

As for the element implied by exploration and experimentation, the level of exploration of material can be understood as the functional premise for the activation of creative processes, in the sense that exploration leads to the knowledge of the properties of a particular material and how the objects can be used and therefore to their possible subsequent use even in a creative sense. The explorative phase of a material, for example, precedes that of symbolic play and of imaginative transformation of the material itself. In this way, the knowledge acquired through exploration and experimentation is used by the children in the creative processes of combining materials, of invention and "creating wholes", that is, when children put together and integrate different materials, in relation to a particular project, so as to produce a coherent whole (Adams, Chen 2012).

The possibility of exploring and experimenting is particularly important in stimulating the creative use of unstructured and recycled materials that do not have a predefined use and that can be given new significance in many different ways by the children; materials with which there is an initial exploratory phase, that can be long and chaotic, then follows or can follow an active use and creative phase. The use of unusual and unstructured material is in fact often underlined as important by authors who are involved in identifying the ways in which creativity can be promoted within the pre-school setting (Drew, Drankin, 2004; Smith, 1996); the Torrance test for measuring creativity calls for an activity denominated 'unusual use" in which the subject is required to think of ways to use cardboard boxes that would normally be thrown in the bin (Meazzini 1992). The eventual creative use of such material implies however, that the child appropriates it, exploring its possibilities and constraints and bringing forth an inevitably significant work. If the teacher then, promotes and supports the exploration and experimentation of the material by stimulating the children to see new elements and to imagine possibilities, by soliciting the creation of projects and mobilizing them through a series of choices, then the same possibilities of the material can be

investigated even in the light of specific questions and within the context of constructive activities that are characterized as open problem-solving situations. These are situations which, while open to a plurality of solutions, initiate the inventive use of material and are therefore functional in activating children's creativity.

## Extended and relaxed time

Connected to the opportunity for exploration and experimentation of a variety of spaces and materials is a second element that is significant for the provision of educational contexts able to encourage creative processes. The temporal dimension of the experiential context and in particular, the possibility to take advantage of extended and relaxed time, to have time for reflection and re- elaboration and continuity of action on things, so as to develop in depth research and to evolve activities, represents a condition that can influence the manifestation of creative behaviour and in general, the expressive quality of children's play. Time represents an element whose importance has been highlighted by different research that has investigated creative processes (Runco, Cayirdag, 2009). In this sense, the activity should be planned in such a way as to guarantee an ample quantity of uninterrupted time for investigation and discussion (Smith 1996). In fact, the possibility of having time constitutes a relevant condition for the associative component of creative thinking, in as much as an individual, even when the discovery seems improvised, needs time to spend to go beyond the obvious idea, to find the remote association and therefore produce an original idea (Runco, Cayirdag, 2009). Lack of or constraint on time can negatively affect the incubation phase of an idea that is a typical phase of the creative process characterized by a more or less aware flow of thought. The creative process is often characterized by the loss of awareness of the temporal dimension and therefore of timelessness (Mainemelis,2002), because the intrinsic pleasure taken in carrying out the activity , the total involvement in it and the strong concentration on the task attenuates the perception of time passing. Even the availability of a protected space that is protected from interruptions and of a place where one can leave what one is doing and then take it up again later can encourage concentration on an activity, the continuity of action and its eventual creative development (Harrington, 1999, Laslocky, Winefield, 2011).

It is necessary therefore that the organization of daily time and the different educational proposals is thought out in a way that gives the children the possibility of understanding the experiential context and of acquiring competence in the experimented activity. It is an extended time, in which it is possible to hesitate, re-elaborate, and investigate in a non-superficial way, that which should characterize the experiences that are supposed to encourage childhood creativity. Time which is not pressing, not hurried, but a time that can be modulated in a flexible manner so as to respect the rhythms of the children and therefore the different ways and times for elaborating the situations that they are experiencing .

This is also concerned with allowing the children to construct a temporal perspective in the activity by offering them the possibility of creating connections between what they are doing and what they have previously done. Encouraging 'thinking that connects' means giving time and providing occasions, even in small groups, for the revision and re-elaboration of experiences, allowing the children to construct links, associations and significances that would otherwise be impossible in an experience that is perceived as fragmented and disconnected.

## Social collaboration among children in open problem-solving situations.

If the first two elements considered refer to matters related to organizational aspects of a context in favour of individual or group creativity, the third element underlines the importance of the social component as a possible force in encouraging creative processes when children are faced with problematic situations open to a variety of solutions. Social interaction and collaboration between children in open problem solving situations represents a condition for the activation and promotion of creative thinking. Children are called in fact to face a problem that can be resolved through contributions of original thought, within a collaborative work that provides exchange of ideas, analysis of a situation from different perspectives and angles, a dialogue between different hypotheses of solutions and points of view. This is a process that can even be mediated and supported by the teacher, which is extremely pertinent to creativity, that is founded both on associative and analogical thinking and on the ability to examine in a critical manner the ideas produced; elements that can be valued and strengthened by the social dimension of the process.

Within a pre-school context, problem-solving is configured as an area which, in connection to play and investigation, interacts and is connected to creativity (Blake, Giannangelo, 2012). Being faced with open problems, that is problems that do not have one single correct solution, but a variety of possible solutions, seems to be largely linked to the activation of divergent thinking, and creative processes (Ward, 2009). The proposal of experiential contexts that facilitate the emergence of problematic situations of this nature, promoting investigative processes, the expression of hypothetical thinking and the taste for discovery, represents therefore an element that can encourage creative attitudes. In this sense, by facing problems which presuppose the possible activation of creative processes, even the teacher can support the children in their mental passages that they use when trying to find a solution to a problem. The creative process does in fact entail the alternation of logical and divergent thinking: if moments of incubation of ideas and insight, i.e., the moment in which the solution to the problem is intuited, are at least in part, those where mainly divergent thinking is at play in as much as they are characterized by associations and flux of apparently chaotic ideas, then the preliminary phase, in which useful information for resolving the problem, and the final one, where the adequacy of the ideas and the hypotheses of solutions produced are verified, appear to be the phases in which logical reasoning and the ability to direct thinking and action appear most relevant. The teacher can therefore, both support the children in acquiring knowledge and information in relation to a specific field of the problem, and solicit them to make hypotheses for a solution and to find strategies for checking them. These strategies should stimulate them in different ways to avoid limiting attention to a single aspect of a problem; to examine the problem from different angle; to abandon unpractical hypotheses of solutions; and to explore mentally other alternatives. It is a process that can be strengthened by facilitating a dialogue of ideas between children and promoting group exchange and discussion.

## Combining different symbolic languages and codes.

An ulterior factor emerges that regards available material and children's action and which we have entitled 'combination of different symbolic languages and systems'. By this title we refer to a crucial characteristic of creative thinking and precisely the process of transition between a system of expression and another, or rather, the action of multiple coding of meanings. It is not concerned in this case with ensuring the children have merely a variety of materials, spaces and experiential environments, whose importance we have already discussed, but rather to encourage the use of multiple codes in their (the children's) expression and production. It is a more subtle aspect than the simple variety of materials because it consists of the variety of languages or codes in reference to the same experiential context. If the children are allowed to experiment with a content of knowledge or experience through graphic drawing but also through sound, and bodily expression, through narration (one could continue on and on) a favourable condition for creative thinking and behaviour is created. First, children experience the relative languages as connected rather than separate areas and therefore gain a representation of human codes and languages that is not separate or segregated. Secondly, they are encouraged to imagine (i.e. to prefigure) different ways of manifesting an idea or object, and therefore they nourish their ability to imagine. In the end, such an experience supports the disposition to 'play' with the possible expressions and it nourishes combinatory thinking definitively. In its most simple form the successive adoption of different languages in the course of an activity constitutes a useful scenario for the activation of the aptitude for connecting, translating, and so combining thinking and representations.

When the construction of an object (for example a castle), however it originated, fuses symbolic play with the constructed object, and is followed by the invention of a story, and ten perhaps graphic representations of the story, we are in the presence of a context that is favourable to supporting abilities and aptitudes for connecting and translating in different codes the same experiential contexts (Antoinetti Colombo Pizzingrilli 2011).

In an even more peculiar and specific form of creative thinking, the combination of different codes is based on synaesthesia (Cacciari 2002), the process of transferring from one sensorial field to another through an experience or perception "Creative people have more articulated neural connections and connect more remote events. The neurological condition known as synaesthesia appears to be related to creative associations. Synaesthesia occurs when two or more of a person's sensory modalities (taste, smell, touch, seeing, and hearing) get mixed. For example, a synesthete may experience colours when perceiving numbers or smell words" (Feist, 2011, 297). From this point of view the stimulation of creativity can require 'games' and focused activities for mixing together sensorial perceptions, as occurs when the teacher proposes games involving visualization of sound and music or gestural translation of sound and music.

Within the same genre of connections and translation of one sensorial plane to another, synesthetic metaphors also belong: these poetic metaphors are especially vivid because they express

cross-sensory mappings that are constrained by a cognitive principle whereby mappings go from lower sensory modes to higher ones (e.g. touch>taste>smell>sound>sight" (Gibbs 2011, 116 ). In general, it should be remembered that rendering metaphorical an experience is at the heart of the creative process and therefore, in some way, the child is invited to render metaphorical their reality and look for expressive analogies and they are encouraged to travel along a creative path.

It should be underlined that when faced with a metaphorisation or analogical research task each individual has a variety of unlimited possibilities available and therefore an open problem with multiple solutions. We are therefore in the presence of a concrete and viable direction for cultivating possibility thinking (Craft, McConnon, Matthews 2012), and proposing those open problem-solving tasks that we have just discussed.

**The role of the educator**

We arrive, at last, at the principal of the most crucial elements for the promotion of creativity: it is represented by the role and behaviour of the adult who is involved in the education of children. At the basis of an education system that promotes creativity there remain certain general assumptions already recalled in preceding chapters: of these and the criteria listed above, the adult must be a conscious interpreter. The first condition of awareness is certainly the adhesion to the idea that creativity is the heritage of everyone and that the educator should not so much be a talent scout of the creative child but rather a figure who supports the promotion of creativity in each child. Another important and unescapable aspect they must be aware of is represented by going beyond a simplified vision, in which creativity coincides only with fantasy and imagination. But the interpretation of general and specific criteria requires also that the adult adopts a precise behaviour and stance.

In terms of the planning of activities, the educator must be aware of the importance of the paces, and time given to the children (as previously stated) and must understand and recognize the factors and conditions that uphold children's creative thinking (from material to expressive languages, problem solving, and group collaborations as already highlighted).

In terms of the specific activities, they must dedicate particular attention to the situation of play, even free play, which is often either totally ignored or managed legislatively by the educators. Play, and symbolic play in particular, represents concentrated occasions for development of creativity, in which it is possible identify many of the conditions that have been recalled here (Jalongo, Hirsch 2012). As well as promoting free play, the adult must support imaginative and symbolic production supporting the children in their expressions without taking their place but rather, stimulating and supporting divergence, or more specifically "possibility thinking" (Craft, McConnon, Mathews 2012). In this way, on a communicative plane, asking the children open-ended questions, questions that guide the imaginative process rather than block it, are useful instruments. Questions such as "what could this be?" and "what could you do with this?" are preferable to teachers' closed questions such as 'what is this?' (Craft, McConnon, Mathews 2012, p.50.). Questions such as these, which need not be understood as precise or as recipes, are a good metaphor for the behaviour of the adult who intends to provide stimulus and suggestions in making the child creative. But most of all, positive behaviour in the adult consists in the adult's ability to listen and observe what the children say and do: this is an indispensable condition for giving the children freedom of expression and at the same time, nurturing, without force or extrinsic barriers, their possibility of inventing and imagining. Listening to children, welcoming their ideas, demonstrating understanding and relaunching them back: this is the way the adult should act in harmony with the children and able to aid them in the evolution of their thinking.

It must be remembered also just how important the relational climate is, in which the adult is a basic ingredient in trying 'to take risks'. In fact, among the conditions that allow innovation and encourage creativity we must remember the importance of the perception of self-efficacy of the child and their willingness to 'take risks' (Plucker Waitman Hartley 2011, p. 439; Craft, 2001, p. 10). An encouraging educator then, will be able to give positive feedback to all the children's expressions and initiatives, to create an emotional and cognitive context in which making mistakes, attempts, and failures are all equally valued, and in which it is therefore easy to run the risk of failing which is connected to any innovative experiment (Craft, McConnon, Matthews, 2012).

The relational dimension carries out an important function for any educational process. In the case of creativity, the relationship with the adult must guarantee the children's safety, guarantee them a relaxed and encouraging climate that allows them to 'dare' to experiment, to 'take risks' in inventing new things that can be potentially criticized or be failures. For all this, the grade acceptance of the adult of any behaviour is decisive and is a vital condition for strengthening creative thinking, which is indeed a risky thought.

The educator who wants to support creativity must learn to recognize not only canonical activities or activities carried out explicitly for that aim, but also the processes of daily life, in the typical routines of educational institutions, such as for example, lunch-time, or the moment of arrival or end of the day. Even in such situations, children can express their inventiveness and their force for 'free and imaginative transfiguration' and from the reaction of the adult they can receive encouragement. In other words, it is not only necessary to set up and plan complex projects in support of creativity. At times, it is easily triggered by the imaginative and playful transformation of lunch, or the moment in the bathroom, or when tidying up. Knowing how to see their processes of creative innovation in these moments is perhaps even the most relevant, and certainly the most incisive, in orienting the child towards creative thinking. When it is said that adults must be creative themselves in their approach to education, perhaps it means hoping for a subtle dimension of taste for play in their daily routine. At the heart of it all, as [perhaps] Einstein said, 'if one doesn't play, what is left?'

## Notes
1 While the structure of the paper was discussed in full by both authors, Antonio Gariboldi wrote the first three paragraphs, and Roberta Cardarello the fourth anf fifth paragraph.

## References
Adams M.L. e Chen J-Q. (2012), "Understanding Young Children's Kinds of Creating", in O.N. Saracho (ed.), Contemporary Perspectives on Research in Creativity in Early Childhood Education, Charlotte, IAP, pp. 343-354.

Antonietti A., Colombo B. , Pizzingrilli P. (2011) , The WCR Model of Creativity. From Concept to Application , The Open Education Journal, 2011, 4, (Suppl 1:M7) 80-89.

Baer J. (1998), "The Case for Domain Specificity of Creativity", Creativity Research Journal, v. 11, 2, pp. 173-177.

Blake S., Giannangelo D.M. (2012), "Creativity and Young Children", in O.N. Saracho (Ed.), Contemporary Perspectives on Research in Creativity in Early Childhood Education, Charlotte, IAP, pp. 293-315.

Craft A., (2001), An analysis of research and literature on CREATIVITY IN EDUCATION, www.euvonal.hu/images/creativity_report.pdf

Drew W.F., Rankin B. (2004); "Promoting Creativity for Life Using Open-Ended Materials", Young Children, July, pp. 1-8.

Feist G.J. (2011), Creativity in Science, in S.R. Pritzker, M.A. Runco (eds), Encyclopedia of Creativity, Elsevier , 296-302.

Gibbs R.W.Jr (2011), Metaphors, in S.R. Pritzker, M.A. Runco (eds), Encyclopedia of Creativity, Elsevier, 113-119.

Harrington D.M. (1999), "Creative Environments, Conditions, and Settings", in S.R. Pritzker, M.A. Runco (Eds.), Encyclopedia of Creativity, San Diego, Academic Press, pp. 264-272.

Jalongo M. R., Hirsch R. A. (2012), Reconceptualizing creative thought processes in young children, in Olivia N. Saracho (ed), Contemporary perspectives on Research in Creativity in Early Childhood Education, Information Age Publishing, Charlotte (USA), 89-105

Laslocky M., Winefield R. (2011), The Importance of Children's Play to the Development of Creativity and Innovation, Bay Area Discovery Museum.

Mainemelis C. (2002), "Time and Timelessness: Creativity in (and out of) the Temporal Dimension", Creativity Research Journal, v. 14, 2, pp. 227-238.

Meazzini P. (1992), "Il test di Torrance", Psicologia e Scuola, 60, pp. 34-39.

Munari B., Fantasia, Laterza, Bari.

Plucker J.A., Waitman G. R. Hartley K. A. (2011), Education and

Creativity, in S.R. Pritzker, M.A. Runco (a cura di), Encyclopedia of Creativity, Elzevier,  435-440

Runco M.A., Cayirdag N. (2009), "Time", in S.R. Pritzker, M.A. Runco (Eds.), Encyclopedia of Creativity, San Diego, Academic Press  pp. 485-488.

Smith M.K. (1996), "Fostering Creativity in the Early Childhood Classroom", Early Childhood Education Journal, v. 24, 2, pp. 77-82.

Vygotskij L. (1932), Immaginazione e creatività nell'età infantile, Roma, Editori Riuniti, 1972.

Ward T.B (2009), "Problem Solving", in S.R. Pritzker, M.A. Runco (Eds.), Encyclopedia of Creativity, San Diego, Academic Press, pp. 254-260.

Cacciari C., (2002), Il rapporto fra percezione e linguaggio attraverso la metafora, www.sssub.unibo.it/documenti/seminario.../cacciari.do.

# 15 Educational practices as told by the teachers: comments and suggestions concerning the enhancement of creativity

*Chiara Bertolini*

## Premise

This chapter intends to create a dialogue between two elements resulting from the comparison and research carried out as part of the CREANET project. On the one hand, there are the practices aimed at enhancing creativity that were illustrated by teachers from the participating countries and that were discussed during Working Groups with their European colleagues.[1] On the other hand, the indication of educational modes and principles that could encourage creativity in the pre-school age group coming from reflections and theoretical debate taking place over a number of settings during the meetings which took place periodically in different European settings.[2]

It is important to clarify immediately certain aspects that go along with the concept of educational-practice. Laeng (1992) understands it to be an action aimed at achieving a goal through the creation of an educational project. Pellerey (& Grzadziel, 2011) underlines that it concerns a human activity that takes place in school, characterized by interaction between teachers and students, aimed at promoting the development of the same students. Mialaret (1998) defines it as an educational situation, unique in terms of time and space, organized and managed by the teacher. The scholar also underlines emphatically the strong link between practice and theoretical reflection of a pedagogical nature: methodological indications should come from theory, not so much in a prescriptive way but rather as suggestions or educational proposals and even boundaries within which educational practice should be paced so that the expected results may be reached. Regardless, the influence appears to be reciprocal: practice can solicit reflections that are useful to the development of theory itself.

By adopting this perspective, the guidelines presented in the previous paper could be read in a practical-project way, or they could be intended as methodological indications useful to the planning of a context aimed at the promotion of children's creativity through an incisive and valid educational practice (Pellerey, Grzaziel, 2011).

In particular, this chapter will attempt to retrace in teachers' professional practice, the educational indications that emerged during the debate within the CREANET project with the aim of discussing them through examples so as to demonstrate how they can be broken down and translated into concrete action, and to demonstrate the practicality of such indications in early years educational settings.

## Methodology

In order to retrace and render visible a link between the educational indications aimed at promoting creativity and educational practice, the projects carried out at school and described by the teachers during the CREANET encounters were studied attentively[3] and were seen to be representative of educational practice that favours creativity. 36 projects were studied in total.[4] The corpus of this material contains all the presentations carried out during the European Working Groups with the exception of those discussed in the first encounter in Bejà (2011), in which the teachers were asked to describe in general terms the school they belonged to.

The basis made up of the 36 files is varied and composite. Some practices were illustrated through a form (named 'description form') which set out to describe the educational pathway in question through the compilation of particular sections[5], either by Power Point presentation or in video format which was discussed orally with European colleagues during the Working Group sessions. At times, the two different ways of describing saw complementary information emerge, at other times they were found to be redundant from the point of view of content. (Paoletti, 2011).

Certain practices were only described through one of the two required formats.

While the teachers were required to describe an educational practice that had the function of stimulating creativity, could the material gathered be considered in some way a-critical or a-problematic in terms of representing a selection of good practice for the promotion of children's creativity? First, because not all the descriptions adhered to the actual request, focusing at times on creativity in terms of teachers' teaching rather than on that of the children's creativity. Secondly, that body of practice should be thought of as representing not so much the absolute, valid, educational models but rather the multiplicity and variety of concrete contexts and practical actions used by the teachers, which they consider to be useful in soliciting creativity in pre-school aged children.

The 36 examples of practice were examined with the aim of retracing the educational directions presented in the previous paper. This analytical work was not simple, partly because of the dissimilarity of practice and the ways in which they were described. Sometimes, generic educational programmes lasting one year were illustrated, at other times shorter projects were described in detail. Into the presentation of practices, at times photographs assumed a crucial role which allowed for an unambiguous reconstruction of the programme's characteristics. Overall, the descriptions of the learning and teaching processes were not completely transparent and self-explanatory. Moreover, not all gave the same information. For example, some concentrated on the description of the processes and others of the products. At times, the desired indicators were declared verbally but not carried out in action (e.g. it was said that critical reflection on experience was encouraged and yet the way this was actually done was not described), at other times the indicators were not explicitly declared but we do not necessarily consider them as being absent (e.g. an indicator such as character rarely emerges over time. It is possible, however, that certain elements, though not actually declared, were in fact present in practice).

In the following paragraphs certain practices will be used as concrete examples of educational indications in favour of creativity that have been previously presented. They should be seen as representing aspects present also in other practice that remain untold due to lack of space.

## The attitude of the educator in fostering creativity

The first suggestions of an educational nature that emerged from the CREANET debate regard the teacher/educator. The aspects which should characterize both their planning and practice are many. It should be said from the outset that in terms of specific topics in question in the following paragraphs (time, space, material, collective situations of open-ended problem solving and the combination/mix of languages), these are rarely defined explicitly in the teachers' presentations, who even when they declare them, actually struggle to break them down in terms of concrete action; perhaps because they are concerned with aspects which are linked more with attitude and awareness of the adult at a professional level. This is also concerned with characteristics which are woven tightly together, but which for clarity's sake we will attempt to illustrate separately.

The foremost characteristic of effective education for creativity regards the ability and the habit of the teacher to propose tasks which expect open results, or rather, tasks which can be faced in different ways with a number of possible solutions. It is therefore the contexts themselves that solicit in children-project-led thinking which starts from the analysis of the initial situation so as to arrive at its transformation (Castoldi, 2010). This type of task is potentially able to promote creativity, because in carrying it out it is very probable that the children run up against problem solving situations which foresee multiple solutions (which is discussed in detail in paragraph 6).

The second suggestion which emerges from the CREANET debate puts the accent on the importance of accompanying children during the experience, providing them an emotional support (supportive behaviour) .

Many authors in the theoretical debate on educating for creativity indicate the need for providing a psychologically reassuring environment in which it is possible to fail and make errors (de Sousa, Fleith, 2000; Harrington, 1999). If creativity is solicited, in fact, through open-ended problem solving situations, then, precisely due to the absence of one single and conventional answer, children can stumble over obstacles and can even take inadvisable roads. An error, however, should not inhibit thinking, but rather, should become an educational opportunity, or rather, a stimulus for continuing to find alternative and perhaps even divergent paths. By searching for such solutions it is important to promote and maintain the willingness of the children to participate cognitively in the task, to become involved and to express their own thoughts without fear of making mistakes. It becomes necessary therefore, to provide an accepting and non-judgmental atmosphere, in which relationships with peers and with educators are supportive and empathic, rather than based on competition and performance (Travaglini, 2000: Griéger, 2003; Laslock, Winefiled, 2011). Despite the importance of this dimension, however, there are very few presentations discussed in the working groups which declare its use underlining its operative aspects. When the teachers from CREANET cite the need to give emotional support, they speak of it in a more abstract sense, in terms of: help, encouragement for the more timid children and the need to express trust in their abilities to the children (e.g. Christian Pre-school of Liepaja, Latvia; Nossa Senhora de Piadade, Portugal; Puriena, Lithuania; Vikbolandets, Sweden).[6] A useful tool for creating a welcoming and non-judgmental environment could be 'verbal mirroring' (Rogers, 1951, 1982). This is a communicative strategy which allows the adult to centre the conversation on the children's thoughts and tune into their reasoning. When the adult mirrors, they express and show to the speaker active listening, genuine interest, intention and desire to know the other's thoughts without being judgmental. These are the reasons why mirroring can create an environment in which children are more willing to participate cognitively in the activity, express themselves and become involved without hesitation. (Bertolini, Cardarello, 2012).

The discussion relating to the need to provide emotional support during the creative process is linked to the third suggestion of an educational nature that highlights the benefit of recognizing the importance of children's ideas. It concerns a particular adult behaviour which contributes in turn in communicating to the children trust and interest on their behalf, creating a welcoming climate and non judgmental climate which promotes their willingness to participate in the task. Much different practice was discussed in the Working Groups which exemplify ways in which it is possible to translate these suggestions into practice. In some cases, the entire experience came from a particular interest by a group of children in some theme that the planning then pivoted on. For example, the experience presented by the Calimero School (Croatia) had its origins in the children's intense curiosity towards pebbles and stones. Having gathered their interest, the teachers then promoted and supported their exploration of the material through the use of books, audio-visual material, visits to the museum and manual activities. Next, the children were invited to assemble stones and pebbles of different sizes, shapes and colours with the aim of making designs and decorations (like mosaics) and to construct objects for daily use (such as a vase). In other practices, the ideas that the children expressed during their learning journey were gathered, accepted and read by the teachers as practical proposals. In the experience described by the Rodari school (Italy), the children explored, gathered information and created objects, costumes, dramatizations around the story of "Orlando in love" by Boiardo. Throughout the projects, the children even suggested inventing a story using the characters from the work. The teachers welcomed the idea, supporting and encouraging the process of collective invention of a narration. In a similar way, the experience documented by the Luthaa Day Care Centre (Finland) came about from the children's pronounced interest in marine life. Around this theme, the teachers supported the children in gathering new information, in inventing a story set on the seabed and in constructing an animation. During the project a little girl expressed the desire to impersonate the role of a mermaid and the teachers therefore suggested that a small group of children should organize a dance for mermaids and pirates. It seems evident that giving importance to children's ideas requires a flexible and dynamic planning style that is constituted by the practice of active listening (Fratini, 2003) and broadly speaking the dialogues, thoughts and actions of the children so as to discuss them with the team of teachers with the aim of throwing back to the children interesting, seductive contexts and instructions which solicit the creative process well.

Even the fourth characteristic of good practice - recognizing creativity within the daily routine - is concerned with the same style of planning. It is concerned once again with listening to the children with the aim of highlighting interests, and thinking in their spontaneous behaviour and in routine moments, so that they could become useful occasions for encouraging potential creative thought. The Nossa Senhora de Piedade School (Portugal) recounts an interesting experience which came about during lunch when, by accident, a glass full of water was spilled over onto the table and a child began to experiment and list, with the pleasure one experiences when playing, the objects that the mark made reminded him of. His friends were very enthusiastic about the game and began to participate. The teachers decided to use the episode as the motor for a project on creativity. They set up a space where children could explore and experiment with coloured liquids, they played at imagining what it seemed to be and then they imagined what the shape made by the liquid could represent. The experience could have continued on the theme of transformation, for example, with the technique of 'imaginative pairing' (Rodari, 1973), which could have accompanied the children while inventing stories thanks to the unusual combination of what the mark on the table seemed before and after its transformation. One can suppose that the children had seen in the small puddle first a dog and then a wardrobe. The teacher, at that point, could have relaunched the suggestion: What could happen to a dog that always carried his own wardrobe on his back? (Rodari, 1973; p.22). The work would then have been potentially even more productive if the invention had taken place within a small group.

From the point of view of the teachers' behaviour and professionalism in promoting creativity, the latest suggestions which emerge from the CREANET meetings regard knowing and understanding children's development and the development of learning and teaching processes. This is about an indication of general value which, perhaps precisely because of its abstractness and lack of specificity, is highlighted only rarely in the practice presented in the working groups. Undoubtedly, each time that a project is planned with the aim of soliciting certain competencies, certain strategies must be chosen and activities developed that take into consideration both the level of development of the child and the theories of learning and teaching being referred to. This problem emerged in the CREANET teachers' words in the question form.   At times it was concerned with broad generic questions, such as: how is it possible to promote children's learning (Svanen, Sweden; Puriena, Lithuania)? In other experiences, however, teachers asked more precise questions about predisposing and using materials and environments, both without and within the school, with the aim of promoting children's  learning and creativity (Vikbolandets, Sweden; Nyckelpingans, Sweden). In a similar way, other teachers reflected on how to use and propose technology to encourage student growth (Luthaa Day Care Center, Finland; Silverdansen& Vikbolandets, Sweden).


## Organization of time

In promoting creativity an important role is played also by the organization of the experiential context, i.e. from how the adult predisposes and manages time and spaces (that contain the material) into which the children's activities are inserted.

As far as the organization of time is concerned, three characteristics that could favour the development of creative thinking were indicated.

First, continuity of the proposed experiences is suggested. Practice is good when the activities carried out by the children are linked to each other not only by their common guiding aim, that is by the promotion of creativity, but also by that 'fil rouge' or common thread made of the intentionally gradual and logical order of the activities. In some of the practice discussed during the Working Groups, for example, children were invited to participate in different activities that had the aim of supporting creative action by retracing, perhaps unconsciously, the phases proposed by Adams and Chen (2012). The two scholars highlight four types of creative processes, which are, from the most simple to the most complex, the following:

• Exploration and experimentation of materials with the aim of understanding the physical properties. This represents a preliminary and necessary condition for the following steps.

• Making and Constructing, which consists of combining/assembling explored materials without the child necessarily intending to build or make anything definable.

• Inventing something with a function or an aim that is previously planned by the child.

• Creating together which entails peer involvement and dialogue aimed at the construction of something in common and on a large scale.

Proposing experiences in continuity, over time therefore means - as happened in certain practice- making available activities in time with a planned logic that is expected to encourage in the children an attitude of exploration and knowledge of the spaces and materials. Only after this are the children invited to construct something. As already suggested by Munari (1981), it is in fact not possible to plan and create anything creative if we have not first explored and experimented materials and techniques. In this regard, the practice presented by Vikbolandets School (Sweden), lasted for an entire school year and included several stages.

In the first stage, the explorational actions of the children were supported and promoted in different contexts (internal and external) and with respect to a variety of natural materials (sand, leaves, etc.). In the second, the children had the possibility of experimenting solutions and actions with the aim of facing certain open ended problems of different types (how to get a trunk up to the top of a slide, how to cross over an axe balanced on top of a truck tyre). In the last stage of this practice the children were invited in different moments, both individually and as small groups, to assemble natural, unstructured material with the aim of constructing something planned.

In other practices, as well as the gradual logic of the activities proposed, even a certain continuity in the content, reminiscent of the programming logic of the integrating background (Cristanini, 1997). In this experience, exploration, experimentation and construction are concerned with the same argument.

This is the case of the project carried out and described by the Luhtaa Day Care Centre (Finland), centred entirely on the theme of marine life. The project began by inviting the children to recount, have a dialogue and exchange knowledge concerning marine fauna and flora. In this phase, as it occurred in certain other practices, one could have proposed differing types of explorations into the theme, both directly - e.g. through a trip to the sea or to an aquarium - or indirectly - e.g. through stories, photos, video documentaries. Afterwards, the children designed marine life using different pictorial techniques. Thanks to the suggestions of their teachers projected onto the wall, a small group of children invented a story about mermaids and pirates that they then made an animation about. First, the small group drew the scenes then they listened to, chose and added the music and then they constructed the characters and brought the dramatization to life. At the end of the experience, the children danced together their own mermaid dance accompanied by the animation sound track.

In other practices, the concept of continuity over time was also embedded in the educational format of the proposals made, such as, for example, the experience described by the Kalimero School (Croatia), during which the children worked on the theme of autumn. First they explored the argument by listening to certain stories about animals and sprites that took place in autumn and then by observing the woods directly throughout the autumn months. The visit to the woods was repeated several times and each time, the children found the same fruit basket including a letter from a sprite who invited them to produce something new each time: a story that the sprite could have read during the long winter period, an autumn drawing, etc.

By continuing to face the theme of organization of time within an education perspective, it is suggested to expect a time for reflection that corresponds to time in which the children are able to think about the experience had, to re-elaborate and revise it. According to Runco and Cayirdag (2009), this relaxation of time that foresees even long extended moments of sedimentation and articulation of thoughts, is an essential condition for the emergence of processes of recombination and creative association. As suggested by certain practice, envisaging time for reflection can be translated in practice by proposing periodically and throughout the whole length of the project, occasions for dialogue between children (Nossa Senhora de Piedade, Portugal; Christian Pre-school of Liepaja, Latvia). This concerned peer discussion that could be carried out both in pairs and in small and big groups, during which the children had a dialogue on the experience taking place so as to construct a collective memory; so as to give shared significance; so as to create dialogue between different ideas and viewpoints (Christian pre-school of Liepaja, Latvia; Rodari, Italia); and to arrive at the shared planning of something to construct and create together (public pre-school "I Gelsi", Italy). Such discussions can also constitute an occasion for teachers to collect the children's interests and thoughts so as to then relaunch projections that are adherent to their propensities (Nossa Senhora de Piedade Portugal; Rodari Italy), as already partly discussed in paragraph above concerning the indicator recognizing the importance of children's ideas.

The discourse surrounding the opportunity to offer time for reflection is directly linked to the third characteristic of effective time management in terms of the promotion of creativity: the distention /extension of time. The possibility of having at disposal a great length of time, that is not limited or finite in a brief amount of time, certainly encourages the emergence of creative processes which mature when the experience taking place has the time to mature due to children's reflections and revisions. Moreover, often creative thinking and action are connected to a strong intrinsic motivation to participate cognitively in the experience that brings about the loss of awareness of the time passing (Mainemelis, 2002). Extended time is a characteristic that does not emerge easily in the practice described by the teachers, who often define the total amount of time given to the project without indicating how it is managed in terms of each activity. Indeed, one might not consider the practice that includes many activities during many months (sometimes over even more than a school year) to be extended, but even a short experience that sees within it activities that can be carried out over long extended periods of time can also be seen as extended. From this point of view, the experience described by the public pre-school I Gelsi (Italy) is exemplary, in which small groups of children had the opportunity to work for a week in a space dedicated to constructiveness. On the Monday the children went into the space where they found, divided in an ordered fashion, a variety of unstructured, natural and recycled materials. The task involved constructing a city together. In order to create it the children needed time and space to explore and experiment with the materials individually. They then needed to make comparisons, to share their experiences, to make projections about constructing the city, they had to decide how to combine the individual products and to face together the problems of construction which they gradually came across. During the week the city took life, it grew and changed. Day after day, the children continued to think, make projections, and construct this collective city, which became the basis even for pretend play and eventually the stimulus for inventing stories. Only on the Friday, was the city eventually destroyed by the children who then reordered the space.

**The possibility of exploring and experimenting with different spaces and materials.**

The discussion on time management is connected to that relative to space and materials. According to Gariboldi (Gariboldi, Cardarello, 2011), in fact, creativity finds fertile terrain when certain conditions co-exist: the presence of materials that offer multiple opportunities for use, the possibility to explore, experiment and reflect in extended time and the presence of an adult capable of making available adequate environments, i.e. environments that guarantee once again the possibility of a plurality of experiences of exploration and discovery. The attention given to organizing spaces and material is certainly a crucial element in the promotion of creativity. In this respect, Harrington (1999) puts the accent on the need to plan and organize spaces in a targeted manner so as to give children occasions in which to find, explore and utilize different materials, which are structured, unstructured, natural and recycled. During the Working Groups, some practices underlined exactly this aspect. The project from the Grafenhausen School (Germany) is interesting from this point of view, as it required particular care in the predisposition of spaces which were rich in materials where the children could explore, experiment and construct. On this occasion, the teachers set up a number of different contexts: a space where it was possible to work with wooden and glass objects which were unstructured or semi-structured, such as cubes, cylinders, pieces of tracking, marbles, etc. In another space, the children could explore and construct with coloured straws and string. Then there was a room dedicated to the construction with semi-materials such as Lego Duplo. There was a room dedicated to symbolism and role-play. By continuing to think along these lines, it would have been possible to dedicate space even to natural materials (such as branches, leaves, stones, shells), another to recycled plastic material (spoons, bottles, yoghurt pots) or to cardboard (empty toilet rolls, wooden reels, etc.).

Certain schools even underlined the importance, not only of making a variety of material available, but also of organizing it in an ordered fashion by type, colour and material (Patronato Santo Antonio, Portugal; public pre-school I Gelsi, Italy).

Another important suggestion in terms of education regards the transformability of spaces. Children's creativity is facilitated in fact, when the adult is willing and able to change the space in light of the children's interests by proposing flexible and dynamic contexts that are potentially able to support and solicit cognitive involvement for the duration of the whole period. The experience of the I Gelsi public Pre-school (Italy), described in the previous paragraph, is also interesting from this point of view. Not only was an extended amount of time envisaged during which the children discussed and constructed the city together as a work in progress that lasted a whole week, but a physical space in which the children's work was maintained day after day was also needed. A space which was transformed and changed over time due to the specific attention given by the teachers both in the choice of materials and in the periodic substitution of the same so as to support and encourage creative processes - of exploration, experimentation and construction - that were being developed within the small group context.

Within this discussion on space and materials one finds another suggestion in terms of teaching that came from the CREANET discussions: the promotion of exploration/experimentation with different spaces and materials. Such an indication finds an explanation in the fact that exploration and experimentation, according to many authors, constitute a necessary step in the creative process towards reaching that final goal of invention and construction of something (Adams, Chen, 2012; Harrington, 1999; Arieti 1979). In the practices discussed in the Working Groups it is possible to retrace this indicator which can be broken down in different ways. Certain experiences were entirely and only dedicated to the promotion of exploratory behaviour. This is the case of the practice presented by the Pink Panther Infant Toddler Centre (Italy), during which the children had the possibility to meet, explore and experiment in different contexts: first a large space whose floor was covered with newspapers, then the same space was changed and set up with large pieces of coloured material. Next, the material was substituted with medium-sized open cardboard boxes and then by different sized coloured balls. In each situation, the children interacted freely with the material and with their peers. This represented an interesting experience that we may consider to be a good, first step towards the promotion of creativity, in so far as it did not bring the children to associate the material with the aim of creating something. Not by chance, it is concerned with a practice that is destined for children in the 0-3 age group. The experience carried out in the Gintarélis School (Lithuania) is also interesting. The children's exploration was solicited by pivoting on the plurality of the senses: children touched different materials with their hands and feet (rough, smooth, dry, wet), they worked with objects of different colours (black, grey, white, flamboyant) and they listened to sounds from nature. In another project children worked with fruit and vegetables, looking at them, touching, smelling and tasting them (Rodari, Italy).

In other practices, however, the teachers set up spaces and proposed materials that were destined to promote experimentation most of all. In the experience of the Nossa Senhora de Piedade School (Portugal), for example, a laboratory corner was set up for the children. The children demonstrated interest, in a creative sense about the coloured liquids and the shapes they made when poured onto a surface. The teachers prepared a space in which the children could prepare solutions with solvents and solutions of different types, so as to experiment with pouring them onto different coloured surfaces and observing the consequences.

In the majority of practices, exploration and experimentation of materials was functional for the construction of something. In this experience, children used materials of different types: structured, unstructured, natural and recycled. These were objects with an undefined use with a great deal of potential in terms of promoting creativity. However, as already underlined, when you want to use them to build something , you need to first explore them and experiment with them in order to be able to understand their functional characteristics and discover the possible ways of using them (Smith, 1996). In this regard, for example, in the practice discussed by the Santo Antonio School (Portugal), the children first had the opportunity to explore a variety of recycled materials autonomously, over an extended time. In particular, they observed, touched, manipulated, smelled and sometimes even bit, plastic cups, spoons and bottles as well as supermarket trays (which had previously contained steaks from the supermarket), milk containers and aluminium foil rolls. After having left the children to discuss the experience together the teacher asked them to invent a story about the objects they had examined. The children then constructed a story together and assembled recycled materials to construct the characters from the story as snakes and giraffes. In the end they used the characters to act out the story itself.

Good practice in terms of creativity should therefore include occasions for exploration not only relative to the material but also to the spaces themselves. In the practices discussed in the Working Groups, the exploration of the spaces often concerned the interior and exterior of the school building (the school garden), only rarely was it concerned with the neighbouring area such as the local park, forest, beach, town centre, zoo, etc. The experience described by the Munksnas School (Finland ) is interesting: the children were able to experience certain outside spaces of the school and the surrounding area throughout the whole four seasons. In winter they observed the ice and worked with the snow in a number of different ways: the slid on the snow, they filled buckets with snow, they could have used it to construct something. In spring and autumn they gathered leaves, stones and pieces of wood that they then used in compositions. In summer they used sand to construct castles in pairs. In a similar way, in the school garden of the Kite School (Lithuania), the children constructed labyrinths in the snow. At first, each child worked individually constructing their own labyrinth. Then, in small groups they observed and compared their own works so as to plan one labyrinth in the snow that they then constructed in a collaborative manner. At the end of the project one child proposed colouring the labyrinths. The teachers accepted the proposal and provided a variety of materials for colouring the snow constructions. It should be underlined then that it is the possibility of using and considering exploration of space as functional to the gathering of information that is useful to the next phase of invention /construction of something. In another experience presented by the Kite School (Lithuania), for example, the children together with their parents were invited to construct a school on a reduced scale using recycled materials. In order to allow and encourage the development of creative processes, the teachers prepared for an initial phase in which the children and adults could not only explore the material but also the different environments of the school, both internal (such as the kitchen, the pantry, the offices, the other classrooms) and external.

**Interaction and collaboration between children in open-ended problem solving situations.**

By retracing the considerations of the previous chapters and thanks to the testimonies of practices gathered in the Working Groups, the characteristics that an education system which fosters creativity should benefit from become increasingly clear, both from the point of view of theoretical argument and from that of translation into operative terms. The promotion of creativity in the pre-school requires that an adult assumes the role of director, as supporter and facilitator of the children's creative processes; that there is extended time to allow the exploration of a variety of materials and contexts; and, that there is the possibility for sedimentation and maturation of their individual and collective experiences. The CREANET experience has continued to express this framework by suggesting the importance of encouraging peer collaboration in open-ended problem-solving situations.

Many of the practices discussed within the European context present this characteristic, breaking it down in different ways. The first reflection regards the task to pose to the children. Facilitating the emergence of problem-solving situations does not only mean creating an adequate environment from the point of view of space, materials and of the welcoming and supportive behaviour of the adult where the children can do whatever they like. It requires also, inventive, open-ended tasks. This entails putting the children in problematic situations that are definite and defined and at the same time ill-formed, as mentioned by Ward (2009), that is, that they are able to be addressed by following different paths of reasoning so as to reach results that may differ. In this regard, the practice discussed during the Working Groups give interesting examples. Many tasks regarded the construction of something with unstructured materials (models of buildings, animals, people, types of transport, environments, frames, candelabra, necklaces, for example as in the practice presented by Stiftelsen Sedmigradsky, Finland; Kite, Lithuania). Constructivity is always, undoubtedly a potentially creative context in as much as it is often an occasion for highlighting and facing problematic situations of a physical nature (that can be concerned with measuring distance, balancing weights, etc.). However, examples of tasks in other settings come out of the practices, such as inventing stories and animations (e.g. in the practice described by the schools: Jardim de infancia Nossa Senhora da Piedade, Portugal; Figueira de Cavaleiros, Portugal), dramatizing narrations - with puppets, through shadow play, by dressing up as characters (e.g. in the experiences described by the following schools: Christian pre-school of Liepaja, Latvia; Puriena, Lithuania), representing phenomena in the graphic form, events, emotions and sounds (e.g. in the experience discussed by the Jardim Nossa Senhora da Piedade, Portugal) and organizing dance and music (e.g. in the practice presented by the Bitute School, Lithuania). The experience described by the Silverdansen School (Sweden) is interesting and bears witness to the possibility of facing problems of a scientific kind in a creative manner. The project foresaw some visits to the forest, during which the children soon began to use both logical and analogical thinking. A large mark on the ground became a dinosaur's footprint for the children. The teacher proposed measuring its surface and the children worked together to work out how to do this. Then the teacher proposed constructing something for hiding themselves in case the dinosaur should arrive, proposing a task of a constructive type. The children then decided to make a mountain with leaves. The teacher accepted the proposal and then proposed again a measurement problem this time in terms of the vertical dimension: how high should the mountain be to cover us? Throughout the experience the children worked in different open-ended problem solving situations, which - generally and potentially - encourage creative thinking in so far as they require an analysis of the initial situation, planning and verifying a solution in order to be resolved, so as to bring about a transformation into its final state (Castoldi, 2010).

The motives at this point are clear: when one intends encouraging creativity in children it is useful to propose open-ended tasks that have the potential to give rise to problematic situations. Such a context is even more fertile however, when the problem is faced in a group. Many examples of practice from CREANET foresaw peer interaction, both in pairs and in small groups of 4-8 members (e.g. in the experience discussed by the following schools: Alice, Abracadabra, Mongolfiera & Soleluna Italy; Nyckelpigans, Sweden). The group works as a sounding board for re-elaborative and creative thinking of the individual. The problem is faced collectively by the group: different points of view and hypotheses are faced up until negotiation and the approval of a solution that is accepted by all the children (Arieti, 1979). Each student expresses their thoughts, suggesting ideas and suggestions to their peers; so that gradually a unique process of resolution of a creative kind takes shape (Gariboldi, 2012). The experience of the Svanen School (Sweden) is representative of other similar CREANET practices and illustrates how a project can be imposed that expects multiple occasions for the resolution of a problem within a small group setting. The project came about from the interests of the children towards the story of a squirrel that had been read to them by an adult. The teacher throws back to the group the proposal that they draw first the events they had listened to and then the desires and feelings of the squirrel, posing therefore, the problem of their representation and representability. These last drawings were then discussed and compared within the peer group. After this, the teacher proposed to small groups of children to invent another story about the squirrel. In the encounters that followed the children proposed, exchanged, combined and negotiated their ideas so as to eventually make a common and shared narrative. Then the adult invited them to construct the scenes and the characters of the story and dramatize it. So again, the children decided together which elements and which characters to construct. They explored different materials so as to decide which ones to use. They discussed how to construct the scenes and characters by facing different kinds of problems (e.g. how to represent in model form a character trait, in which way could round objects be used to construct the wheels of a car). At the end of the project they had created a dramatization and discussed the experience together.


**A mix of different symbolic languages and systems.**

The last suggestion in terms of education regards the promotion of the association and combination of different symbolic languages and systems. Vygotsky (1932) has already spoken on creativity in the combined sense when he defined it as the activity that produces something new, either material or immaterial, combining elements with additive ends. In this sense, creativity is seen to be a thought which connects as the ability to bring out associative links and connections and gathers together unusual associations between ideas and objects, referring also to the different domains of consciousness (Gariboldi; 2012; Minerva, Vinella; 2012).

Perhaps, in the light of considerations made in the previous paragraph it is possible to think of the combinatory character of creativity even in social terms, or rather, when it implies the connection between the thoughts of different children. As previously discussed, the comparison and interaction within a small group seems to encourage the emergence of more complex creative processes than those of the individual, thanks to the construction of a common thought that is the result of the combination and reciprocal influence of the contribution of each individual child.

By continuing to reason about this connection, it seems reasonable that creative education should include, among its various ingredients that accompany it, even an internationality to develop different symbolic systems so as to make them communicate and integrate (Pinto Minerva, Vinella, 2012). Some practices discussed in the Working Groups indicate certain possible ways of facing this concern.

One way, perhaps insufficient but none the less useful, is that of encouraging the exploration of spaces and material through all of the senses (as already discussed in paragraph 5).

A second possibility however regards the possibility of facing a thematic knot by proposing, in an organized manner, a sequence of activities that pivot around different symbolic systems and languages. In this regard, it is useful to remember the experience carried out at the Rodari School (Italy), which centred on the story of Orlando in Love (by Boiardo). The project started from the reading of different parts of the work (that had been revisited linguistically so as to render them understandable to pre-school children). Then the children were invited to represent the events graphically. After this, in a small group, they explored and used different recycled materials to build Orlando's castle. The teacher therefore continued to encourage combinatory thinking, but also imagination and the assumption of different points of view (creating almost a sort of confusion), inviting the children to both describe verbally and draw as though they were some of the characters from the story. After this, in small groups, they constructed some characters from the events with recycled materials. The transit from one symbolic language to another brought the children to visit even the Boiardo Castle (located near the school) and then to dramatize a war scene in one room and to dance party dances in another (episodes contained in the original work). Within the experience, the story then, witnessed different transformations: the children re-elaborated them graphically, constructively and physically. The project ended with the proposal coming from the children to invent a new story with the characters from Orlando in Love which was another occasion for supporting the comparison and combination of the children's thoughts and of the well-known characters from the work of literature.

The third possibility regards, on the other hand, the possibility of translating and experimenting an experience that was pivotal to a certain perceptive sense and a certain language through another sense and another symbolic language. The Christian pre-school of Liepaja (Latvia) proposed tasks of this type to the children. On certain occasions, the pupils explored certain external spaces of the school - such as the public park and the beach - listening to the sounds of nature with their eyes closed, then the teacher invited them to draw the sounds that they had heard. On other occasions, they listened to certain pieces of original music, and drew individually the emotions they had experienced whilst listening and they discussed with their peers the meaning of the drawings they produced. It was decided to invite the children to graphically represent the elements that escape from sight - such as sounds and the emotional state of people - in a type of open problem-solving situation in which it was not possible to predict right or wrong answers. By continuing to reason in this synesthetic logic of contamination of sensorial spheres (Pinto Minerva, Vinella, 2012) it would even have been possible to solicit the children to combine the languages in other ways with respect to those exemplified, such as, by inviting them to express a colour with a sound.

Another possible way of enhancing the combined use of symbolic systems consists in allowing the children to weave together logical and analogical thinking, as occurred in the experience already described in the previous paragraph, by the Silverdansen School (Sweden), during which teachers and children, solicited from the experience in the wood, invented an imaginative story together about dinosaurs that also required resolving certain problems of a scientific type. Analogously in the experience at the I Gelsi public school (Italy) the children had the possibility of interweaving and experiencing side by side activities of a logical-rational type (such as exploring the physical characteristics of an object, facing problems of measurement of distance, combining unstructured materials so as to construct something) with activities that centred on analogical thinking (such as pointing out the imaginative similarity of an object or participating in symbolic play).

## Some conclusive reflections

The exploration of the CREANET experiences in search of methodological indications discussed in the preceding paper allows for certain reflections.

On the one hand, it demonstrates the possibility of putting into practice such suggestions within the context of the school and illustrates a variety of ways in which they can be translated into operative practice. On the other hand, it contributes to outlining increasingly clearly the characteristics of educational practice in terms of creativity. The central role of the adult emerges, who should continually listen to the children in an active manner so as to gather their interests and processes on the basis of which they should relaunch proposals and contexts that are intrinsically motivating and efficient in terms of the promotion of creativity, within an education style that is flexible and centred on the children. The teacher should be a director of the experience through their predisposition of psychologically and non-judgmental, welcoming spaces in which the children are willing to express their own thoughts without the fear of making mistakes.

To act in a creative manner requires, in fact, the willingness to put oneself in the game and therefore it implies taking the risk of making mistakes. Education for creativity should therefore, provide for the predisposition of a context in which an error is seen as an occasion for soliciting children's divergent thinking. The adult is even called to organize the physical space in which the experience takes place; a space that should contain and offer an organized and usable variety of different unstructured and semi-structured materials to the children. They should also know how to choose and change the materials over time and in light of the interests and processes activated by the children. Creativity-based education moreover, needs to structure a pathway in which the activities proposed to the children present logical and planned continuity. It is necessary therefore to prepare initially contexts for exploration and experimentation of a theme, of material and /or a technique and only afterwards, tasks of an inventive-constructive type. Alongside this, they should propose activities centred on different channels and languages so as to encourage their contamination. The promotion of creativity does not mean simply leaving the children free to explore and act in environments that are rich in material. It is necessary also to propose open, inventive tasks - such as how to construct a character, draw a sound, invent a story - that puts the children in a problem-solving context that allows and provides a number of possible solutions. In such a context, the children are forced to examine the initial situation so as to plan a solution. Moreover, the role of the peer group emerges as crucial as at different times during the experience they compare, discuss, negotiate and revise ideas. In order to emerge and be properly trained, creativity requires an extended amount of time in which children can continue to think of the experience, construct ideas and material products but where they can also correct themselves when they make mistakes.

**Notes**

1. The practices presented in CREANET have been collected and can be consulted at the following link: http://www.creativityinpre-school.eu/creanet/bestpractices.htm

2. In the previous paper Roberta Cardarello and Antonio Gariboldi illustrated and described the educational principles and methodologies that emerged from the European meetings.

3. The analysis of the practices was carried out by the author.

4.The material was downloaded from the following link:

http://www.creativityinpre-school.eu/creanet/bestpractices.htm

5. For each project, the description form asked to explain: title, goal of practice, time, spaces, procedure/methodology (role of teacher/distribution of groups /documentation), materials, conclusion (final reflections) and which of the seven key words were highlighted in Beja (2011) as being characteristic of creativity and recognized in the practice and the reasons given.

6. Each practice was named and identified through the name of the school and of the nation of origin. Due to lack of space the section of the Working Groups in which each practice was discussed has not been included.

**References**

Adams M.L., Chen J-Q. (2012), Understanding Young Children's Kinds of Creating, in O.N. Saracho (Eds.), Contemporary Perspectives on Research in Creativity in Early Childhood Education, IAP, Charlotte, pp. 343-354.

Arieti S. [1979 (1976)], Creatività. La sintesi magica, Il Pensiero Scientifico Editore, Roma.

Bertolini C., Cardarello R. (2012), Leggere insieme per comprendere un testo: descrive e valutare i processi comunicativi, Giornale Italiano della Ricerca Educativa, 8, pp.13-24

Castoldi M. (2010), Didattica generale, Mondadori, Milano.

Cristanini D. (1997), Programmare e valutare nella scuola materna, Milano, Fabbri editori.

De Sousa Fleith (2000), Teacher and Student Perceptions of Creativity in the Classroom Environments, Roeper Review, 22, 3, 143-153.

Fratini C. (2003), La dimensione comunicativa, in F. Cambi, E. Catarsi, E. Colicchi, C. Fratini, M. Muzi, Le professionalità educative, pp. 67-94, Carocci, Roma.

Gariboldi A., Cardarello R. (2012), Pensare la creatività. Ricerche nei contest educativi prescolari, edizioni junior, Bergamo.

Griéger P. (2003), Lo sviluppo della creatività, Rivista Lasalliana, 1, pp. 37-49.

Harrington D. M. (1999), Creative Environments, Conditions and Settings, in S. R. Pritzker, M. A. Runco (Eds.), Encyclopedia of Creativity, Academic Press, San Diego, pp. 485-488.

Laeng M. (1992), Enciclopedia pedagogica, Brescia, Editrice la Scuola.

Laslocky M., Winefiled R. (2011), The Improtance of Children's Play to the Development of Creativity and Innovation, San Francisco: Bay Area Discovery Museum.

Lumbelli L. (1982), Psicologia della comunicazione 1: la comunicazione, il Mulino, Bologna.

Mainemelis C. (2002), Time and Timeless: Creativity in (and out of) the Temporal Dimension, Creativity Research Journal, 14, 2, pp. 227-238.

Mialaret G. (1998), étude scientifique des situations d'éducation, L'année de la recherche en sciences de l'éducation, 5, pp. 7-30.

Munari B. (1981), Da cosa nasce cosa. Appunti per una metodologia progettuale, Laterza, Bari.

Paoletti G. (2011), Comprendere testi con figure, Franco Angeli, Milano.

Pellerey M., Grzadziel D. (2011), Educare. Per una pedagogia intesa come scienza pratico-progettuale, Las, Roma.

Pinto Minerva F., Vinella M. (2012), La creatività a scuola, Laterza, Bari.

Rodari G. (1973), Grammatica della fantasia. Introduzione all'arte di inventare storie, Einuadi, Torino.

Rogers C. R. [2000 (1951)], La terapia centrata sul cliente, Psycho, Firenze.

Runco M.A., Cayirdag N. (2009), Time, in S. R. Pritzker, M. A. Runco (Eds.), Encyclopedia of Creativity, Academic Press, San Diego, pp. 485-488.

Smith M.K. (1996), Fostering Creativity in the Early Chldhood Clasroom, Early Creativity Research Journal, 24, 2, pp. 77-82.

Travaglini R. (2000), Riflessioni pedagogiche sullo sviluppo della creatività nella ricerca-azione, Ricerca e Sperimentazione, 6, pp. 887-898.

Vygotskij L. S. [2011 (1932)], Immaginazione e creatività nell'età infantile, Editori Riuniti, Roma.

Ward T. B. (2009), Problem Solving, in S. R. Pritzker, M. A. Runco (Eds.), Encyclopedia of Creativity, Academic Press, San Diego, pp. 254-260.

# 16 Conclusions

*Antonio Gariboldi and Roberta Cardarello[1]*

## The creativity debate

There is no doubt that the term creativity carries purely positive significance which induces us all to adhere to it. Moreover, since 2009, the year in which the EU solicited the member countries to research, reflect and have a dialogue on the theme of creativity, the initiatives on the theme, which mark a renewed interest and study into creativity, have multiplied. And so, in this way the theme is analysed in reference to the economy and to sociology, to productive innovations as well as institutional and political ones. From this renewed interest and research it is clear that many different meanings can be associated to the argument and to the theme of creativity, that are not always well-defined or interrogated in depth, precisely because of this halo of positivity that surrounds the theme.

Even within the pedagogical field, the condition of criticality of the education systems, both with reference to the world of work and production and to the significance of school and knowledge, constitutes terrain that nurtures recent attention given to creativity. Creativity within this context is complimented with changes in the traditional ways of schooling, it is linked to a critique of traditional systems of teaching in favour of innovative strategies and methodologies that favour motivation. The intention is to innovate the content and the objects of study: moreover, the cultural world is vastly enriched by new forms of communication, entertainment, and technology. Despite the undoubted interest in such themes regarding education, it would be reductive to see creativity as a mere receptacle of innovation or as opposed to everything that does not work in education systems.

Creativity is, in fact, a concept that can be precisely defined, with the overriding aim to make it a relevant but non generic objective to pursue in educational terms. The shared assumption today is that creativity does not only connote actual geniuses or individuals of exceptional talent, but rather belongs in some way to the repertoire of resources of each individual and emphasizes the interest and responsibility of who is involved in education, called upon to reflect on how they promote thinking and creative behaviour. This implies that it is possible to educate towards creativity and that in this way it is useful to acquire a less generic point of view on the theme and to attempt to highlight the conditions favourable to its promotion.

## Creativity: a concept with 'soft edges'

Despite research's numerous attempts in various areas to define creative thinking and to identify unanimously the characteristics of such a process, creativity appears, at least still today, to be a construct that remains difficult to define, with ambiguous meaning and is therefore open to interpretation, a concept of 'soft edges' (Wittgenstein 1953).

It is true that it seems arduous to determine clearly what creativity is, on the other hand one may also ask: "is it always possible to substitute advantageously a blurred image with a clear cut one?

Is it not often exactly the blurred image that we need most? (ibid, p. 49). It is not by chance that Wittgenstein's questions concentrate on play, an element that has close ties with the argument of creativity, and he suggests that in order to approach the theme of creativity, particularly within education, it is necessary to problematize and keep open and flexible the referred definitions, in as much as this can help to bring together the changing aspects of a phenomenon that appears to be multi-formed and complex. This is all the more so, when the cultural contexts are as diverse as with the CREANET project, and are called to debate on the theme of creativity and considering, as underlined in one of the book's papers referring to Glaveanu (2011), that "creativity is not just influenced by immediate social and contextual factors, but it is the very nature of this process to be relational and as such could not exist outside of certain cultural resources and dialogic relations" (Pugnaghi, p. 105)

However, as Wittgenstein underlines once again, tracing a frame and outline, however imprecise, around a concept can even be a way, if temporary, to activate a discourse for a specific purpose, to render the concept useful in terms of a particular aim. In this sense, dealing with education for creativity within the pre-school context implies the need to attempt to circumscribe what is intended by creativity, in order to avoid conceiving it as something that characterizes the words and the behaviour of the children and to attempt to render it, therefore, the object of analysis and reflection that can encourage cultural growth in the area.

## Creativity and childhood

One does in fact run a risk when the theme of creativity is faced with reference to childhood. Educational publications and common sense convincingly support the fact that creativity is systematically present in early childhood and that it disappears or it decreases rapidly in the successive years, whether due to psychological dynamics, such as the prevalence of 'literalism', or due to the direct action of the school system and education that suffocates and represses it in children. In reality, in order to ascertain the consistency of such opinions, it is better to elucidate what conduct they are referring to, so as to avoid referring solely to spontaneous conduct and reducing creativity to a certain few behaviours such as play, that takes on different manifestations, nature and frequency at different ages, which are connected differently to learning and development. If not well-defined, the term creativity risks becoming a mere synonym for exploration and play that simply connotes children's development.

The risk, therefore, is that creativity is made to coincide with only a determinate type of conduct , of which expressive manifestation and play are almost exclusive examples, that are so connected to early childhood years to be little functional to the support of the promotion of thought and of learning in successive age groups and schooling. Hence, the risk that creativity is 'something for little children' is symmetrical to that creativity is a quality reserved to very few geniuses and people of talent, or that it is quality exclusive to artists and the expressive arts. This is why it is necessary to reflect on the characteristics and the manifestations of creativity in childhood and try to propose them congruency with the ideas accredited to creativity today. The aim is two-fold. On the one hand, to prevent a theoretical fracture between explanations that are put forward about creativity, and on the other hand, and even more relevant, to find educational lines and forms of children that consider them in continuity with their future as permanently creative individuals.

**Imagination and logic**

In this sense one of the definitions of creativity that seems to avoid the afore-mentioned risk is that which interprets it as "the ability to produce work that is novel (original, unexpected) and at the same time appropriate so that the outcome meets the constraints and requirements of a task at hand" (Kaufman, Baer, 20014, p. 3). One definition that, while not being without problematic elements, highlights how in the creative act the element of novelty and originality, that is the ability to express new ideas and recognize unusual connections between thought and object, must be integrated to that of adequacy to the task or to the implied activity, to the usefulness and effectiveness of the proposed idea or solution. Originality therefore represents a necessary condition but is not sufficient for creativity, which requires an interpretation that is original and benefits from experience (Runco, 2008). Children, for example, produce many original ideas, in the sense that they are unusual or new ideas with respect to those produced by themselves in the past or by their peer group. They are however ideas which can be original but not always necessarily creative. In fact creative ideas, inventions or solutions also have to be in some way effective, appropriate, suitable or useful and this implies the ability to direct thinking and action towards a certain objective (ibid).

A connection of this type, that sees creativity as the integration between ability to be original and to direct thought and action, can have significant implications for those concerned with education, particularly when included in a perspective that considers creative potential as being universally distributed and not as a talent that belongs to only a few exceptional people (Runco, 2004). If creative potential is intended solely as the ability to think outside the box, then it appears difficult for a teacher "to acknowledge the contribution of a knowledge base in developing creative outcomes" (Andiliou, Murphy, 2010, p. 216). If however, creativity is not conceived only as divergent thinking, imagination, ability to think outside the box, then it becomes important to stimulate and support in the children, both individually and as a small group, a process which considers alternating between logical and analogical thinking, between moments in which information and knowledge is gathered and organized in a methodical way; moments in which situations or problems are seen from different perspectives and angles - by encouraging the ability to ask questions that go beyond what is evident, by encouraging the emergence of associative links, perceiving unusual combinations and relationships between ideas and objects - and moments in which the appropriateness of the ideas that have been generated are analyzed and evaluated in function of the ongoing task. As a teacher who was interviewed regarding research carried out for the CREANET project underlines, it becomes fundamental to guarantee "the possibility of giving space to divergent thinking and at the same time keeping everything you do in order".

It is a vision of creativity that seems to be in line with a famous motto of Bruno Munari (1977): "don't tell children what to do but how to do it"; but most of all it is a connection that is not limited to assigning importance to the possibility of free expression in an environment rich in stimulus and material, conferring major responsibility to the action of the teacher and soliciting deeper and more knowledge based projections of the contexts of experience (intended as interacting sets of time, space and relations) in which the children are involved.

## CREANET activities and indications for organizing 'creative contexts'

In this sense the activities that have characterized the CREANET project, the results of which are published in the book, had as one of their basic objectives that of bringing out the different ideas of creativity and of activating a dialogue between researchers and teachers in different countries about how to promote creative processes within the educational environment, in order to be able to share certain common conceptions about creativity, while respecting cultural differences and approaches. This included practices that can favour its emergence and development.

The first step therefore entailed studying the most recent literature on creativity in the various countries involved in the project so as to look more deeply in a thematic sense (creativity and scientific thinking, creativity and teaching, etc.) into the topic of creativity. The aim was to explore and reconstruct the main lines of research and study that characterized the investigation into creativity in these years, so as to identify possible and varied categories of analysis and interpretation of the creative phenomenon in early childhood centres. This meant, then, constructing greater theoretical knowledge concerning the ways of understanding creativity and education for creativity, sharing the results of this work through the many conferences and seminars that were organized at both a national and international level throughout the length of the project.

In this sense an important element of the work was represented by the investigation carried out in the different countries involved in the project on the ideas and opinions of the teachers with regard to creativity and on the ways to promote it within a pre-school context. The research revealed diverse representations and awareness, as documented in the book, giving extra material for the dialogue that was developed during the meetings between researchers and the teachers' working groups.

The whole of the research activity was in fact carried out with the constant collaboration of teachers' working groups, in which practices in favour of creativity carried out in the different participating CREANET schools were presented and discussed with reference to certain previously defined thematic areas. These working groups significantly involved the teachers and allowed them to discuss on a working educational plane, comparing experiences carried out in the different countries and bringing out the differences in terms of culture and educational approach, thus providing important points for reflection on the practice that can best facilitate and support creative processes.

At the end of this project the indications presented in the last part of the volume were elaborated. While aware that the intention to encourage creativity within the pre-school setting implies the necessity to plan in depth the characteristics of the different educational experiences that are proposed to the children, the indications elaborated by the project coordinating group lay out the aim of defining certain elements of reference for the organization of 'creative contexts'. These elements emerged in different ways in the different activities envisaged by the project and bring together, in part, what had come out of the literature on the theme.

The conditions and the strategies useful in the promotion of creative thinking are in fact the object of specific reflection within the area of pre-school education, in as much as is it thought that education for creativity can be greatly valued within the area of a formative curriculum which is less centred on formal knowledge. This highlights the importance of putting emphasis on the process rather than on the product; of proposing creative problem-solving situations that come from problems that come about naturally in daily life; of conceding time to the child to explore all the possibilities (from the most common ideas to the most original); of creating a climate that allows children to perceive that mistakes are accepted and in which the ability to take risks is encouraged; of guaranteeing abundant, useful and interesting resources and material at the children's disposition; and, finally, of creating a welcoming environment (Laslocky, Winefield, 2011). These are indications which focus therefore on the importance of creating an atmosphere in which children feel emotionally safe and not judged, that they have a variety of spaces and stimulating material and extended time that allows exploration and the development of thoughts and actions, of giving value to the activities and projects that encourage children to face problems to be solved in a creative manner.

These are, however, aspects which imply precision in the role that the teacher must assume within the context of the experiences that are meant to facilitate creative thinking. In general, the opportunity to ask open-ended questions is underlined; to give value to the children who give unexpected answers; to tolerate ambiguity; to encourage experimentation; and to make an example of creative thinking and behaviour (Blake, Giannangelo 2012). Within the various activities of a creative nature, the teacher should also help the children to express their creative ideas in the clearest way possible and to give pointers, when they demonstrate creative thinking, so as to encourage others on the imaginative plane (Mellou, 1996).

If within the context of early years education, so as to encourage and sustain the development of creativity, it appears fundamental not only to propose activities linked to artistic expression but also give value to play, to problem solving and investigative thinking (Blake, Giannangelo 2012), the planning of a context that is really able to promote creative processes requires reflection that is not superficial in terms of the role of educational direction carried out by the teacher. It requires reflection on the way in which the teacher 'frames' the creative process and suggests possibility (Adams and Chen 2012), avoiding the superimposition of the children's ideas with their own cognitive schemes and supporting the emergence and development of creative thinking. It seems important to reason both on the characteristics of space, time and materials and on the ways of managing the relationship between adult and child and between child and child. Creativity, in fact, can be strengthened through social interaction. Within the group, children are faced with different knowledge, ability and perspectives and they therefore have the possibility of acquiring elements for constructing new connections and combinations.

If creativity is linked essentially to the ability to "think in terms of connections" and "make connections between heterogeneous components" (Pinto , Minerva, Vinella, 2012, p. 57), i.e. as a teacher interviewed in a focus group affirms, creativity is "uniting things that seem unlinked in order to obtain new solutions [...] making a leap that unites things so as to arrive at something new", so it is useful that the children "are encouraged to dedicate particular attention to the ability to identify the interconnection between expressive languages and knowledge, in the plot and modes of understanding", so as to progressively construct "a vision of reality profoundly integrated, that is both one and plural at the same time" (ibid. pp. 56-57). In this sense it would appear to be important to promote the sequential and multi-functional use of different symbolic systems, to create situations and projects where children can translate ideas that they have generated and developed through different languages.

Heuristic abilities and divergent thinking, that represent elements that are at play in creative processes, can be encouraged through the integration and weaving between the real and the imaginary, between logical and analogical thinking, feeding this metaphoric productivity that can be understood as "connections of zones and aspects of experience, initially disjointed, through synthetic procedures belonging to art are used even in heuristic procedures in science" (Bondioli, 1996, p. 408).

The organization of creative contexts brings with it then the need to consider and plan not only the physical and functional characteristics of the environment, but also to use and reason on the quality of the processes, reflecting on the different roles that the teacher can take on and on the strategies that they can contribute in giving value to these processes in a creative sense.

The indications elaborated by the CREANET coordination group do not cover all the aspects cited but rather solicit attention on some of these, proposing a synthesis of a series of elements that may be seen as a guide for the activities that are planned in schools or in early childhood centres. We believe, in fact, that dialogue on the theme of education for creativity, while complex in so far as it concerns even cultural and pedagogically different visions, acquires real significance if it is able to bring contributions, however small, on how to improve practice in the early years educational settings.

While aware of the difficulty of giving back the variety and richness of the reflections that were stimulated by the CREANET activities, and also of the impossibility of giving a full account of the differing formative implications of the project, this volume, as a whole, documents the principal results of the project as carried out. We believe, in any case, that the greatest value of the project lies in the possibility to construct real occasions for dialogue between people who work in very different situations on a theme - education for creativity- that seems to equate significantly with the professional commitment of those who are involved in childhood. In this sense, the exchange activated by CREANET is intended as the basis on which to found other collaborations and initiatives, in as much as it represented one way of creating relationships and collaborations on relevant educational questions between teachers and researchers who work within different European countries.

## Notes
1 Antonio Gariboldi wrote paragraphs 2, 4 and 5 ; Roberta Cardarello wrote paragraphs 1 and 3.

## References

Adams M.L. e Chen J-Q. (2012), "Understanding Young Children's Kinds of Creating", in O.N. Saracho (ed.), Contemporary Perspectives on Research in Creativity in Early Childhood Education, Charlotte, IAP, pp. 343-354.

Andiliou, A., Murphy P. K. (2010), "Examining variations among researchers' and teachers' conceptualizations of creativity: A review and synthesis of contemporary research", Educational Research Review, 5, pp. 201-219.

Blake S., Giannangelo D.M. (2012), "Creativity and Young Children", in O.N. Saracho (Ed.), Contemporary Perspectives on Research in Creativity in Early Childhood Education, Charlotte, IAP, pp. 293-315.

Bondioli A. (1996), Gioco e educazione, Milano, Franco Angeli.

Glăveanu, V. P. (2010), "Paradigms in the study of creativity: Introducing the perspective of cultural psychology", New Ideas in Psychology, v. 28, n. 1, pp. 79–93.

Kaufman J.C., Baer J. (2004), "Hawking's Haiku, Madonna's Math: Why it is hard to be creative in every room of the house", in R. J. Sternberg, E.L. Grigorenko, J.L. Singer (Eds.), Creativity: From potential to realization, Washington DC, American Psychological Association, pp. 3-19.

Laslocky M., Winefield R. (2011), The Importance of Children's Play to the Development of Creativity and Innovation, Bay Area Discovery Museum.

Mellou E. (1996), "Can Creativity be Nurtured in Young Children?", Early Child Development and Care, v.119, pp. 119-130.

Munari B. (1977), Fantasia, Bari, Laterza.

Pinto Minerva F., Vinella M. (2012), La creatività a scuola, Bari, Laterza.

Runco M.A. (2004), "Everyone has creative potential", in R. J. Sternberg, E. L. Grigorenko, J. L. Singer (Eds.), Creativity: From potential to realization, Washington DC, American Psychological Association, pp. 21-30.

Runco M.A. (2008), "Creativity and Education", New Horizons in Education, v. 56, 1.

Wittgenstein L. (1953), Ricerche filosofiche, Torino, Einaudi, 1967.

www.ingramcontent.com/pod-product-compliance
Lightning Source LLC
Chambersburg PA
CBHW071052280326
41928CB00050B/2222